THE PRESIDENCY
AND RHETORICAL LEADERSHIP

NUMBER SIX
Presidential Rhetoric Series
Martin J. Medhurst, General Editor

*A complete listing
of books in print in this series
appears at the back of the book.*

THE PRESIDENCY AND RHETORICAL LEADERSHIP

Edited by Leroy G. Dorsey

TEXAS A&M UNIVERSITY PRESS • COLLEGE STATION

Library of Congress Cataloging-in-Publication Data

　　The presidency and rhetorical leadership / edited by Leroy G. Dorsey.—
1st ed.
　　　　　p. cm.—(Presidential rhetoric series ; no. 6)
　　Includes index.
　　ISBN 1-58544-178-3 (cloth : alk. paper)
　　1. Rhetoric—Political aspects—United States.　2. Political
oratory—United States.　3. Presidents—United States—Language.
I. Dorsey, Leroy G., 1959–　II. Series.
PN239.P64 P74　2002
808.5'1'0883512—dc21　　　　　　　　　　　　2001004113

CONTENTS

ACKNOWLEDGMENTS

The chapters appearing in this volume were first presented at the fifth annual conference on presidential rhetoric held at Texas A&M University's Presidential Conference Center, March 4–7, 1999. These conferences are sponsored by the Program in Presidential Rhetoric, a research unit of the Center for Presidential Studies in the George Bush School of Government and Public Service. The editor wishes to acknowledge the assistance of then Center Director George C. Edwards III, the Department of Speech Communication under the leadership of Richard L. Street, Jr., the Office of the Vice President for Research and Associate Provost for Graduate Studies, and the support of Linda and Herman Giesen of Dallas, Texas, and Emil and Clementine Ogden of College Station, Texas.

The editors' special thanks go to the members of the Program in Presidential Rhetoric who planned this conference: James A. Aune, Vanessa B. Beasley, Martin J. Medhurst, Tarla R. Peterson, Enrique D. Rigsby, and Kurt Ritter. We also wish to thank the graduate and undergraduate students who served in a number of key roles and helped to facilitate the successful administration of the conference. The committee members are indebted to the many scholars who chaired panels or served as paper respondents. Their critical insights inspired many provocative conversations.

Finally, it may seem strange to many readers that a book about rhetorical leadership and the presidency omits a chapter on one of the most successful rhetorical presidencies of all—that of Abraham Lincoln. Actually, we considered Lincoln so central to the conference topic that we devoted an entire roundtable discussion to his rhetorical prowess. Selected papers from that roundtable have now been expanded into scholarly articles and published as a special issue of the journal *Rhetoric & Public Affairs* 3 (spring, 2000), under the guest editorship of Prof. Michael Leff. We commend that special issue and the articles in it by David Zarefsky, Kirt H. Wilson, Martha Watson, Edwin Black, and Michael Leff and Jean Goodwin, all of which originated at the 1999 Texas A&M Conference on Presidential Rhetoric.

THE PRESIDENCY
AND RHETORICAL LEADERSHIP

Introduction

The President as a Rhetorical Leader

Leroy G. Dorsey

WHAT IS RHETORICAL leadership? At face value the term appears fairly straightforward: it is leadership exerted through talk or persuasion. This definition, however, masks the complexities and scope of rhetorical leadership. To best understand the nature of rhetorical leadership, its fundamental elements must be explicated, particularly since leadership itself is an elastic concept that moves among a bewildering array of meanings.

The last half-century has seen over sixty different systems developed in an attempt to describe the psychological, sociological, and organizational dimensions of leadership.[1] Given that the scholarly literature and popular press on this centuries-old concept is voluminous, an exhaustive treatment of it is beyond the scope of this introduction. Even so, there are several widely recognized descriptions of leadership that need to be highlighted.

Some scholars believe that leadership stems from certain physical and mental qualities that an individual possesses. Exhibiting these "traits"—persistence, personal appearance, and sociability, for example—helps a leader to induce action in others. Contrary to the trait perspective of "born leaders" is the suggestion that leadership stems from a person's formal position in an organization. With an officially sanctioned title, the holder of that title can legitimately direct others for the achievement of a goal. Other conceptions of leaders cast them as wielders of some kind of personal power granted to them by their followers (what some call "charismatic leadership"). When subordinates feel good about an aspect of the leader's behavior or attitude, such as the leader being seen as passionate about the welfare of the people working for him or her, they allow the leader the power to direct them. Some scholars view leadership as a process, one that involves the leader's attempt to maintain the role relationships of the group. By ensuring a stable relational structure, the leader can better influence the group's behavior. Still others describe the effective leader as a person who can seize the moment by articulating a "vision" for his or her organization, a vision that would lead to long-lasting institutional change. The leader's vision of the organization's future casts that future in an attractive and pragmatic light, making it an appealing destination that is worth the effort.[2]

Treatment of leadership in the popular press also spans hundreds of publications. For the most part, these self-help books provide primers on the techniques of leadership. For example, the *Leadership Secrets of Attila the Hun* (a *New York Times* bestseller) reveals that contemporary leaders who, among other things, delegate wisely, choose lofty goals, and understand that "Huns only make enemies on purpose," would be successful. Other books describe leadership as simply having common sense. These books present a number of rules that the accomplished leader follows, including being patient, encouraging cooperation, exhibiting maturity, being specific in giving instructions, and gathering a competent staff for support.[3]

Regardless of the venue through which the concept has been examined, and the multitude of meanings generated, most appear to intersect at a basic definition of leadership. Generally, leadership represents a means whereby a person influences another person or group to achieve a common aim.[4] Furthermore, most of these works, either explicitly or implicitly, link the means of influence to communication. Gail Fairhurst and Robert Sarr summarize this line of thinking when they write that "leadership is a language game" whereby a person frames reality in such a way as to "manage meaning."[5] In other words, the concept of leadership is grounded in the nature and practice of rhetoric.

In the political dimension, however, the link between leadership and rhetoric has been an uneasy one. Since ancient times, political leadership via rhetoric to influence the public has often been seen as dangerous. Examples are numerous, but let two suffice for illustration. Sen. Henry Cabot Lodge took issue with Pres. Woodrow Wilson's public leadership when the president called for American participation in the League of Nations. According to Lodge, Wilson's attempt to use rhetoric to lead politically created a risky illusion. "The mechanical appliances of the rhetorician designed to give a picture of a present which does not exist and of a future which no man can predict," Lodge warned in 1919, "are as unreal and short lived as . . . the angels suspended on wires and the artificial lights on the stage. They pass with the moment of effect and are shabby and tawdry in the daylight. Let us at least be real."[6] Today, one can pick up virtually any popular critique about such discourse and it will bemoan the unreal nature of political leadership by rhetoric. For instance, the *New Republic*'s Jonathan Rauch observed wryly that people unknowingly "think a really fine president soars on majestic wings of inspiring rhetoric. . . . [However], lofty rhetoric is no substitute for sound judgment in a tight corner."[7] Under these conceptions, rhetoric is not about a union between a speaker and an audience who have the responsibility to share the means to define and to enhance their existence at any particular moment in time. Instead, being rhetorical appears to mean that someone is verbally creating a deceptive and ultimately detrimental reality in order to maintain control over someone else, the latter a hapless dupe in the process—leadership at its worst.

Even with the supposed realization that the modern presidency has shifted from a largely administrator-based to a more rhetoric-based institution, leadership via public communication still has an unsavory taste for many. In "The Rise of the Rhetorical Presidency," James Ceaser, Glen Thurow, Jeffrey Tulis, and Joseph Bessette argue that twentieth-century presidents have been more willing than their predecessors to employ rhetoric to achieve both legislative and, particularly, nonlegislative goals. A rhetorical presidency, they assert, reflects a chief executive who engages in a "form of presidential speech that soars above the realm of calm and deliberate discussion of reasons of state or appeals to enlightened self-interest. Rather, the picture of leadership that emerges . . . is one that constantly exhorts in the name of a common purpose and a spirit of idealism."

Ceaser and his colleagues argue that the "rhetorical" evolution of the presidency represents a bane rather than a boon. When the president attempts to exert pressure on Congress by appealing to the public, or tries to lead by providing moral leadership for a spiritually flagging country via high-sounding visions, the president is actually doing a disservice to his constituency. Echoing the concerns expressed by Lodge about Wilson's public leadership, Ceaser and his associates believe that modern presidents raise expectations with their high-blown rhetoric, expectations that too often result in public disappointment and confusion. They grudgingly admit there is a place for rhetoric in presidential leadership, but not an exalted place or even a particularly important one. As Ceaser and his colleagues note, "What the continued use of inspirational rhetoric fosters is not a simple credibility problem, but a deep tension between the publicly articulated understanding of the nature of our politics and the actual springs that move the system."[8] Their concern highlights the assumption of a disconnect between being rhetorical and the "actual springs that move the system"—the Constitution. Stated another way, rhetoric has no meaningful place when the president is envisioned as primarily a constitutional leader.

For others who examine political leadership, the chief executive becomes a sort of superadministrator, one who eschews the flash of *rhetorical tricks* in a public forum for the intellectually substantive coordination of the government's constituent parts. Richard Neustadt observes that the presidency does not automatically guarantee the chief executive the power or the ability to lead his cabinet officers and legislative leaders. Of importance to Neustadt is the notion that the president be an effective negotiator with his political colleagues. The president "does not get action without argument," Neustadt writes, since "presidential power is the power to persuade."[9] Given this conception, it is not surprising that most of the scholarship on political leadership, particularly presidential leadership, limits rhetoric to a form of reasoned discourse among elites. "The essential job of the President," James MacGregor Burns notes, "is to mobilize support within government. . . . This calls less for public relations gimmickry than for establishment of clear priorities, intensive consultation with congressional leaders, willingness to compromise . . . and the capacity, both intellectual and institutional, to follow through after decisions are reached." Burns disdains the "President of all the people" who seeks the "artificial atmosphere" of leadership by employing "some kind of electronic pulpit that would enable him to draw people across party lines" in lieu of establishing solid policy between institutional constituencies.[10] Lance Blakesley also emphasizes the president's place as the leader of a complex organization who should be more concerned with process than rhetoric. Like Burns, Blakesley concludes that the successful presidential leader will be an administrator who focuses solely on the development of policy within the organization, assigning only the most administratively and technically competent to assist in the endeavor.[11] Fred Greenstein, in his 1988 book, makes a similar point. For him, the president no longer represents one man, but a complex policy-making organization that the chief executive attempts to influence. Greenstein portrays presidential leadership as the "chief executive's capacity to control his aides and employ them to make informed, considered political choices."[12] Essentially, these themes dismiss a larger public as a potential audience, reflecting the idea that presidents who engage the public rhetorically are not effective leaders.

Yet, as Martin Medhurst has noted, attempting to keep rhetoric apart from presidential leadership—taking the "rhetorical" out of the rhetorical presidency—brings with it its own set of limitations. For example, scholarship that assumes the negative connotations of rhetoric as being emotional rather than enlightening, or that rhetoric's only merit comes from its use in the realm of policy talk among elites, unnecessarily constrains the perspective of presidential leadership.[13] Embracing the dynamic changes in society—technological, cultural, and spiritual—and examining how such changes affect a president's public and private messages, allows for richer and more diverse perspectives on the act of human communication as a means of political leadership.

Scholars who are comfortable including rhetoric within the orbit of political leadership exhibited by the chief executive can substantively broaden the understanding of that fluid and complex dynamic. Erwin Hargrove, for instance, believes that presidential leadership is realized when the chief executive utilizes particular skills to "present effective and politically appealing remedies for public problems." He notes that Franklin Roosevelt's success came from his ability to assess his public audiences and the situation they found themselves in and to craft an appropriate message. "Discernment of the historical possibilities for action," Hargrove writes, "is the master skill that provides guidance for . . . rhetoric. Rhetoric is the chief instrument of strategy because it is used to convey a sense of purpose." Furthermore, the president can lead by teaching his constituents about "reality." Not a static or an objective sense of reality, Hargrove explains, but a more probability-based reality: an interpretation of the past as it might impact on the present, and the choices that are available for guiding future policy.

Roderick Hart examined presidential communication from 1945 through 1985 and concluded that speech making by the chief executive represented a key tool in his ability to lead. In fact, the president's discourse is the verbal equivalent of chess: "Presidents are extraordinarily active players in the game of public opinion, and all of their public statements . . . are strategically designed to position the president for the next one in an endless series of moves and countermoves." Using such public rhetoric, Hart asserts, presidents have led the nation on any number of legislative and cultural issues. While he bemoans the increasing lack of eloquence in presidential communication and leadership, Hart also believes the audience is powerful enough to "determine what will be regarded as the sound of leadership in the modern age."[14]

In his latest book, *The Presidential Difference*, Greenstein identifies the qualities exhibited by presidents from Franklin Roosevelt to Bill Clinton that mark a successful leadership style. Chief among these qualities is the president's "effectiveness as a public communicator." For him, many chief executives have not addressed the "public with anything approximating the professionalism of countless educators [or] members of the clergy." When presidents consistently give "short shrift to the teaching and preaching side of presidential leadership," defeat follows. The other qualities Greenstein lists, including organizational capacity, vision, and political skill, highlight the essentially rhetorical nature of political leadership: A leader must be able to communicate compellingly the goals, and the means to achieve those goals, with any number of diverse audiences.[15]

Yet other studies have examined particular rhetorical strategies employed by presidents to lead the nation. Mary Stuckey labels the president an "interpreter-in-chief" who uses television as the means to disseminate stories about the community; the president uses such stories not only to promote policy but also to influence the conscience of the community. Samuel Kernell discusses how the chief executive "goes public," strategically managing the press as a means to generate support for his agenda by holding staged rallies, releasing selected information at designated times, and delivering major addresses. Marcia Whicker and Todd Areson identify the leadership behaviors that determine if the chief executive can be an effective persuader. Successful presidential leaders, they hold, construct messages for audiences that are simple, timely, clear, informed, and emotional.[16]

Suffice it to say that political leadership and rhetoric constitute a complex dynamic. What, then, is "rhetorical leadership?" Is it simply merging the definition of rhetoric and leadership as an explanation for what presidents do? If so, rhetorical leadership could be defined as the process of discovering, articulating, and sharing the available means of influence in order to motivate human agents in a particular situation. In some regards we do not have to go any farther than this: to be rhetorical means to attempt leadership of some sort; to lead requires an ability to be rhetorical. To stop here, however, limits the deeper appreciation of rhetorical leadership.

Perhaps the more intriguing perspective revolves around how the president can be a *successful* rhetorical leader. At one level, voters ask: Can the leaders we choose do the job? Can they assess a complex situation and explain it both to elites and to the public in such a way that the opportunity for political, cultural, and social influence can be realized? In other words, can the politician rationally decide upon a course of action and lead others to follow it? Regarding this conception of leaders, it is not who they are that is of utmost importance to the audience at that moment, it is what they can do that becomes the benchmark for successful rhetorical leadership. Jeff Greenfield made this point when he observed sardonically that the 1972 promotion for Richard Nixon's foreign policy contained an implicit message: "*Okay, you don't like the son of a bitch, but maybe he's so secretive because he's planning bold moves.*"[17] For a period of time the public and the president's colleagues were content with Nixon the deliberator as leader. In 1974, however, they rejected that rational persona and deemed Nixon the person unpalatable as a leader.

Perhaps fortunately for chief executives, there exists a parallel understanding of successful leadership that emphasizes not "what can leaders do" but rather "who are they?" Are the leaders we choose good people? Commonly speaking, does the leader have a virtuous character? Theodore Roosevelt emphasized this point repeatedly in his rhetoric. For example, "in the great battle of life," he wrote in 1900, "no brilliancy of intellect . . . will count when weighed in the balance against that assemblage of virtues . . . of moral qualities, which we group together under the name of character."[18] But this persona is not always welcomed either. As Eugene Garver writes in interpreting Aristotle's *Ethics*, the latter understood that "there is no universal rule that [one] should always prefer a courageous person over a professional soldier. . . . Sometimes a professional skill detached from character is just what we want in accountants and soldiers."[19]

So what is the lesson for accountants, soldiers, and presidents? Successful rhetorical leadership comes from the demonstration of, at any given moment, the artful balance of superior decision-making skills *and* the exhibition of the requisite character. Thus, contemporary chief executives who are seeking to lead rhetorically should embrace the classical notion of prudence, a concept central to the rhetorical tradition from classical to contemporary times.[20]

Aristotle, for example, defined the prudent person as being able to "deliberate finely about things that are good and beneficial for himself . . . about what sorts of things promote living well in general."[21] The successful political leader particularly needed what Aristotle considered this virtue of thought.[22] Prudential leadership, then, represented a practical intelligence, coupled with the ability to reason soundly, in order to accomplish the goals necessary for the livelihood of all. A prudent leader was not required to have wisdom, Aristotle wrote, because wisdom derived from the "principles of a science" and the "truth about the principles." Wisdom concerned the scientific understanding about the divine nature of the universe; in contrast, a leader's job centered on bettering the life of his charges by finding a reasonable mean between existential choices. "Prudence," Aristotle observed, "is about human concerns, about things open to deliberation. . . . The unqualifiedly good deliberator is the one whose aim accords with rational calculation in pursuit of the best good for a human being that is achievable in action." A prudent leader, then, is deliberate and rational, choosing among options that can be realized in the world as it is and that would likely insure the community's well-being.[23]

Echoing Aristotle, Cicero likewise believed prudence meant having a sort of practical knowledge, or what he called the virtue of "good sense." "When a man is extremely good at perceiving what is most true in each particular thing," Cicero noted, "and when he is able with great acuity and speed to see and to explain the reason, then he is rightly considered extremely sensible and wise."[24] This trait appeared essential for the effective leader: if that person did not exhibit the ability to anticipate the future and choose the correct actions accordingly, disaster would follow. Someone leading an army into battle, for instance, would be imprudent if he had not previously calculated the best means for success. As Cicero observed, a leader must never act in such a way "that one will need to say, 'I had not thought of that.'"[25]

But Cicero extends this aspect of practical knowledge. Whereas Aristotle argued that prudence related to deliberating on the ways to enhance human affairs, excluding the scientific knowledge of the divine as a resource in that deliberation, Cicero believed that the community could only reach its goals with such "knowledge of all things human and divine." Knowledge of the divine had a place in the prudent governing of men and women. By reflecting on the divine and having good sense about what measures to take to lead the community politically, Cicero maintained, a leader would adopt practical actions "most clearly in the protection of men's interest."[26]

Aristotle's and Cicero's writings on virtue are extensive, but two of their observations on the intersection between the virtue of thought and the virtue of character are of particular note. According to Aristotle, a political leader "cannot be fully good without prudence, or prudent without virtue of character."[27] Without those character traits Aristotle defined as virtuous, such as generosity, fairness, decency, and honesty—traits that people today consider the benchmarks of good character—a person's vices would prevent reasoned deliberation and lead to outcomes contrary to the success of the group. Cicero concluded likewise. It was virtuous behavior, he believed, that originally determined who would lead: "once upon a time men of good character were established as kings in order that justice might be enjoyed. For when the needy masses were being oppressed . . . they fled together to some one man who excelled in virtue." In fact, of all the virtues of character, Cicero believed that "justice" was central since it involved the maintenance of fellowship between the members of the group.[28] A person exhibiting the virtues of character, along with the virtues of thought, embodied the great leader. Cicero wrote: "This, therefore, is manifest: the men who are usually chosen to rule are those who have a great reputation among the masses for justice. If in addition, indeed, they were thought also to be men of good sense, there was nothing that men would think they could not achieve under their leadership."[29]

Prudence, for both ancient writers, involved more than coming to a *reasonably correct* answer via the virtue of thought (whether inspired by the divine or human means). It also meant more than coming to the *ethically right* answer because the person possessed the virtue of character.[30] Both virtues had to be balanced in order to find the best means for all involved. Perhaps even more critical, then, a person must be able to *demonstrate* this balance, this combination of good sense and good character, in order to be recognized as an effective leader. Prudence, then, is displayed in action.

According to Robert Hariman, prudence is about performance. "Prudence," he writes, "is the art of making the right gesture in a public space with whatever are the available means for political action."[31] This definition, which seems to center around creating "mere appearances," does not mean that prudence is divorced from the rigors of rationality and character. Along with this performative nature of prudence, Hariman and Francis Beer argue that a politician needs to possess what they call "calculative prudence": the ability to "optimize the acquisition of knowledge to make valid predictions about specific actions" (the classical virtue of thought). Likewise, they note, the politician also needs "normative prudence": a "deliberative process . . . [to] determine how to attain what is good and avoid what is bad" (the classical virtue of character).[32]

Essentially, "performative prudence" acts as a sort of hybrid of the other two. Performative prudence as the "social performance of a role," Hariman and Beer believe, also "has to be both normative and calculative if it is to be 'realistic.'"[33] Thus, conceptualizing prudence as performance means that political actors must balance their calculative and normative attributes appropriately. The prudent politician actually represents a person who understands how "matters of calculation . . . are modulated and constrained by questions of performance, including questions of characterization, timing, tone, and the like."[34] By demonstrating the right balance between their virtues of thought and character, prudent leaders exhibit their awareness of what is possible and appropriate for any number of contingent issues involving any number of groups and situations. Simply put, they are successful rhetorical leaders.

Perhaps, then, it is best to understand successful rhetorical leadership as a politician's ability to perform well the sometimes conflicting virtues of thought and character—to understand how, when, and in what manner to balance being strategic and saintly, reasonable and righteous. The chapters in this volume, either explicitly or implicitly, recognize the importance of how the chief executive expresses these virtues as a means for political action. In other words, these chapters examine, from different perspectives, the notion of presidential prudence and rhetorical leadership.

David Zarefsky asserts that rhetorical leadership extends directly from the concept of prudence. According to Zarefsky, from the beginning presidents have employed rhetoric to extend the power constitutionally granted to them by their office. As a result, they have engaged in two broad strategies in what could be considered prudence as performance. Early presidents transformed existing rhetorical practices, such as ceremonial occasions, into forums for their policy agendas; they also developed innovative rhetorical strategies, such as using their election as the occasion for action or inaction regarding a particular policy. Both approaches, Zarefsky argues, reflect the president seizing traditional moments and transforming them into forums to demonstrate their virtues. From George Washington to Ronald Reagan, Zarefsky illustrates how the chief executive's improvisational skills allowed him to express artfully his good sense and good will for political effect.

Stephen Lucas's essay supports Zarefsky's claim that early presidents understood rhetoric as a viable means to empower their leadership. George Washington, Lucas shows, was keenly aware of the performative dimensions of his office. Washington adapted the traditional rhetorical forms of his day into new forums that gave him license to demonstrate his political and personal commitments in ways that influenced his audiences on numerous issues. Stated another way, Lucas concludes that Washington understood the need to be prudent. According to Lucas, the first president strategically used his inaugural address, annual messages, his regional tour appearances, and his Farewell Address to embody the quintessence of the politically sound and virtuously stalwart public leader. As Lucas notes, Washington struck the perfect balance between reason and emotion "that allowed him to educe awe and reverence even as he inspired confidence in his character, judgment, and trustworthiness with power."

James Farrell's essay on John Adams reveals the second president as a man consumed with ensuring that his presidency would be viewed as a sterling example of prudent leadership. Both during and after his presidency, Adams wrote extensively to explain his presidential decision to send a second peace delegation to France in 1799. When the negotiations from that mission were not well received by the public, Adams began a decades-long rhetorical campaign. Targeting not just his contemporary audience, but future historians as well, Farrell notes, Adams argued that his presidency was the epitome of the prudential ideal. Inspired by the writings of Cicero on the virtuous public servant, Adams believed that excellence in presidential leadership included, among other things, moral behavior and dispassionate deliberation. By consciously portraying himself as an exemplar of the Ciceronian ideal, Adams hoped that the force of his performance would become his audiences' warrant for their acceptance of his presidential decisions as the embodiment of good leadership.

Lawrence Kaplan's essay on Thomas Jefferson reveals the president's inability to perform effectively the role of a prudential leader. Jefferson demonstrated on several occasions his flawed reasoning ability to his chief foe, Napoleon Bonaparte, while negotiating the acquisition of Louisiana and Spanish Florida. When Bonaparte agreed to the sale of Louisiana in 1803, Jefferson believed that his diplomatic threat of a British-American alliance had convinced the French emperor to concede the land. Kaplan believes that Jefferson failed to comprehend that certain external factors outside of his rhetoric had forced Bonaparte to release the territory. Blinded by his own hubris (a vice Aristotle would argue prevents good deliberation and, by extension, leads to a banal performance), Jefferson employed the same rhetorical strategies in 1808 to pressure France into forcing its Spanish satellite to relinquish control of Florida to the United States. Even when France continued to seize American ships illegally during this time, Jefferson chose not to rebuke Bonaparte, hoping instead that his diplomatic deliberations would win the day. Instead, Bonaparte rejected Jefferson's demonstration of prudence, believing it to be gullible and pitiable.

H. W. Brands's essay depicts Theodore Roosevelt's successful performance as a man of strong character. Roosevelt's career as a Dakota rancher, frontier cowboy, "Untouchable" police commissioner, and rough-riding military hero illustrated that he would do anything to uphold a sense of right. Brands acknowledges that Roosevelt was a "genuine intellectual," but he also emphasizes that it was the president's "compelling persona as a man of action" that gave him the righteous ability to lead successfully on controversial issues. For example, when a wintertime coal strike threatened the northeastern states in 1902, President Roosevelt interceded without the benefit of constitutional authority. He demanded that the owners of the mines settle the strike or face losing control of the mines to the U.S. Army. While unheard of for a chief executive to take such an action, the mine owners believed Roosevelt to be a prudent man who would do what he believed was right; consequently, the strike was settled. "The wonderful thing about being perceived as a man of action," Brands concludes, "was that it lent authority even to what might have been bluffs."

James Andrews observes that Woodrow Wilson believed that leadership resulted from the articulation of an epideictic message, a vision that could unify diverse individuals into an American nation that understood its greatness and its responsibilities at home and abroad. Wilson brought his own noble character to the public stage, reaffirming his vision in the American consciousness and demonstrating the prudential ideal of thought and character in service to the good of the community. Whether addressing a group of naturalized citizens in the wake of the *Lusitania*'s sinking in 1915, or a Fourth of July audience at Gettysburg in 1919, Wilson embodied the divinely inspired leader that called for his followers to stand together against the profane forces of selfishness and sectionalism. His prudential performance influenced his audiences then and continues to influence American policy today.

Thomas Benson examines Franklin Roosevelt's 1934 and 1938 commemorative speeches at Gettysburg as exemplars of rhetorical leadership. Even though the president intentionally subordinated Abraham Lincoln and the issue of slavery as an element of the Civil War in 1934, and remained silent on the struggle for African American civil rights in 1938, Roosevelt made what could be considered prudent choices for a leader. He believed that the means to increase the livelihood of *everyone* lay in economic revitalization. To use those forums for social agitation for a portion of the community would have been counterproductive. Thus, the president articulated a prudent position: He offered the

New Deal as the reasonable solution to the economic problems, and he demonstrated his graciousness of character by remaining silent on race relations.

In their essay on Dwight Eisenhower, Meena Bose and Fred Greenstein observe that the problem facing any president is the public's perception of him in the "dual capacity as head of state and principal national political leader." This observation reflects the dual conception of classic prudence. On one hand, the president must be a "symbol of unity" (have good character). On the other hand, the president must be a capable problem-solver (have good sense). To be a successful rhetorical leader, the president must demonstrate these virtues of character and of thought at the right time and with the right balance. For most of his presidency, Eisenhower performed his role, becoming effective as a leader and quite popular as well. Bose and Greenstein argue that Eisenhower took on the public persona of a plain and upright man who employed simple language and who tried not to criticize other politicians by name. Eschewing the persona of a reasoned deliberator at press conferences, the president "sometimes professed ignorance," which they say "went over well with the public." Eisenhower's private communications, however, were models of reasoned discourse. The president's leadership behind the scenes, his "hidden hand presidency," demonstrated to recipients of this discourse that he possessed a "keenly analytical mind."[35]

The final two essays in this volume provide a fitting conclusion to the notion of rhetorical leadership as prudential performance. The essays deal with the two most controversial presidents of the late twentieth century: Ronald Reagan and Bill Clinton.

Scholars have generally been confounded by Ronald Reagan's acumen as a political strategist in dealing with the Soviet Union, while also showing his obvious disinterest in leadership, as evidenced by falling asleep in cabinet meetings. But according to G. Thomas Goodnight, Reagan was simply being prudent. When necessary, Reagan performed as a reasoned deliberator who was able to meet the expectations of various political exigencies. He appeared as a practical leader, blaming the liberals for any setbacks and arguing that reason dictated that he secure what he could when he could. When necessary, Reagan ignored the standards for political competence and demonstrated prudence by *ingenium*—the mark of wit applied against the tediousness of rationality. He maintained an aura of command even while performing the role of a bumbling but concerned neighbor by dismissing his many gaffes as inconsequential, consequently making those who challenged his gee-whiz errors seem smug by comparison.

For many, Bill Clinton is the most confounding of presidents. As John Murphy wonders, how can a chief executive simultaneously evoke feelings of awe and despair, wonder and disgust? Murphy argues that Clinton possesses *metis*—a "wily and expansive sort of intelligence"— that accounts for Clinton's popularity and acknowledged leadership. A "kissing cousin [of] prudential conduct," Murphy asserts, this cunning intelligence allowed Clinton to maneuver successfully within an American community "marked by multiplicity"—a nation composed of diverse experiences, inconsistent narratives, minimized moralities, and cultural anxieties. Clinton's performance of *metis* (or prudence if you will) demonstrates that he is a cunning agent who adapts to the moment, which in turn offers hope to the people trying to likewise survive in their fractured culture.

Ultimately, Murphy's assessment of Clinton's performance echoes how the successful rhetorical leader, ever aware of the audience and the particulars of the moment, acts to balance the classical conception of prudence: "We may not love such a cunning character, but we believe that he will lead us through trouble."

While the executive office obviously bestows the status of leader and voice of the nation on whoever holds the office, simply occupying the position does not necessarily mean that successful leadership will follow. What each essay in this volume illustrates is the inventiveness and awareness presidents need to demonstrate so that they are recognized as reasonable and ethical leaders. To lead rhetorically and to be successful, then, presidents must not only be cognizant of the pitfalls lurking in the social and political landscape, but they must also be aware of the opportunities to craft the appropriate expression of their character as a symbol for overcoming those troubles. Thus, presidents who can gracefully adapt their performance to balance both their virtues of thought and character in the moment will be seen as prudent leaders. And prudence, as these essays will demonstrate, is the centerpiece of rhetorical leadership.

NOTES

1. Peter G. Northouse, *Leadership: Theory and Practice* (Thousand Oaks, Calif.: Sage, 1997), 2.

2. See, for example, Northouse, *Leadership*, 1–6; Bernard M. Bass, *Bass & Stogdill's Handbook of Leadership: Theory, Research, and Managerial Applications*, 3d ed. (1974; reprint, New York: Free Press, 1990); Jay A. Conger and Rabindra N. Kanungo, *Charismatic Leadership in Organizations* (Thousand Oaks, Calif.: Sage, 1998); Burt Nanus, *Visionary Leadership: Creating a Compelling Sense of Direction for Your Organization* (San Francisco: Jossey-Bass, 1992); Noel M. Tichy and Mary Anne Devanna, *The Transformational Leader* (New York: John Wiley and Sons, 1986).

3. See, for example, Wess Roberts, *Leadership Secrets of Attila the Hun* (1985; reprint, New York: Warner Books, 1987); Roger Fulton, *Common Sense Leadership* (Berkeley, Calif.: Ten Speed Press, 1995); and Kenneth Blanchard, Patricia Zigarmi, and Drea Zigarmi, *Leadership and the One Minute Manager: Increasing Effectiveness through Situational Leadership* (New York: William Morrow, 1985).

4. See Northouse, *Leadership*, 3.

5. Gail T. Fairhurst and Robert A. Sarr, *The Art of Framing: Managing the Language of Leadership* (San Francisco: Jossey-Bass, 1996), xi, 3.

6. *Congressional Record*, 66th Cong., 1st sess., 3784 (Aug. 12, 1919).

7. Jonathan Rauch, "Our Greatest Modern President: Father Superior," *New Republic*, May 22, 2000, 25.

8. James W. Ceaser, Glen E. Thurow, Jeffrey Tulis, and Joseph M. Bessette, "The Rise of the Rhetorical Presidency," *Presidential Studies Quarterly* 11 (1981): 163, 170.

9. Richard E. Neustadt, *Presidential Power and the Modern President: The Politics of Leadership from Roosevelt to Reagan* (New York: Free Press, 1990), 11.

10. James M. Burns, *The Power to Lead: The Crisis of the American Presidency* (New York: Simon and Schuster, 1984), 158–59.

11. Lance Blakesley, *Presidential Leadership: From Eisenhower to Clinton* (Chicago: Nelson-Hall, 1995), 98–99.

12. Fred I. Greenstein, "In Search of a Modern Presidency," in *Leadership in the Modern Presidency*, ed. Fred I. Greenstein (Cambridge, Mass.: Harvard University Press, 1988), 351.

13. Martin J. Medhurst, "A Tale of Two Constructs: The Rhetorical Presidency versus Presidential Rhetoric," in *Beyond the Rhetorical Presidency*, ed. Martin J. Medhurst (College Station: Texas A&M University Press), xiii–xv.

14. Erwin C. Hargrove, *The President as Leader: Appealing to the Better Angels of our Nature* (Lawrence: University Press of Kansas, 1998), 38, 175; Roderick P. Hart, *The Sound of Leadership: Presidential Communication in the Modern Age* (Chicago: University of Chicago Press, 1987), 2, 210, 212–14.

15. Fred I. Greenstein, *The Presidential Difference: Leadership Style from FDR to Clinton* (New York: Martin Kessler Books–Free Press, 2000), 195.

16. Mary E. Stuckey, *The President as Interpreter-in-Chief* (Chatham, N.J.: Chatham House, 1991); Samuel Kernell, *Going Public: New Strategies of Presidential Leadership*,

2d ed. (Washington, D.C: Congressional Quarterly Press, 1993); Marcia L. Whicker and Todd W. Areson, "Presidential Persuasiveness and Public Sector Leadership," in *Executive Leadership in the Public Service*, ed. Robert B. Denhardt and William H. Stewart (Tuscaloosa: University of Alabama Press, 1992), 65–72.

17. Jeff Greenfield, *Playing to Win: An Insider's Guide to Politics* (New York: Simon and Schuster, 1980), 186.

18. Theodore Roosevelt, "Character and Success, Mar. 31, 1900," in *The Works of Theodore Roosevelt: American Ideals/The Strenuous Life/Realizable Ideals*, National ed., vol. 13 (New York: Charles Scribner's Sons, 1926), 381.

19. Eugene Garver, *Aristotle's Rhetoric: An Art of Character* (Chicago: University of Chicago Press, 1994), 190.

20. In Aristotle's time, prudence was known as *phronesis*. During Cicero's time, prudence was called *prudentia*.

21. Aristotle, *Nicomachean Ethics*, trans. by Terence Irwin, 2d ed. (Indianapolis: Hackett, 1999), 89.

22. For Aristotle's requirement for the good leader, see Aristotle, *The Politics of Aristotle*, trans. by Peter L. Phillips Simpson (Chapel Hill: University of North Carolina Press, 1997), 83. For Aristotle's division between virtues of thought and virtues of character, see Aristotle, *Nicomachean Ethics*, 353.

23. Aristotle, *Nicomachean Ethics*, 91–92.

24. Cicero, *On Duties*, ed. M. T. Griffin and E. M. Atkins (Cambridge: Cambridge University Press, 1991), 7–8.

25. Ibid., 32.

26. Ibid., 59–60.

27. Aristotle, *Nicomachean Ethics*, 99.

28. Cicero, *On Duties*, 9.

29. Ibid., 78–79.

30. Although the popular conception of virtue aligns it with good character (being truthful, fair, etc.) and not necessarily with rational thinking, both Aristotle and Cicero included prudence as one of several virtues.

31. Robert Hariman, "Prudence/Performance," *Rhetoric Society Quarterly* 21 (1991): 28.

32. Robert Hariman and Francis A. Beer, "What Would Be Prudent? Forms of Reasoning in World Politics," *Rhetoric & Public Affairs* 1 (1998): 305–307.

33. Ibid., 310.

34. Hariman, "Prudence/Performance," 27–28.

35. See also David Henry, "Eisenhower and Sputnik: The Irony of Failed Leadership," in *Eisenhower's War of Words: Rhetoric and Leadership*, ed. Martin J. Medhurst (East Lansing: Michigan State University Press, 1994), 223–49.

CHAPTER 1

The Presidency
Has Always
Been a Place
for Rhetorical
Leadership

David Zarefsky

FTER HIS EXTENDED STAY at Camp David in July, 1979, Pres. Jimmy Carter delivered a speech in which he did not use the word "malaise." However, in examining why national unity on energy policy seemed impossible, he spoke of a crisis of confidence. Early in the speech, he quoted advice he had received from his guests at Camp David, beginning with a southern governor who had told him, "Mr. President, you are not leading this Nation—you're just managing the Government."[1]

Had the framers of the Constitution heard these remarks, they would have been hard pressed to understand them as criticism. Their concern was precisely that the president should *not* become the leader of the nation, for that might make him a demagogue or tyrant, but rather that he be the manager of the government, responsible for executing policies devised by Congress. Selecting the president was not a matter of selecting this or that policy or ideology, but of selecting the best person to carry out congressional decisions. The expectation of presidential leadership came later, but not much later. The original constitutional system excluded the possibility of meaningful political conflict. The public good was thought to be self-evident and virtuous people could see and act upon it. Electors would demonstrate their own virtue by identifying the most virtuous to hold the presidential office. George Washington amply, indeed unanimously, met the need.

But political factions—nascent parties—developed early in the Washington administration, in the conflicts between Alexander Hamilton and Thomas Jefferson about the nature of American society and government. Washington instinctively recognized that the presidency should be kept on a higher plane than either faction, and at least until the Whiskey Rebellion he succeeded in doing so. Even when he later took Hamilton's side of the argument, he equated Federalist ideology with national interest. His successors, of whatever persuasion, also have proved adept at construing their own interests as synonymous with the national interest and thereby at standing for the whole people.

The president could not just "stand," though. He had to move, to defend the national interest against special interests and to assert the national interest preemptively, before special interests could prevail. Certainly by the time of the Jefferson administration, a modicum of presidential leadership was expected. But what, exactly, is meant by leadership?

The term is often poorly defined or undefined in the literature on presidential studies, but there are persistent themes about leadership and its relation to rhetoric. In his now-classic work, Richard Neustadt suggests that leadership involves exceeding the baseline role of national clerk. He goes on to note that the means for doing so are not provided in the Constitution and that therefore presidents must find them through persuasion.[2] James MacGregor Burns finds the essence of leadership in a president's purposefully deploying organizational resources to bring about discernible changes in processes and institutions.[3] Taking a sharply different tack, Bruce Miroff focuses on the enactment of spectacle to create the image of control and decisiveness.[4] In a particularly insightful book, Stephen Skowronek regards leadership as the ability to negotiate constraints and opportunities in order to resolve a paradox: presidents must disrupt a preexisting order even while affirming the value of order and creating a new one.[5] Skowronek stresses that the situation—in his phrase, our location in political time—will affect the opportunities available to a president and hence the standard against which the president should be judged. Successful leaders, while responding to their situation, are those who can "control the political definition of their actions, the terms in which their places in history are understood."[6] In this view, leadership is the control of meaning or interpretation given to actions.

A similar view to Skowronek's is offered in Erwin Hargrove's recent book on presidential leadership. Hargrove identifies leadership with the ability to discern the possibilities emerging from the mix of opportunities and constraints at a given time, to "teach reality" by conveying a persuasive interpretation of unresolved problems, and to suggest plausible remedies by reinterpreting shared beliefs and values. These shared beliefs and values—the content of a culture—represent a constraint on presidential action, and the ability to interpret them is the corresponding opportunity.[7] Finally, Hargrove explains that presidential leadership requires prudence, or the practical wisdom to discern the appropriate action in a given case.[8] To state the matter another way, there are no rules for sizing up a situation or responding to it. Rather, these skills are developed in particular contexts and through practice.

This brief survey of the relevant literature suggests several recurrent themes. First, presidential leadership involves rising above some baseline notion of the minimal constitutional requirements of the office. Second, this result is achieved by bringing about change—not necessarily reversal, but change. Third, the change is transformative. It outlasts the immediate circumstances and reconstructs the nature and expectations of the office over the long term. Finally, this effect often is achieved by discovering and using the available means of persuasion in a given case.

This last statement, of course, reproduces almost verbatim Aristotle's classic definition of rhetoric. It is worth remembering that rhetoric is not bombast and ornamentation, nor a noun to be preceded with adjectives such as *empty* and *mere.* It does not stand in opposition to reality because it, too, is real. Rather, it represents the old and useful art of discovering in a particular situation the means available to influence others to perceive, believe, or act differently than they otherwise would.

It is called into being by an exigence, a problem for which persuasion can provide the solution. Thus, it constitutes the means by which the president, as "leader of the American people," can "shape and mobilize public opinion."[9]

It is probably going too far to assert that all presidential leadership is rhetorical. Yet rhetoric is intimately involved in its exercise. Timothy Cook, a political scientist who studies news coverage of political institutions, helps to explain why this is so. In his recent book *Governing with the News,* he accounts for politicians' increasing reliance on the news media to attract an audience. Media strategies, he says, "become increasingly useful means for political actors to pursue governance—and become an increasing focus of their attention and their activities—as the disjuncture between the power of those actors and the expectations placed on them grows."[10] With specific reference to the presidency, Cook observes that there is a gap between "the expectations placed on the office and the actual resources that presidents are able to control."[11] Power and resources are limited by the Constitution, which reflected the framers' fears of a strong executive who would lead the country rather than manage the government. The increasingly complex demands of modern life and the centrality of the presidency to the political system create much larger expectations. To fill the gap, presidents turn increasingly to rhetoric, regarding persuasion as a source of power that might restore equilibrium: constitutional power plus rhetorical leadership *together* would be commensurate with the needs.

Cook's thesis is a tenable explanation for the significance of rhetoric to presidential leadership. But arguments such as his often are given an unfortunate spin when it is suggested that reliance on persuasion distinguishes more recent from earlier presidents. The "modern presidency" sometimes is said to have begun with World War II, and presidential scholarship sometimes seems preoccupied with the last eleven presidents to the neglect of the first thirty-one. Jeffrey Tulis has distinguished between nineteenth- and twentieth-century presidents, suggesting that this century's presidents, more so than their predecessors, saw their principal responsibility as evoking and responding to the will of the people.[12]

Such accounts rely on the assumption of an epochal shift between earlier and later presidencies. The difficulty, as Richard Ellis notes, is that they "have the unfortunate consequence of flattening nineteenth-century presidential history."[13] They highlight similarities rather than differences among presidents, both those before and those after the supposed epochal moment, and they make us less sensitive to either recurrent patterns or long-term evolutions in rhetorical leadership.

Therefore, I wish to defend an even grander version of Cook's thesis. Almost from the beginning, certainly from the time that political conflict became a fact of life, presidents needed more power and resources than the Constitution offers, and they found in rhetoric the means to at least narrow if not close the gap. They have done so either by transforming existing rhetorical practices (for example, transforming ceremonial addresses into speeches advocating policies) or by developing new ones (such as interpreting election results as a mandate for a specific action). Moreover, their goals and strategies have been remarkably stable even while the technology for pursuing them has changed with the culture. I would like to illustrate each of these approaches, beginning with the transformation of the ordinary.

Nowhere does the Constitution require that the president deliver an inaugural address. But George Washington began the practice, modeling it on British custom, and it was quickly established as the norm. The prospect that a newly elected president would not deliver an inaugural address is unthinkable. But from an almost purely ceremonial ritual, the inaugural evolved quickly into a hybrid with deliberative and ceremonial aspects—a speech that reunites a politically divided country, previews the policy agenda for the new president's term in a general way, and situates the launching of a presidency within a historical context. These and other generic aspects of the inaugural address developed through the example of Thomas Jefferson's first inaugural address.[14]

Aside from our most recent election, it is hard to imagine a more divisive contest than that of 1800, in which Jefferson opposed John Adams, under whom he had served as vice president. Republican charges that Adams sought to return the country to Great Britain were met with Federalist insistence that Jefferson sought to deliver America to the revolutionaries in France and that he was an atheist besides. Electors were chosen at different times and, with only South Carolina remaining to vote, the candidates were tied at sixty-five each. After intense politicking, South Carolina voted for the Republican ticket. But each elector cast two votes and one elector forgot to "throw away" his second vote. As a result, Jefferson and Aaron Burr, nominally running mates, tied with seventy-three each, so the election went to the House of Representatives. Die-hard House Federalists, sensing an opportunity for mischief, voted for Burr. It took thirty-five ballots for Jefferson to emerge the winner, and that did not happen until February 17, barely two weeks before Inauguration Day. To complicate matters further, this was the first occasion on which power would pass from one political faction to another. Who knew whether peace or revolution lay ahead?

Jefferson answered that question in his inaugural speech. In the manner of a "rhetorical performative," he proclaimed that a higher unity transcended the bitter party divisions, and by saying it he made it so. "Every difference of opinion," he insisted, "is not a division of principle. We have called by different names brethren of the same principle. We are all Republicans, we are all Federalists."[15] The clearly implicit message is that the election season was over and that it was time to rise above the partisanship that contest had engendered. Jefferson defined a stance amidst ambiguity. He used the inaugural not just to mark his accession to office but to establish a norm for the people's postelection behavior: partisan divisions at election time are well and good, but once the election is over we must all rally behind the winner.

Not all subsequent inaugurals are so memorable or transformative. But the features Jefferson introduced have remained—so clearly that they are now expectations that a well-crafted inaugural is expected to meet. Another way to say this is that Jefferson's rhetorical leadership permanently changed the nature of the inaugural address. It is hard to imagine an inaugural that did not fit into Jefferson's basic framework.

Some subsequent presidents have also used the inaugural address to structure an ambiguous situation to their advantage. One thinks immediately of Abraham Lincoln in 1861 or Franklin Roosevelt in 1933, for example. Each sought to define a crisis in such a way as to offer reassurance. One thinks of John F. Kennedy in 1961, whose speech suggested that despite or because of his youth, he had the gravitas to wage a Cold War against the Soviet Union. One thinks of Lincoln in 1865, whose speech placed the Civil War in biblical perspective in order to pave the way for healing after a time of deep division, and of Richard Nixon in 1969, who sought the same goal but had less success. One thinks of Ronald Reagan, whose 1981 inaugural captured both the political conservatism and national optimism that would mark the ensuing decade. The transformative effect of some of these speeches did not outlast their own time. But the notion that the inaugural is a strategic resource, not just a ceremonial occasion, seems secure.

The one presidential message that *is* prescribed in the Constitution is the State of the Union address, referred to until recent times as the Annual Message. It, too, is a ceremonial occasion that presidents have used strategically to enhance their political position. With few exceptions, such as James Monroe's Annual Message of 1823 or Abraham Lincoln's of 1862, the innovative use of the State of the Union address is of more recent origin. Jefferson downgraded the Annual Message by abandoning the tradition of delivering it to Congress orally in person, a tradition that was not revived until Woodrow Wilson took office. Wilson's decision to appear before a joint session was not just an opportunity for spectacle; it was an implicit argument that the executive branch, not Congress, is the source of governmental leadership. Attention is focused on the president; he initiates the legislative agenda; he has the active role while members of Congress passively receive the message. Wilson's rhetorical demonstration was no accident. His goal was precisely to reverse the congressional dominance that had characterized nineteenth-century politics.[16] Before Wilson, presidents had given an annual report to Congress on how well they had carried out congressional instructions; now it was he who challenged them to act.

Since State of the Union messages are highly contextual, few are remembered long after their delivery, even when they announce major initiatives—such as Franklin Roosevelt's "Four Freedoms" in 1941 or Lyndon Johnson's declaration of war on poverty in 1964. But it is worth noting some of the innovations employed by recent presidents to enhance the capacity of this speech to exalt their own political position. Perhaps most notable was Lyndon Johnson's 1965 decision to shift the hour of the speech to television's evening prime time so that he could use it not only as a message to Congress but also as an appeal to the American people. Ronald Reagan began the practice of celebrating American heroism in the persons of those invited to share the First Lady's box, people to whom the president referred during the speech as exemplars in whose honor all Americans could unite. The 1998 and 1999 State of the Union messages offered vivid examples of Bill Clinton's ability to use the speech to shift the agenda, to distract attention from personal scandal, and to enact through his performance the argument that his leadership of the nation remained strong despite his own travail.

A final example of a ceremonial occasion transformed into a strategic asset is the acceptance speech at the national nominating convention. The Anti-Masonic Party held the first nominating convention in

1831, and they quickly became common practice. Candidates were not present, of course, thereby maintaining the convenient fiction that the office sought them rather than the other way around. Instead, they sent a message to party officials accepting the nomination after it had been formally tendered by a delegation sent from the convention. Originally they were perfunctory replies, but James Buchanan—otherwise undistinguished rhetorically or in other respects—in 1856 began the practice of using the acceptance letter to articulate his views about the party platform, and his successors followed the practice.[17] In 1892, Grover Cleveland changed the mode of delivery from an acceptance letter to a speech, making it a public event, and since 1900 all but one major presidential nominee has done the same.[18] The significance of this move, of course, is that it removes the mediating role of the party leadership and places the candidate in a direct relationship with the people. In 1932, Franklin D. Roosevelt took the next step: appearing at the convention to accept the nomination in person. Not only did this move, as he said, break with the foolish tradition that the candidate should act as though he did not know he had been nominated, but it visibly displaced the party leadership and established the candidate as the focal point of the campaign. Since then, the speech has focused more on the candidate's vision for the country than on specific planks in the party platform. Just as Roosevelt's 1932 acceptance speech was the source of the phrase, "New Deal," so Kennedy's in 1960 was the origin of the "New Frontier."

Sometimes the acceptance speech has infused a divided and dispirited party with hope. This was the theme of Harry Truman's acceptance speech in 1948, Hubert Humphrey's in 1968, and George McGovern's in 1972. (On the other hand, sometimes it is a means to stake out one's position even at the cost of polarizing the party, as Barry Goldwater did in 1964.) In recent years, as conventions have become ritual occasions to ratify choices of candidates that effectively had been made months before, the acceptance speech—usually preceded by a film—has become the candidate's means of self-introduction to the broader national audience who had not focused much on the campaign.

Inaugural addresses, State of the Union messages, and acceptance speeches are all examples of conventional rhetorical occasions that presidents can transform. My second category is different. Here I want to focus not on prescribed or evolving *occasions* but on the use of rhetorical invention to enhance presidential leadership. At key moments, presidents either explicitly or through practice have claimed significant new powers that are rhetorical in nature; as a result, they have helped to bridge the gap between public expectations and political necessity, on the one hand, and the limited grant of constitutional authority, on the other.

Perhaps the clearest example is the theory of the presidential mandate, for it most sharply draws the distinction between managing the government and leading the country. A presidential election is often seen not just as the choice of one chief executive over another but also as the impetus to particular policy outcomes. Such a view was anathema to the founders, who distrusted popular judgment on policy matters. The word *mandate*, in fact, traditionally referred to orders such as royal decrees that would be given by a superior to a subordinate.[19] The notion that elections were mandates began during the administration of Andrew Jackson, a president who deserves far more attention from scholars seeking to understand rhetorical leadership.

Jackson believed that, by virtue of his election by the whole people (rather than local or state constituencies), he embodied the popular will. This fact, in turn, was a warrant for the actions he proposed. He knew he was right because the people had elected him and because his correspondents told him that the people supported him. That he had been elected was a reason for Congress to do his bidding—and this was the new rhetorical element. There was little danger of error because, if he guessed wrong, the people could remove him at the next election.

Jackson did not act immediately upon these beliefs, and when he did it was in response to the initiative of his political opponents. He had opposed the Bank of the United States but had done nothing to harm it during his first three years in office. In his 1831 Annual Message, he made a neutral statement suggesting to some that he might be altering his position and to others that he was waffling. His secretary of the treasury favored the Bank. Hoping to capitalize on discord within the administration and to raise an issue that would embarrass Jackson in the coming election, opponent Henry Clay introduced a bill to renew the Bank's charter—four years before it was scheduled to expire. If Congress passed the bill, it would place Jackson in a compromising position. No president had exercised a veto on anything but constitutional grounds, and the Supreme Court in *McCulloch v. Maryland* had held the Bank to be constitutional.[20]

Jackson not only vetoed the legislation, he also issued a veto message unlike any that had been seen before. Politically besieged, he responded to the situation by finding new means of presidential power in a rhetorical act.[21] Three features of the veto message stand out. First, Jackson argued that the Bank was unconstitutional, notwithstanding the Supreme Court decision. He thereby claimed a role for the executive branch in determining constitutionality. The Court might declare an act unconstitutional, but if they ruled that it was constitutional, the president was not obliged to agree. Second, Jackson did not confine himself to constitutional objections as his predecessors had done. He also argued that, for a host of reasons, the bill was bad policy. Without justifying his decision to do so, by his performance he enacted presidential prerogative to veto legislation on substantive grounds. Third, he appealed to the people to sustain his decision at the next election. Toward the end of the message, he denounced the Bank as a tool of the rich and powerful, who were "not content with equal protection and equal benefits," and he indicated that he would be "grateful and happy" if the people supported his decision by their votes in the coming election.[22]

Upon his reelection, Jackson was slow to characterize the results as a referendum against the Bank, probably because at the same time he was dealing with South Carolina's threat to nullify the tariff of 1832. Nevertheless, he resolved to act. He would not wait until the Bank's charter expired in 1836; he would withdraw the government's deposits at once. He claimed that his action was justified by the Bank's continuing effort to obtain a recharter in opposition to the will of the people. In his statement announcing removal, Jackson cited the 1832 election results as his mandate for doing so. Referring to himself in the third person, he said, "Whatever may be the opinions of others, the president considers his reelection as a decision of the people against the bank. . . . He was sustained by a just people, and he desires to evince his gratitude by carrying into effect their decision so far as it depends upon him."[23] This was the first time that a president invoked the outcome of an election as his reason for a course of action.[24]

In this message, Jackson was responding to a specific political and rhetorical problem. His solution, anticipating the writing of E. E. Schattschneider, was to enlarge the scope of conflict by bringing additional resources—in this case, the appeal to popular will—into the fray.[25] There is no evidence that he considered how he was altering political theory and rhetorical situations for the long term, but he was doing nothing less than redefining the concept of virtue. Formerly associated with disinterested Republicans who focused only on the public good, it now became linked to the politician who mirrored the will of the people.[26] As this nineteenth-century definition took hold, discerning the people's will became increasingly important, and the early forms of straw polling were not far in the future.[27]

When Congress reconvened after the removal statement, the National Republicans were livid. Clay excoriated Jackson for finding a "new source of executive power" not in the Constitution and the laws but "in the result of a presidential election."[28] Others charged him with usurpation of power, and the Senate formally censured him—the only time in history that this action has been taken against a president.[29] But Jackson remained firm, and in the process established for subsequent presidents the claim that their actions are called for by the will of the people.

It is a claim Jackson's successors have made often. John Tyler and James K. Polk both regarded the 1844 election results as a mandate for the annexation of Texas. Abraham Lincoln saw the 1864 election results as a mandate for ratification of the Thirteenth Amendment. For Grover Cleveland, the 1892 election was a mandate for tariff reform; for William McKinley, the election of 1896 was a mandate for reinstituting high tariffs.[30] In this century, the 1920 election was a mandate to stay out of the League of Nations; the 1932 election was a call for government activism in the face of the Great Depression; the results in 1964 were seen as a mandate for Medicare, and those in 1980 as a mandate for deep cuts in personal income taxes. In some years, congressional election results have likewise been seen as a mandate for action. Even poll results today are sometimes taken as a mandate.

Of course, some popular understandings of mandates have been mistaken. The election of 1860 was not a mandate for Civil War; the election of 1916 was not a mandate to stay out of World War I at all costs; and the election of 1992 was not, as many had thought, a mandate for comprehensive health-care reform. Moreover, in the pursuit of public approval for the sake of a mandate, presidents are tempted to oversimplify complex issues and to make promises they cannot keep.[31] But Jackson's successors have not repudiated his innovation; they continue to find in the claim of a popular mandate the rhetorical means to enhance their power and their ability to lead.

In addition to the claim of a mandate, presidents have used the strategy of "going public" to enhance their leadership position. Going public means appealing directly to the people for support, bypassing their representatives. It is often thought to be a recent innovation, associated with the declining influence of political parties and the growing prominence of communication technology. In his book on this strategy, for example, Samuel Kernell associates it particularly with Presidents Carter and Reagan.[32] In fact, although the tactics have changed, the strategy of "going public" is very old. It can be traced back to George Washington's first term. Alexander Hamilton and other prominent Federalists launched a newspaper, the *Federal Gazette of the United States*, in order to have a reliable political organ. Alarmed by its success, Thomas Jefferson and his allies soon established the rival *National Gazette*. The former received the printing business from the Treasury Department; the latter, for the State Department.[33] The two papers presented the public face of the conflict between Hamilton and Jefferson over the Washington administration's policies. Constrained by the conventions of the time from speaking publicly to promote their interests, political leaders quickly developed the sponsored newspaper as a surrogate.

The two original papers died during the 1790s, but Jefferson quickly established a new one, the *National Intelligencer*, during the 1800 presidential campaign. While in office, he used this paper to present the administration's position on issues to the public, although he tried to conceal his relationship with the paper and to respect it as an impartial source. Madison and Monroe continued the relationship with the *Intelligencer*, albeit in a less intimate way.

The heyday of the partisan newspaper came during the Jacksonian era. The number of post offices grew rapidly, as did the number of eligible voters, and the newspapers were heavily subsidized so that the price to the reader was modest. Jackson's administration paper was the *Washington Globe*, which began publication in 1830. In league with the editor, Amos Kendall, Jackson used the *Globe* to communicate with the public during the Bank war, explaining his decision to withdraw the deposits. Later, James K. Polk used coverage in the Washington *Union* to mobilize support for his foreign policies, chiefly his action during the Mexican War.[34]

By the 1850s, the partisan newspaper was in decline because of the development of large independent papers such as James Gordon Bennett's *New York Herald* and Horace Greeley's *New York Tribune*.

Accordingly, presidents gave less attention to direct management of opinion through party papers and instead tried to curry favor with the independent editors. Lincoln typified this approach, which predominated at the end of nineteenth century. The logical next step, pioneered by Theodore Roosevelt, was presidential speaking to mobilize the public over the heads of both newspapers and parties. Roosevelt began the practice of making presidential statements about matters of public policy.[35] But he and Woodrow Wilson—to say nothing of Carter and Reagan—did not invent the idea of "going public." It was a rhetorical instrument to enhance presidential leadership from the beginning.

"Going public" is not without its risks, as Daniel Stid noted in his study on Wilson.[36] In order to enlist public support, presidents may define routine problems as crises and promise more than they can deliver to solve them. Referring to the public appeals of Presidents Kennedy and Johnson, John Kenneth Galbraith called this rhetorical style "Dawnism": promising that one's proposed course of action will herald the dawn of a new day.[37] The danger in such inflated rhetoric, of course, is not only that it may court failure and sow disappointment when actual results do not match the level of the idealized visions, but also that it may desensitize the people so they will fail to recognize a true crisis when (or before) it arrives. It also fosters a view of presidential omnipotence that can lead to hubris. Alternatively, it can make the president appear unpresidential, no longer above the fray when he descends to do battle with his adversaries in the public forum. Finally, the knowledge that the president is crafting his appeals to match public opinion leads one to question the sincerity of his policy commitments. When every line of a policy speech is known to have been tested against public opinion, the sincerity of presidential commitments is open to doubt. Nevertheless, from the beginning presidents have seen appeals to the public as one way to broaden the context of a message and to claim greater power by means of rhetorical behavior.

In addition to claiming mandates and "going public," presidents have sought to enhance their leadership through a rhetorical approach to foreign policy. The belief that there is power in American words is also of long standing. It derives from the inherent ambiguity in the Puritans' conception of Americans as the chosen people. That premise could lead to active involvement in the affairs of other nations in order metaphorically to spread God's word. But it also could lead to withdrawal from the world on the theory that, since we were the chosen, we had no business sullying ourselves with the politics of lesser nations. The beauty of a rhetorical foreign policy is that it compromises this question. It permits active involvement on the rhetorical plane while avoiding the large commitments of men and money that military or diplomatic intervention would require. What held things together was the unstated belief that, because of our moral force, others would attend to our proclamations and do what we wanted.

This premise was developed early. Certainly one of its most successful applications was the promulgation of the Monroe Doctrine in 1823. This act was precipitated by false but credible fears of British or Russian colonization of the Oregon Territory and Spanish reconquest of Latin America. Invited to join the British in a joint declaration, Monroe chose instead to put forward a unilateral declaration during his 1823 Annual Message. He warned the nations of the Old World to keep clear of the Western Hemisphere: "we should consider any attempt on their part to extend their system to any portion of this hemisphere as dangerous to our peace and safety."[38] Other countries, presumably influenced by the force of our argument and the superior morality of our position, would take heed.

The nations to whom the Monroe Doctrine was directed greeted it with ridicule and contempt. The Russian government responded that "the document in question enunciates views and pretensions so exaggerated, it establishes principles so contrary to the rights of the European powers that it merits only the most profound contempt."[39] British conservatives called it "blustering," "arrogant," and "monstrous," and Metternich said it was "indecent."[40] The French and Latin Americans generally supported it, but they were not the sources of potential threat.

Nor did the major European powers scrupulously adhere to the doctrine. Britain established colonies in the Falkland Islands, Honduras, and Guiana without reprisal. But neither Russia nor Britain tried to recolonize Oregon, nor did Spain seek to retake Latin America. They may not have planned to anyway, but Americans attributed the facts to the Monroe Doctrine. Blessed with moral superiority, established as the "beacon on the western shore," we have the mission of persuading others by precept and example. And, because of our unique position, other nations will listen to us. By proclaiming what we wish to achieve, we have the power to make it so.

The apparent success of the Monroe Doctrine, enhancing presidential leadership through rhetorical proclamation, had two long-term consequences. First, it became a rhetorical touchstone to which later presidents appealed. James K. Polk, while professing adherence to Monroe's intent, transformed the doctrine from a defensive to an active program by appealing to popular fears of potential European influence in order to gain public support for the Mexican War.[41] Grover Cleveland's secretary of state, Richard Olney, maintained in 1895 that the Monroe Doctrine entitled the United States to dominate the Western Hemisphere.[42] The Roosevelt Corollary of 1904 used the doctrine to justify preemptive intervention by the United States.[43] In 1940, Franklin Roosevelt appealed to the Monroe Doctrine as the basis for his insistence that the United States would not condone the transfer of French or Dutch colonies in the Western Hemisphere to the Axis powers. John F. Kennedy referred to the doctrine as one of the reasons that the placement of Soviet missiles in Cuba in 1962 must not be allowed to stand. Ronald Reagan cited it as justification for the American invasion of Grenada in 1983. It is not too bold a claim to state that Monroe's doctrine was used in contexts that the fifth president never would have contemplated.

The second effect of the doctrine's ascendancy was to encourage the belief that American words had special power in foreign affairs. The Open Door notes of William McKinley's secretary of state, John Hay, established the principles of access to Chinese markets and the integrity of Chinese territory. Successful American relations with China for the next fifty years were attributed by many Americans not to geopolitical considerations but to the rhetorical force of the Open Door notes. Yet anyone who held that view would have been hard-pressed to explain the Communist takeover of China in 1949 other than by reference to American sabotage or treason, since earlier events supposedly had established the power of our word.

For that matter, much of the Cold War was conducted as a rhetorical war, on the assumption that American vigilance and "posturing" could induce the Soviets to back down.[44] To cite but one example, Senate Republicans during the Eisenhower administration supported the "captive nations resolution" to signal people behind the Iron Curtain that we expected them to be free. This would embolden them during their "long, twilight struggle" to throw off their yoke at an appropriate time. When events went well, we attributed the results to our vigilant rhetoric; when they went against us, we concluded that we had not been vigilant enough. In this case, a rhetorically grounded foreign policy became a self-sealing argument that shielded us from analysis and critique. It took the Vietnam War to call into question the assumptions of Cold War rhetoric.

The final case of innovative rhetorical leadership I wish to examine is the rhetorical reconstruction of history in order to contextualize present issues in a historical trajectory. The working assumption is that the past does not speak; it must be spoken for. If, as Hargrove suggests, the president's job is to teach reality through rhetoric,[45] then the president emerges as the chief national definer of situations. This significant activity, like the other rhetorical moves described here, can be found in the work of the early presidents.

Once again the case of Andrew Jackson is instructive. During the nullification crisis, he stipulated that the union of the states was perpetual. Since the Constitution did not speak to the possible dissolution of the Union, Jackson's stipulation of what the document meant made it possible for him to denounce nullification as a violation of the sacred text.

The nullification crisis ended in a way that did not unequivocally confirm Jackson's view. South Carolina rescinded its nullification ordinance, which rendered the Force Bill moot. The Palmetto State then nullified the Force Bill. Since the Force Bill was a dead-letter law, the action went unchallenged; it had no immediate practical consequences. But the nullifiers believed it validated their theory. The same arguments therefore could be resurrected to justify secession in 1860.

Abraham Lincoln followed a line of reasoning similar to Jackson's, and he attributed to the founders a belief in the perpetuity of the Union. The Union was older than the Constitution, he insisted, so the states in ratifying the Constitution did not create it, they only made it more perfect. Since the states had not created the Union, they could not dissolve it either. Lincoln also attributed to the founders a decidedly antislavery conviction. The historical record was ambiguous, and Lincoln's opponents, such as Stephen Douglas, read it very differently. But as Lincoln repeatedly told the story, the founders did not establish slavery in America. Rather, they saw it already among them. They did not like it, but they could not figure out what to do about it. They resolved to contain it by proscribing it from new territories, as is epitomized by the Northwest Ordinance. They also carefully avoided using the word *slavery* in the Constitution, so that the great document would be un-blemished on that future day when the "peculiar institution" had disap-peared.

This exercise in historical reconstruction, which characterized Lincoln's speeches beginning in 1854 and culminated in the Gettysburg Address, portrayed the founding in a very different light from that offered by William Lloyd Garrison, who had burned the Constitution on the grounds that it was a proslavery document. In Lincoln's view, the founders were antislavery men—a fact everyone understood until Stephen Douglas muddied the waters with his deceptive doctrine of popular sovereignty—and the task of the Civil War was to reclaim the original vision.

Just as Lincoln appropriated the history of the founding for his pur-poses, later generations have appropriated his memory for theirs.[46] Woodrow Wilson, for example, saw the Civil War as the triumph of nationalism and Lincoln as the master of "interpretive leadership" who had explained that transition to the American people; Wilson wanted to follow in the same path.[47] Franklin Roosevelt made repeated refer-ences to Lincoln, disassociating him from the contemporary Republi-can Party and suggesting that, were he alive, he would support the nationalism of the New Deal. Roosevelt, while failing to dismantle southern segregation, also associated himself with what he took to be Lincoln's advanced views on race, and thereby promoted the shift in the political allegiance of African Americans from Republican to Demo-crat that continues to this day. Much as Ronald Reagan would say about American workers in a different context, Roosevelt convinced African Americans that they were not deserting the party of Lincoln; the party had deserted them.

Roosevelt also appropriated the ideals of Thomas Jefferson. The Jeffersonian liberalism of the nineteenth century emphasized individual autonomy and limited government as the best protection for the people. Beginning with his Commonwealth Club speech during the 1932 cam-paign and then throughout his presidency, Roosevelt reformulated this view. He followed a line of argument that had been introduced by Herbert Croly during the Progressive Era.[48] In an age dominated by big business, the people needed big government as a counterweight. Rather than being the enemy of the people, government was their pro-tector. As has often been said, FDR adapted Hamiltonian means to Jeffersonian ends.[49] Aside from the political feat of portraying himself as a descendant of *both* Lincoln and Jefferson, Roosevelt also was able to portray the New Deal as conservative rather than radical. As Sidney Milkis explains, his "use of the term 'liberalism' gave legitimacy to progressive principles by embedding them in the language of constitutionalism and interpreting them as an expansion rather than a subversion of the natural rights tradition."[50]

Just as Roosevelt sought to appropriate Lincoln, so Ronald Reagan among others sought to appropriate Roosevelt. Roosevelt was not a deep thinker and not all of his statements were consistent. Reagan emphasized the 1932 campaign pledges of limited government and a balanced budget, and reminded his listeners of Roosevelt's opposition to the dole. He endorsed many of the limited reforms of the early New Deal, reminded his audiences that his first political allegiance was to the Democrats, and insisted that he had not deserted the party; the party had deserted him. In office, he and his successor so demonized the post–New Deal conception of liberalism—from which they excluded Roosevelt—that erstwhile liberals took to calling themselves progressives instead.

Reagan's invocation of Roosevelt angered Democrats. In his 1980 convention address, Sen. Edward Kennedy (D-Massachusetts) thundered that the Republican candidate had "no right" to quote him. But the whole point of this analysis is to stress that no one has a monopoly on public memory. It is a resource that inventive rhetors can use not to engage in antiquarian controversy but rather to frame the context in which audiences see themselves and their own time. It has been a means of rhetorical leadership by which presidents can enhance their own power, stature, and effectiveness.

To recapitulate, then, I have suggested that presidents exercise rhetorical leadership either by transforming existing rhetorical conventions or by inventing new rhetorical resources, to make up for the fact that the formal powers they are granted are insufficient for the challenges they must face. The new or changed resources alter the balance and outlast the immediate situation, enhancing the position of subsequent presidents.

The reader may have noticed that I have focused particularly on presidents we traditionally regard as activists, such as Jefferson, Jackson, Lincoln, and Franklin Roosevelt. (Reagan is something of an anomaly.) These are the presidents Skowronek identifies with the task of political reconstruction—repudiating an old order, establishing a new one, and celebrating the principle of order itself.[51] This is perhaps the situation in which the potential for rhetorical leadership is greatest. The presidents who followed them—such as James Madison, Martin Van Buren, Ulysses S. Grant, Harry S. Truman, and George Bush—typically were eclipsed by the rhetorical leadership of their predecessors. Those who carry a political regime to its logical conclusion—including such presidents as James Monroe, James K. Polk, and Lyndon B. Johnson—despite their other strengths, usually do not build appreciably on the record of *rhetorical* leadership of those whose legacy they strive to complete. (Theodore Roosevelt is an exception.) Finally, those who come at the end of an era, whom Skowronek identifies with the problem of disjunction—presidents such as John Quincy Adams, Franklin Pierce, James Buchanan, Herbert Hoover, and Jimmy Carter—usually fare worst of all. Unable to navigate quickly changing currents, they tend to constrict the public sphere and to reduce great issues to technical problem solving.

There is something to this observation. All presidents must play the hand they are dealt, and not all situations lend themselves equally to rhetorical leadership as I have described it here. But, as Richard Vatz has reminded us with respect to the rhetorical situation, no situation is completely determined. Any rhetor faces a mix of opportunities and constraints, and the rhetors' choices do much to shape the very situations to which they supposedly respond.[52]

To consider two recent examples, neither Jimmy Carter nor George Bush was predetermined to hold the rhetorical position he did. Carter's "trouncing" by Reagan in 1980 is a retrospective judgment. The election was close. Carter was leading going into the final weeks, but his disappointing debate performance turned the tide against him, and the election was seen at the time as a rejection of Carter and his personal style rather than a shift in regime. And George Bush was not predestined to remain in Ronald Reagan's shadow. It was Bush, after all, who presided over the end of the Cold War and the military success in the Persian Gulf. It was he, not Reagan, who enjoyed a 91 percent approval rating, the highest ever. In my judgment, Bush's rhetorical failings are of his own making: the artless way in which he abandoned the "no new taxes" pledge, his failure to see that the end of the Cold War changed the whole political landscape and to exploit his popularity in 1991 to rally support for a compelling domestic agenda, and allowing himself to be trapped in dilemmas that led him to denounce the 1990 Civil Rights Act as a quota bill and to claim disingenuously that race played no part in his nomination of Clarence Thomas to the Supreme Court.

I mention these examples to emphasize a point made much earlier. Rhetorical leadership is not predetermined. It comes about through the exercise of prudence, the practical art of balancing and accommodating competing interests to maximize opportunities and minimize constraints. If the task sometimes seems difficult in the face of a fragmented public, weakened political parties, difficult issues, an accelerating news cycle, and the other characteristics of modern politics, it is worth reexamining earlier presidencies—not only to appreciate them more and to see from whence we came, but to realize striking similarities and recurrent patterns of rhetorical invention.

At least in one respect, however, things have changed dramatically. So much of the expansion of presidential power over the past two hundred years has been the result of rhetorical leadership that we can never go back to the day when the statement, "Mr. President, you are not leading this Nation—you're just managing the Government," would be a positive statement rather than a harsh criticism.

NOTES

1. *Public Papers of the Presidents: Jimmy Carter, 1979*, vol. 2 (Washington, D.C.: GPO, 1980), 1235–36.

2. Richard E. Neustadt, *Presidential Power: The Politics of Leadership, with Reflections on Johnson and Nixon* (New York: Wiley, 1976), 100.

3. James MacGregor Burns, *Presidential Government: The Crucible of Leadership* (Boston: Houghton Mifflin, 1973), 194.

4. Bruce Miroff, "The Presidency and the Public: Leadership as Spectacle," in *The Presidency and the Political System*, 4th ed., ed. Michael Nelson, (Washington, D.C.: Congressional Quarterly Press, 1995), 274.

5. Stephen Skowronek, *The Politics Presidents Make* (Cambridge, Mass.: Harvard University Press, 1993), 20.

6. Ibid.

7. Erwin C. Hargrove, *The President as Leader: Appealing to the Better Angels of Our Nature* (Lawrence: University Press of Kansas, 1998), vii, 25, 38.

8. Ibid., 7.

9. William E. Gienapp, "Abraham Lincoln and Presidential Leadership," in *"We Cannot Escape History": Lincoln and the Last Best Hope of Earth*, ed. James M. McPherson (Urbana: University of Illinois Press, 1995), 77.

10. Timothy E. Cook, *Governing with the News: The News Media as a Political Institution* (Chicago: University of Chicago Press, 1997), 119.

11. Ibid., 130.

12. Jeffrey K. Tulis, *The Rhetorical Presidency* (Princeton, N.J.: Princeton University Press, 1987).

13. Richard J. Ellis, ed., *Speaking to the People: The Rhetorical Presidency in Historical Perspective* (Amherst: University of Massachusetts Press, 1998), 2. See also Stephen Skowronek, "Notes on the Presidency in the Political Order," *Studies in American Political Development* 1 (1986): 287.

14. For a discussion of the generic elements of the inaugural address, see Karlyn Kohrs Campbell and Kathleen Hall Jamieson, *Deeds Done in Words: Presidential Rhetoric and the Genres of Governance* (Chicago: University of Chicago Press, 1990), 14–36.

15. Thomas Jefferson, "First Inaugural Address," in *American Voices: Significant Speeches in American History, 1630–1945*, ed. James Andrews and David Zarefsky (New York: Longman, 1989), 116.

16. James Bennet, "The Speech, the Trial, and the State of the Politics," *New York Times*, Jan. 10, 1999, sec. 4, 1.

17. Richard J. Ellis, "Accepting the Nomination: From Martin Van Buren to Franklin Delano Roosevelt," in *Speaking to the People: The Rhetorical Presidency in Historical Perspective*, ed. Richard J. Ellis (Amherst: University of Massachusetts Press, 1998), 115.

18. Ibid., 118, 121.

19. Richard J. Ellis and Stephen Kirk, "Jefferson, Jackson, and the Origins of the Presidential Mandate," in *Speaking to the People*, ed. Ellis, 36.

20. Robert V. Remini, *Andrew Jackson and the Course of American Freedom, 1822–1832* (New York: Harper and Row, 1981), 342, 366.

21. Skowronek, *Politics Presidents Make*, 133.

22. James D. Richardson, ed., *A Compilation of Messages and Papers of the Presidents, 1789–1897*, 10 vols. (Washington, D.C.: GPO, 1897), 2:590–91.

23. Ibid., vol. 3, 7.

24. Ellis, "Jefferson, Jackson, and the Origins," 56.

25. E. E. Schattschneider, *The Semisovereign People* (New York: Holt, Rinehart, and Winston, 1960), 16.

26. Perry M. Goldman, "Political Virtue in the Age of Jackson," *Political Science Quarterly* 87 (Mar., 1972): 46.

27. For a study of the early forms of polling, see Susan Herbst, *Numbered Voices* (Chicago: University of Chicago Press, 1993).

28. Ellis, "Jefferson, Jackson, and the Origins," 58.

29. This was written while the Clinton impeachment trial was still in progress, but censure already appeared an unlikely option. The Jackson censure was repealed later, after the Senate was in Democratic hands. This experience led some senators during the Clinton trial to fear that any censure of President Clinton likewise would be repealed by a future Congress.

30. Ellis, "Jefferson, Jackson, and the Origins," 56.

31. For a critique of the theory of the mandate, see Robert A. Dahl, "The Myth of

the Presidential Mandate," *Political Science Quarterly* 105 (autumn, 1990): 355–72.

32. Samuel Kernell, *Going Public: New Strategies of Presidential Leadership* (Washington, D.C.: Congressional Quarterly Press, 1986).

33. Mel Laracey, "The Presidential Newspaper: The Forgotten Way of Going Public," in *Speaking to the People*, ed. Ellis, 67, 79.

34. Ibid., 72, 78.

35. Gerald Gamm and Renee M. Smith, "Presidents, Parties, and the Public: Evolving Patterns of Interaction, 1877–1929," in *Speaking to the People*, ed. Ellis, 92.

36. Daniel Stid, "Rhetorical Leadership and 'Common Counsel' in the Presidency of Woodrow Wilson," in *Speaking to the People*, ed. Ellis, 162.

37. John Kenneth Galbraith, *Who Needs the Democrats?* (New York: Signet Books, 1970).

38. Richardson, *Messages and Papers*, 2:218.

39. Dexter Perkins, *A History of the Monroe Doctrine* (Boston: Little, Brown, 1963), 57.

40. James MacGregor Burns, *The Vineyard of Liberty* (New York: Knopf, 1982), 251.

41. Frederick Merk, *The Monroe Doctrine and American Expansionism, 1843–1849* (New York: Knopf, 1966), 277.

42. "Richard Olney's Claims to American Suzerainty over the Western Hemisphere, July 1895," in *Ideas and Diplomacy: Readings in the Intellectual Tradition of American Foreign Policy*, ed. Norman A. Graebner (New York: Oxford University Press, 1964), 251–55.

43. Richard W. Leopold, *The Growth of American Foreign Policy: A History* (New York: Knopf, 1962), 205–206.

44. On the Messianic nature of Cold War rhetoric, see, for example, Eric Foner, *The Story of American Freedom* (New York: Knopf, 1998), 254.

45. Hargrove, *President as Leader*, vii.

46. For a comprehensive treatment of uses of the memory of Abraham Lincoln, see Merrill D. Peterson, *Lincoln in American Memory* (New York: Oxford University Press, 1994).

47. Terri Bimes and Stephen Skowronek, "Woodrow Wilson's Critique of Popular Leadership: Reassessing the Modern-Traditional Divide in Presidential History," in *Speaking to the People*, ed. Ellis, 155.

48. Foner, *Story of American Freedom*, 161.

49. On Roosevelt's redefinition of "liberal," see Sidney M. Milkis, "Franklin D. Roosevelt, Progressivism, and the Limits of Popular Leadership," in *Speaking to the People*, ed. Ellis, 189; Alan Brinkley, *Liberalism and Its Discontents* (Cambridge, Mass.: Harvard University Press, 1998), 1-62, passim; Foner, *Story of American Freedom*, 204.

50. Milkis, "Franklin D. Roosevelt," 191.

51. Skowronek, *Politics Presidents Make*, 20.

52. See Richard Vatz, "The Myth of the Rhetorical Situation," *Philosophy & Rhetoric* 6 (summer, 1973): 154–61.

CHAPTER 2

George Washington and the Rhetoric of Presidential Leadership

Stephen E. Lucas

T HE FINAL YEAR of the twentieth century marked the bicentennial of the death of George Washington. He died on December 14, 1799, laid low by a streptococcal throat infection and the repeated bloodlettings that were a routine element of eighteenth-century medical science. His passing touched off a spectacle of national grief in which, as Benjamin Rush observed, "the whole United States mourned for him as a father."[1] Today we still refer to Washington as the father of his country, but we do not feel a strong sense of kinship with him. Although we cannot escape his visage, which peers at us from the one-dollar bill and the pages of every American history textbook, as well as from countless pop-art representations and Presidents' Day advertisements, virtually all of those likenesses are based on the stiff, formal portraits by Gilbert Stuart that strip Washington of the all-too-human traits we associate with the likes of his contemporaries such as Benjamin Franklin and Thomas Jefferson. The same is true of the moralistic biographies that, from Parson Weems forward, have shaped Washington's popular image as a paragon of moral virtue. Who in a postmodern age can easily relate to anyone—even a president of the United States—who is reputed to have said, "I cannot tell a lie"? Even the Washington Monument, which dominates the skyline of our nation's capital and ranks with the Statue of Liberty, the Eiffel Tower, and the Empire State Building as the most recognizable structures of modern Western architecture, is stunningly stark and inhuman, with nary a visible nook or cranny, twist or turn, to mar its sleek facade, an edificial metonymy of the flawless nature of Washington's personal and civic character.

In his presidency as well Washington seems, at first glance, to be remote in ways other than those marked merely by the passage of time. None of the major issues facing his administration—getting the new nation off to a smooth start, establishing its credibility in the community of nations, solidifying the union created by the federal Constitution—have even vestigial resonance today. Once venerated as the greatest of American presidents, Washington has not only been replaced in that exalted ranking by Abraham Lincoln but is also locked in competition with Franklin Roosevelt for second place.[2] Even Washington's maxims of neutrality and autonomy in foreign affairs, which provided first principles for generations of American statesmen, seem more than a trace anachronistic in an age of global interdependency that requires a far different political science from that which dominated Enlightenment thought.

Nor was Washington a rhetorical president in the same manner as chief executives from Woodrow Wilson onward. Typically circumspect in his public statements and exceedingly respectful of the prerogatives of the House and Senate, he did not campaign for legislation or appeal over the heads of Congress directly to the people as do modern presidents. Neither did he hold press conferences or take to the hustings in behalf of specific policy initiatives, domestic or foreign. All of this was consistent with Washington's adherence to what he saw as the constitutional restrictions on his office, as well as with his limitations as an orator. "Vastly more a listener than a speaker," even in private company, he possessed, in Jefferson's estimation, "neither copiousness of

ideas, nor fluency of words."[3] Lacking the spellbinding delivery of oratorical luminaries such as Patrick Henry, Richard Henry Lee, and Fisher
Ames, he was "a tolerable Speaker" whose "elocution had no glaring
fault, and no high excellence."[4]

Yet, as Washington understood, the presidency is inherently a rhetorical institution in which effective leadership depends not just upon
the constitutional exercise of the duties of office but also upon the persuasive powers of the president vis-à-vis Congress, the people, foreign
nations, the press, and even the remainder of the executive branch.
As Jeffrey Tulis explains: "All presidents exercise their office through
the medium of language, written and spoken. Even brute power is expressed in words, through orders, through commands."[5] Although we
do not customarily think of Washington as a man of words, he was
remarkably well prepared to fulfill the rhetorical, as well as political,
duties of the office he assumed on April 30, 1789. After serving as an
officer in the Virginia militia, he became actively involved in the politics of the colony's tidewater gentry, won election to the House of Bur-
gesses at the age of twenty-seven, sat on a number of important com-
mittees in that august assembly, and came, by 1775, to be one of the
most respected figures in the Old Dominion. In all these enterprises he
was acutely aware of his public persona, and he took care to write and
speak so as to create a favorable view of his motives, character, and
achievements. Although he never attained—or aspired to—literary
distinction, he did become a clear, forceful, economical stylist. A shrewd
observer of people and events, he had a sharp eye for detail, and he
was capable of producing richly textured narrative and descriptive
prose. He also learned early the importance of precision in discourse.
As a young commander in the Virginia militia, he was deeply embar-
rassed by putting his signature to a public document that characterized as an "assassination" the death of a French emissary at the hands
of Washington's troops in a frontier skirmish. Washington blamed his
translator—an explanation that was better accepted in America than
in Europe—but he never forgot the lesson that carelessness in language
can have grave consequences.

Above all, however, it was Washington's eight years leading the Continental Army during the Revolutionary War that prepared him for
the challenges he would face as president. Deeply respectful of the
Anglo-American tradition of civil control of the military, he was remarkably adept at adjusting the needs of his troops to the wiles and

wishes of the Continental Congress. He also knew, as one of his biographers has noted, that the most crucial battles of the war were those fought in the arena of public opinion.[6] Like most successful military leaders in a republican society, he needed as much rhetorical acumen as martial skill. As commander in chief, he faced the discursive tasks of persuading Congress and the states to provide adequate men and materiel, of recruiting new enlistments and convincing soldiers already in the army to reenlist, of communicating orders clearly and precisely, of maintaining discipline and morale, of keeping civilian authorities informed about military operations, of sustaining a positive attitude toward the army among the general population, and, after the entry of France in 1778, of carrying out a delicate diplomatic correspondence with America's first foreign ally. All told, Washington issued some nine thousand letters on military business during the war, many of them of considerable length. He even proposed at one stage that the Continental Congress provide him with a portable press and a printer so he could keep up with "the multiplicity of writing, and other business" that occupied so much of his time.[7]

Moreover, for a man who was always diffident about his abilities as a writer and speaker, Washington achieved a series of stunning rhetorical triumphs during his tenure as commander in chief, triumphs that dramatically increased his stature as a heroic figure and revealed his keen understanding of the nature of leadership in a republican society. His first act as commander in chief was not military, but rhetorical: the presentation of a speech to the Continental Congress accepting his appointment. This address, in which Washington renounced any pecuniary compensation beyond expenses, forged the first link in his reputation as a disinterested patriot who placed the good of his country above personal reward.[8] His most famous wartime speech was addressed to the potentially mutinous officers at Newburgh, New York, in March, 1783. Rejecting all overtures that he lead the army against civil authority, he "prevented this revolution," as Jefferson stated, "from being closed as most others have been by a subversion of that liberty it was intended to establish."[9] Three months later, in June, 1783, Washington issued the last of his circular letters as commander in chief to the governors of the thirteen states. Known at the time as Washington's Legacy, it was widely acclaimed in America, received "the universal applause of Europe," and remained his most celebrated public paper until issuance of his presidential Farewell Address.[10] Washington's last act as commander in chief, like his first, involved the presentation of a speech. On December 23, 1783, he appeared before the Continental Congress to resign his commission and to take leave of public life. Romanticized in John Trumbull's painting "The Resignation of General Washington," Washington's address, punctuated by the physical surrender of his commission, drew tears from members of the audience and secured his fame on both sides of the Atlantic as a modern Cincinnatus.[11]

I mention all of this partly because it reminds us that Washington entered the presidency with a rhetorical résumé matched by very few of his successors. I also stress his wartime rhetoric because it set the tone and, in more than a few instances, established models he would draw upon as he initiated the rhetorical forms and practices of the presidency. We cannot understand Washington's presidential discourse without seeing it as part of a rhetorical trajectory that extends from his speech accepting command of the Continental Army in 1775 through his Farewell Address twenty-one years later. Time and again we find in his addresses as president echoes of his Revolutionary War speeches and writings. Always cognizant of the fact that he walked "on untrodden ground" as the nation's first chief executive, he judiciously adapted traditional rhetorical forms and practices to the new occasions and exigencies faced by the world's first modern republican nation.[12] In the process, he not only met the rhetorical needs of the moment, but he created precedents for presidential discourse that endure to this day. Let me illustrate by looking in turn at his first inaugural address, his Farewell Address, his Annual Messages to Congress, and his three regional tours as president.[13]

FIRST INAUGURAL ADDRESS

Just as Washington had begun his tenure as commander in chief with an address to the Continental Congress, he launched his presidency with a speech to both houses of the newly created United States Congress. Unlike the Annual Message to Congress (known today as the State of the Union address), which is mandated by the Constitution, there is no requirement that the president deliver an inaugural address. Washington's decision to do so was dictated by his reading of the unsettled political situation in April, 1789. Two states—North Carolina and Rhode Island—had refused to ratify the Constitution, and some Antifederalists still hoped to call a second constitutional convention to rectify what they regarded as the calamitous handiwork of the first. Fully aware that many Americans shared the Antifederalists' reservations about the Constitution—especially since it lacked a bill of rights— Washington knew his inaugural address would be of pivotal importance in generating goodwill, trust, and confidence in the new government. He also felt the need to explain why he was reversing the decision he had announced six years earlier, upon resigning his commission, to retire from "the great theatre of Action" and take permanent leave "of all the employments of public life."[14]

In seeking to attain these objectives, Washington turned to a formula that had worked with spectacular success fourteen years earlier in his speech accepting command of the army. Part of that formula, which was also in keeping with the highly ritualized rhetorical conventions of taking office in the eighteenth century, was to downplay his desire and qualifications for office, to stress the "magnitude and difficulty of the trust" to which his country had called him, and to request forgiveness for any errors he might make as president. The other part of the formula was to inform Congress that he would not accept a salary and to request that his remuneration "be limited to such actual expenditures" as he might confront in office. In addition, Washington invoked for Americans the blessings of "that Almighty Being who rules the Universe," urged Congress to set aside all local views and partisan interests in conducting its deliberations, and offered a carefully worded endorsement of amending the Constitution so as to settle "the degree of inquietude" aroused by the absence of a bill of rights.[15]

Consistent with the protocols of the time, Washington's inaugural was delivered to the House and Senate behind closed doors. There is little doubt, however, that it was meant for public consumption, and it was quickly reprinted in newspapers throughout the continent. As one reads through the large volume of responses to the speech voiced in the press and in the letters and addresses sent to Washington from civic and religious groups, it is clear that his words were perfectly suited to the situation he faced in April, 1789. According to a Bostonian, the address contained "sentiments which warm every heart and animate every serious mind. . . . There is but one sentiment regarding it here— UNIVERSAL APPLAUSE."[16] A writer in Philadelphia exclaimed that the speech "deserves to be engraved in letters of gold. Antiquity has handed down nothing to us equal to it. . . . To be the enemy of the Federal Government *now*, is to be the enemy of the great and good General Washington."[17] To yet another writer, "the manly style, and truly democratical simplicity," of the speech brought to mind "the great Fabius addressing the people of Rome, after having saved his country." Praising Washington for "his disinterested refusal of all pecuniary emoluments—his mild, conciliating language—his strongly implied opinion in favour of such alterations as shall improve, and not injure the Constitution," this writer declared with satisfaction that the president remained "the same amiable, honest, and GREAT MAN, the same real and unaffected friend to the PEOPLE, he always has been. In being elevated to the first place in the Union, he does not forget that he is still a citizen."[18]

Washington's first inaugural was so successful in defusing opposition to the new government that today we have lost sight of just how tenuous matters were at the time he assumed office. As Robert Ferguson has noted, "Communal acceptance of the Constitution remains one of the mysteries of early republican life."[19] Yet that mystery is solved, at least in part, when we recognize how skillfully Washington's speech was composed to rally supporters of the Constitution, to assuage the concerns of doubters, and to instill a powerful sense of optimism about the future of the infant republic. It was, in fact, a perfect exemplar of what Ferguson calls the consensual literature of the Founders—a style of discourse designed to produce political cohesion and social stability by forging "artificial unities amidst a contentious, far-flung populace." Consistently seeking "to encompass difference within a consciously communal perspective," the most influential political works of the age "distort the nature of conflict to create order and clarity in the name of authorial calm. . . . Their language deliberately entertains several planes of implication at a time, and it is most successful when the same utterance performs many functions."[20]

In the case of Washington's first inaugural, the deep divisions that had separated Federalists from Antifederalists all but evaporate as he sanctifies the new government with the glory of the revolution and the benediction of heaven, while the contentious issue of a bill of rights is defused with two lengthy periodic sentences that constitute a classic model of strategic ambiguity. No matter how many times one parses these sentences, it is impossible to determine Washington's position on the issue absent clues provided by the historical context. Even the personal subject of Washington's ambivalence about returning to public life after his previous pledge of retirement is discussed in such a detached voice that, to modern readers, he comes across more as a dispassionate observer of his own "anxieties" and "dispondence" than as a man caught in a swirling "conflict of emotions."[21] Yet it was precisely this voice, whose effect was deepened by the speech's labyrinthine syntax, that had such great appeal for Washington's audience, for it helped assure his fellow citizens that, while he drank deeply at the cup of moral sentiment (as any virtuous eighteenth-century gentleman should), he remained fully sober and sensible, in control both of himself and his emotions. The entire first inaugural, in fact, is composed in a kind of code, one that was fully intelligible to Washington's contemporaries but whose nuances remain difficult for us to apprehend across the centuries. This is doubtless one reason why the first inaugural has not received its due from historians, rhetorical critics, or students of the presidency.[22] Yet, I would argue, it is a neglected masterpiece that deserves to be ranked with the first inaugurals of Jefferson, Lincoln, and Franklin Roosevelt for its rhetorical artistry and for its impact on the course of American history.[23]

Farewell Address

Unlike Washington's first inaugural, his Farewell Address has been anything but neglected. Released to the public through *Claypoole's American Daily Advertiser* of September 19, 1796, it was quickly reprinted by other American newspapers, appeared in several European journals, and elicited almost universal praise for its "sentiments of political wisdom, truth and justice."[24] Despite the fact that Washington had come under severe criticism from Democratic-Republicans during his second term, there were few public dissenters to the opinion that the maxims advanced in his Farewell Address ought to be "engraved on the hearts and minds of every American" and "gratefully . . . transmitted by them to posterity as their political creed."[25] For the next century and a half it was revered as a sacred statement of American political principles, and it continued to be read in Congress each February 22 until the 1970s. Although no longer regarded as oracular, it remains one of the most honored—and studied—of all American political discourses.

In his seminal work on the Farewell Address and the evolution of early American foreign policy, Felix Gilbert traces the rhetorical ancestry of Washington's valedictory to the European tradition of political testaments that set down in writing the principles of statecraft guiding the foreign policy of a given nation. Although some testaments were fabricated by "literary men" who purported to publish the last will of a well-known statesman, most were authentic works by "a leading minister or prince who tried to explain the principles which had guided his policy and which he wanted his successor to continue." According to Gilbert, the apogee of this genre was reached with the *Politischen Testamente* of Prussia's Frederick the Great, and there "was hardly an important ruler or statesman in the eighteenth century whose death was not followed by the publication of his Political Testament."[26]

Although Washington doubtless saw his Farewell Address as serving the same kind of function in the United States that political testaments served across the Atlantic, the model he had most clearly in mind was his 1783 Legacy to the governors of the states. Having concluded his military career to great acclaim by making public his thoughts on how best to preserve the independence won in the Revolutionary War, he seized the occasion of leaving the presidency to enunciate the principles that should guide Americans in their relations with each other and with the rest of the world. That the two papers were inextricably linked in Washington's thinking is evident from his statement in 1792, when he first aspired to retirement, that he was contemplating issuing a "Valadictory address" in which he would "take the liberty at my departure from civil, as I formerly did at my military exit, to invoke a continuation of the blessings of Providence" upon the United States and "all those who are the supporters of its interests."[27] Four years later, he referred to his 1783 Legacy in the Farewell Address itself, citing the American people's "endulgent reception of my sentiments on a former and not dissimilar occasion" as a precedent for issuing a comparable document now that he was leaving the presidency. Washington's advice in the address revolved around two broad themes— the necessity of maintaining political union and the importance of neutrality in foreign affairs. Although the second of these themes was unique to the Farewell Address, the former had received attention in 1783 as one of the four "Pillars on which the glorious Fabrick of our Independency and National Character must be supported." Not only did Washington emphasize the same idea in 1796, but he also did so by utilizing the same structural metaphor, referring to the union created by the Constitution as "a main Pillar in the Edifice" of American liberty, independence, and prosperity.[28]

Washington's audience instantly perceived the parallels between the two documents. Only one newspaper of Washington's time—the *Courier of New Hampshire*—headlined his presidential valedictory as his "Farewell Address."[29] Published sans title, with only the salutation "Friends and Fellow Citizens," it was initially seen as a counterpart of his 1783 Legacy. The Massachusetts legislature told Washington that it received his latest work "with the same sentiments of respect and emotions of gratitude which were inspired by that which terminated your military career."[30] Time and again the address was referred to in language that evoked Washington's earlier farewell. The Vermont legislature called it "a legacy so replete with wisdom and sound policy as . . . to be engraved on the hearts and minds of every American," while the citizens of Northumberland, Pennsylvania, thanked Washington for "the inestimable legacy you have left us in your late fraternal address to the People of the United States."[31] Utilizing the same idiom, other respondents characterized Washington's words as "the valuable legacy of good advice, which he has bequeathed on his departure from public life," as "an invaluable legacy to the people of these states," as "the richest Legacy of a Father to his children," as "a most invaluable Legacy from a *Friend*, a *Benefactor*, and a *Father*," and as "a choice Legacy of experience, wisdom and patriotism . . . transmitted as an inheritance to our children."[32]

Like his first inaugural, Washington's Farewell Address was a bold act of presidential leadership. Eager to leave the burdens of office and escape to retirement at his beloved Mount Vernon, he was, at the same time, deeply concerned about the young nation's ability to put aside its divisive quarrels regarding European politics and to maintain the federal union created by the Constitution. Fully aware of his iconic standing as the most admired civic figure in the Western world, he used the moral authority he had acquired through a public life of more than four decades to delineate the political principles he believed essential if the United States were to "progress without interruption, to that degree of strength and consistency, which is necessary to give it, humanly speaking, the command of its own fortunes."[33] He had devoted the major part of his adult life to the cause of American liberty, and he had done all he could during his presidency to guide the nation through the rocks and shoals that threatened the initial leg of its voyage as an independent republic. Now that he was leaving office, he turned, as he had many times before at critical moments during his political and military careers, to the power of words as an indispensable instrument of republican leadership.

We know, of course, that the words of the Farewell Address were indited primarily by Alexander Hamilton. In fact, almost all of Washington's public papers, during the Revolution as well as his presidency, were composed with the assistance of ghostwriters. In this respect he was different from his successors only in the caliber of talent available to him. What other American president has been able to include the likes of Hamilton and Madison among his speechwriters? Yet for all of his reliance upon the pens of other men, Washington was far too concerned about his public persona and the potential impact of his discourse to allow anyone to compose for him without close supervision and correction. His aides and associates were responsible for much of his prose, but he so thoroughly superintended the creation of his major addresses that they unquestionably bore his personal stamp.

In the case of the Farewell Address, Washington began by turning to an unpublished farewell message produced for him by Madison (from Washington's notes) in 1792, before the president had acceded to the requests of Madison and others to serve a second term.[34] Working from this text, Washington composed a draft that was based one-third on Madison's words and two-thirds on his own. Perhaps uneasy about the tone of his draft, which betrayed his bitterness at the attacks on his character by Democratic-Republicans during his final years in office, Washington sent a copy to Hamilton with a letter that left open the possibility of throwing "the *whole* into a different form." Washington's wish, he told Hamilton, was that the address "appear in a plain stile; and be handed to the public in an honest; unaffected; simple garb."[35] Ten weeks later, Hamilton returned two manuscripts, one a revision of Washington's draft, the other a completely new text that was considerably longer and more philosophical in tone. After careful consideration, Washington expressed his preference for Hamilton's new text, which he found "more dignified" and "more copious on material points."[36] This text became the working draft of the Farewell Address.

After transcribing Hamilton's text into his own hand, Washington edited the whole so as to bring it fully into line with his own thinking. In the process, he made several substantive changes, including the addition of a paragraph on the importance of education in a republican society. He also went over the text word by word with an eye toward clarity, precision, and economy. By the time he finished, he had a text in which the ideas, the language, even the syntax and diction were consonant with his own. After showing the text to his cabinet on September 15, he met the next day with David Claypoole, who readily agreed to print the address in his newspaper. Once the address was set in type, Claypoole took the proofs to Washington two or three times (he could not remember which). Washington scrutinized each set of proofs, correcting even the punctuation, in which, Claypoole observed, "he was very minute."[37]

In addition to being deeply involved in the composition of his Farewell Address, Washington stage-managed its release to help ensure a favorable reception. Having learned early in his public life the importance of uttering the right words at the right moment, he typically chose both his words and his moments for public utterance with great care. Although he had resolved to retire months before the publication of his Farewell Address, he had not announced his decision. Through the spring and summer of 1796, as suspense about his future continued to mount, he said nothing. When his Farewell Address appeared in *Claypoole's Daily Advertiser* of September 19, it was perfectly timed to capture public attention. By linking the dramatic announcement of his retirement with the exposition of his political principles, he ensured a massive audience for the latter. Moreover, had he released his advice to his countrymen in a separate document, divorced from the emotional context created by his opening paragraphs avouching his love of country and explaining his decision to seek "the shade of retirement," it might not have had the same impact on readers. As usual, Washington's sense of political and rhetorical timing was impeccable.

Nor should we overlook the significance of his decision to transmit his address directly to the citizenry via the press. His 1783 Legacy had been communicated to the thirteen state governors, to whom he had reported on numerous occasions during the war for independence. For him to have sent it to the population at large would have constituted a serious breach of protocol and might well have been seen as demagogic. As president he took great pains not to exacerbate the fear of executive power Americans had developed during the Revolution. As a result, all of his formal deliberative messages before the Farewell Address had been presented to Congress. Now, however, he took the historic step of speaking without an intermediary to the people, who, said Madison, were his "only constituents."[38] From the outset of his thinking about the Farewell Address, his aim had been to reach "the Yeomanry of this Country . . . in language that was plain and intelligible to their understandings."[39] By making them his central audience via "the commercial networks of his time,"[40] he enhanced the standing of his farewell as a personal legacy to the American people and validated their primacy as the source of all legitimate power under the Constitution.

Annual Messages

Washington's first inaugural and his Farewell Address constitute a set of rhetorical bookends unequaled in any subsequent presidency. Both his assumption of power and his relinquishment of it exemplified perfectly his mastery of the skill Rousseau ascribed to the ideal *législateur*— the "ability to lead without compelling and to persuade without proving."[41] The same skill is evident in his eight Annual Messages to Congress. Modeled on the British monarch's speech from the throne at the beginning of each new session of Parliament and on its American analogue, the governor's speech to the colonial assembly, Washington's messages derived also from the constitutional provision that the president "shall from time to time give to the Congress information of the state of the Union, and recommend to their consideration such measures as he shall judge necessary and expedient." Although presidents from Jefferson through Taft would send their Annual Messages to Congress in writing, Washington delivered his in person. He presented his first five messages in the Senate chamber and the last three in the House of Representatives, with the full Congress in attendance at all.

Knowing there was "scarcely any part of my conduct which may not hereafter be drawn into precedent," Washington took as one of his chief objectives to ensure "that these precedents may be fixed on true principles."[42] In keeping with this objective, he moved cautiously in establishing relations between the executive branch and Congress. Part of that caution is evident in his Annual Messages, the first two of which were substantially briefer than those that came later. As time went on, Washington become more extensive in his policy recommendations as he sought to take full advantage of the occasion provided by the Annual Message to provide direction to Congress and, through press coverage, to the nation as a *whole.*[43]

A master of political ceremony, Washington staged the delivery of his messages with great care. On the day of his sixth message, for example, he rode to Philadelphia's Federal Hall in his imposing carriage, which was drawn by four horses and escorted by a procession of twenty-one constables. Attired formally in black and wearing a dress sword, he entered the chamber of the House of Representatives at precisely twelve noon attended by Secretary of State Edmund Randolph, Secretary of War Henry Knox, and Attorney General William Bradford. The members of Congress rose upon his entrance and remained standing until he took his place between the vice president and the Speaker of the House. After bowing to the audience, Washington reached into his coat pocket and removed his spectacles and a neatly folded text of his speech, which he proceeded to read in a clear and distinct voice. When he was finished speaking, he handed copies of his text to the vice president and the Speaker. He then walked from the chamber as the entire audience stood at silent attention. Washington's "whole appearance," one member of the gallery wrote, "commanded the utmost reverence and attention" and made it seem "as tho' we were addressed by a far superior being than any here below."[44]

The most controversial of Washington's Annual Messages was that of November 17, 1794. Delivered three weeks after his return to Philadelphia from leading a force of thirteen thousand militiamen against the Whiskey Rebellion in western Pennsylvania, it was far and away the most strident speech of his presidency. Although he feared it might fan the embers of party spirit, he decided he had no choice but to be "more prolix in my speech to Congress, on the commencement and progress of this insurrection, than is usual in such an instrument." Concerned about the impact of the rebellion on domestic politics, as well as on international perceptions of American unity and stability, he believed it was better to discuss the matter in full rather than "to let it go naked into the world, to be dressed up according to the fancy or the inclination of the readers, or the policy of our enemies."[45] Having put the uprising to rest militarily, he used his Annual Message to solidify support for his actions. A successful speech, as Edmund Randolph observed, would "establish perfect tranquillity to the Government" and bring the administration "through a trying crisis with dignity."[46]

Addressing a packed audience in the House chamber, Washington devoted almost his entire message to the Whiskey Rebellion. Noting that most Americans had accepted the tax on whiskey, he blamed the troubles in Pennsylvania on a "prejudice, fostered and embittered by the artifice of men, who labored for an ascendancy over the will of others, by the guidance of their passions." After reviewing the history of the excise law, the attacks on federal officials who sought to enforce it, and efforts to quell the rebellion short of coercion, Washington explained that military measures had finally become necessary to "maintain the authority of the laws against licentious invasions." Turning to the Democratic Societies he held responsible for much of the tumult, he castigated "certain self-created societies" that, "careless of consequences and disregarding the unerring truth," had propagated "suspicions, jealousies, and accusations of the whole government." Yet there was a positive side to the uprising, Washington explained, for despite the "machinations of the wicked" and the incendiaries' efforts to instill "a spirit inimical to all order," the American people had shown they were "now as ready to maintain the authority of the laws against licentious invasions, as they were to defend their rights against usurpation" at the time of the Revolution.[47]

Reactions to the speech varied. Representative George Thacher of Maine wrote that Washington "delivered one of the most animating, firm and manly addresses I ever heard from him or any other person. . . . I felt a strange mixture of passions that I cannot describe. Tears started into my eyes, and it was with difficulty I could suppress an involuntary effort to swear that I would support him."[48] Washington's detractors were less impressed. In the House of Representatives, a fierce debate broke out over his condemnation of "self-created societies." From Monticello, Jefferson raged that the government had mounted "an attack on the freedom of discussion, the freedom of writing printing & publishing," while Madison, who by then was firmly in the ranks of the opposition, deemed Washington's assault on the Democratic Societies "perhaps the greatest error of his political life."[49] In the nation at large, however, the president's words carried the day. Resolutions endorsing his position came from every state and from every kind of meeting. Equally telling, within a year the number of Democratic Societies had declined precipitously. Notwithstanding Washington's growing body of critics, his hold on the minds and hearts of the people remained secure.[50]

If Washington's speech on the Whiskey Rebellion was the most controversial of his Annual Messages, his address of December 8, 1795, was his most adroit. Delivered during the prolonged agitation over the Jay Treaty and at a time when Washington was under fierce attack in the Democratic-Republican press, it rose above the strife by focusing attention on America's "numerous and extraordinary blessings." After reviewing developments in foreign policy, the president found cause only for "consoling and gratifying reflections." He took the same approach to domestic affairs, in which he discovered "equal cause for contentment and satisfaction." While many of the nations of Europe were engulfed in foreign wars and domestic convulsions, the United States exhibited "a spectacle of national happiness never surpassed if ever before equalled." Even the region that had supported the Whiskey Rebellion was enjoying "the blessings of quiet and order," and Washington had pardoned the convicted rebels in an effort to "mingle in the operations of government, every degree of moderation and tenderness, which the national justice, dignity and safety may permit." "To cooperate with you" in furthering the nation's happiness and prosperity, he told the houses of Congress, "is a fervent, and favorite wish of my heart." After making several specific recommendations—including the need to protect the Indians from "the violences of the lawless part of our frontier inhabitants"—Washington concluded by stating that temperate discussion and mutual forbearance in the deliberations of Congress were "too obvious, and necessary for the peace, happiness and welfare of our country, to need any recommendation of mine."[51]

A brilliant stroke, the speech left Washington's opponents grasping at air. By studiously avoiding any tone of strife, in contrast to his sharply worded message of the previous year, the president rose so far above the fray as to make his critics look pernicious and small-minded. Free and prosperous, growing rapidly in strength and population, the United States was indeed in an advantageous situation. In driving home this unassailable fact, Washington shifted attention from partisan discord to those elements that united Americans and made their future prospects so bright. By acting as if there were no cause for contention, he helped restore a measure of public harmony at a critical point in the life of the young republic.

Washington's eighth message to Congress, delivered December 7, 1796, two and a half months after publication of his Farewell Address, marked his last public appearance as president and was witnessed by the "largest assemblage of citizens, ladies and gentlemen ever collected on a similar occasion."[52] The thirty-minute speech touched on a multitude of topics, including progress in Indian affairs, the British evacuation of the Northwest posts, implementation of the Jay Treaty, creation of a navy, encouragement of manufactures, relations with the French, and the need for a national university. Most memorable, however, was the way Washington used it to close the circle on his presidency. Exhibiting his sure touch in matters of ceremony, he concluded the address by noting that, as he met with the people's representatives "for the last time," he looked back to "the period when the Administration of the present form of Government commenced." After congratulating Congress and the country on "the success of the experiment," he echoed the religious phraseology of his first inaugural by offering his "fervent supplications to the Supreme Ruler of the Universe, and Sovereign Arbiter of Nations, that his Providential care may still be extended to the United States; that the virtue and happiness of the People may be preserved; and that the Government, which they have instituted, for the protection of their liberties, may be perpetual." When Washington finished, there were few dry eyes in the House chamber.[53]

Despite the vast gulf in time, technology, and political sensibilities that separates us from Washington and his world, the similarities between his Annual Messages and today's State of the Union addresses far outweigh the differences. His well-known reluctance to usurp the legislative powers of Congress notwithstanding, his Annual Messages were far more than ceremonial speeches. He used them not simply as a vehicle for general reflections on the condition of the country, but as an instrument for presenting the policies he wished Congress to pursue in the coming year. In fact, when preparing his messages, he customarily had an aide examine his previous messages to see which of his recommendations Congress had adopted and which it had not, so he could decide whether there were any he should bring forward again.[54] Even in the earliest years of the new republic—and perhaps to an extent unintended by the framers of the Constitution, including Washington himself—the Annual Message focused attention on the president as the symbol of national unity and the voice of national policy. There is, to this day, no comparable regularly scheduled rhetorical event that shines the same bright light on either the judicial or legislative branches of government.

Because Washington did not stump the country in support of his policies, the Annual Message was his primary opportunity to give personal voice to them.[55] In his hands, it became a vital instrument of presidential leadership—even more so because he presented it in person rather than in writing. A charismatic leader whose hold on the imagination of his contemporaries is impossible to recapture today, Washington exuded a powerful personal magnetism. Although his delivery skills were unexceptional, his heroic reputation and commanding physical presence more than made up for—and in some ways were enhanced by—his lack of oratorical polish. It was one thing to receive Washington's ideas on paper; it was quite another to receive them in person. As Wayne Fields has noted, when Woodrow Wilson restored Washington's practice of delivering the Annual Message orally, he affirmed an aggressive approach to presidential leadership "in which Congress has to deal with the person of the president as well as with the office he holds."[56]

REGIONAL TOURS

Given the landmarks established by Washington's first inaugural speech, Farewell Address, and Annual Messages, it is easy to lose sight of the fact that he created yet another rhetorical precedent, one that puts him more in line with modern chief executives than with almost all of his nineteenth-century successors. On October 15, 1789, he left New York on a twenty-nine-day journey that took him through Connecticut, Massachusetts, and New Hampshire. In August, 1790, he returned to New England, this time to visit Rhode Island, which in May had become the thirteenth state to ratify the Constitution. Eight months later, he undertook a two-month excursion through the southern states, traveling 1,887 miles before returning to the capital at Philadelphia. It was the most extensive tour by a sitting president until Andrew Johnson's ill-fated "swing around the circle" in defense of his Reconstruction policies seventy-five years later.[57]

The stated purpose of Washington's tours was to give him a chance to judge "the temper and disposition of the Inhabitants towards the new government,"[58] but there can be no doubt that he also saw them as a way to help cement the bonds of national union. In this regard, the most important element of the tours was the towering presence of

Washington himself. As the *Gazette of the United States* noted, when it came to allaying "uneasiness" about the Constitution, "Seeing him . . . will have a very conciliatory effect, and do more than a thousand arguments from even an Ames or a Gerry."[59] As Washington knew, he could exert a powerful influence simply by "seeing and being seen."[60] Indeed, it is unlikely that any American president has understood better than Washington the rhetorical power of self-presentation. Like many other eighteenth-century figures, he often referred to life as a drama and to himself as "a figure upon the stage." An avid theatergoer, he was especially fond of Joseph Addison's *Cato*, which provided models of republican behavior and discourse that Washington emulated through much of his life.[61] But apart from the influence of any particular exemplar, Washington had an "uncommon awareness of self." His biography, as W. W. Abbot has noted, "is the story of a man constructing himself. . . . Washington at work on Washington."[62] As a young man in Virginia's tidewater gentry, he learned early the importance of bearing, dress, etiquette, and language in the construction of one's public image. In this society, every occasion from horseback riding to dances, election meetings to court days served as a stage "on which individuals, and especially gentrymen, might act out their claims to public honor and have them validated by the community." Nor was this solely a manner of personal display, for the eighteenth-century code of honor that Washington lived his life by "took external appearance as a sign of inner merit," an index to one's character and sense of civic virtue.[63]

By the time of his inauguration, Washington had perfected the roles of military commander, republican hero, and modern Cincinnatus. It was but a small step for him to add the role of president to his repertoire. He certainly looked the part. Over six feet tall and weighing more than two hundred pounds, he had a strong, finely proportioned figure, moved with athletic grace, and seemed uncommonly majestic in bearing. Jefferson considered him the finest horseman in America, but whether seated or standing, on horseback or on foot, he impressed his contemporaries as having "the soul, look, and figure of a hero united in him."[64] "There is not a king in Europe," Benjamin Rush remarked, "that would not look like a valet de chambre by his side."[65] But, of course, America was not a monarchy. Washington's demeanor and appearance were imposing, but in ways that jibed with the republican sensibilities of his countrymen—and women. Abigail Adams, who was not easily impressed, all but swooned upon meeting him for the first time. "You had prepaired me to entertain a favorable opinion of him" she told her husband, John, "but I thought the one half was not told me." She found Washington dignified, noble, and high-minded, but she was equally taken with his amiability and ease of bearing. "Modesty," she admired, "marks every line and feture of his face."[66]

The blend of regality and republicanism that so captivated Abigail Adams was central to Washington's role as president, and he cultivated it with consummate skill. That skill extended even to his choice of attire. On the day of his inauguration, for example, he selected a specially made brown suit brightened with silver buttons decorated with spread eagles that symbolized American liberty. The outfit was completed with white silk stockings, shoes with silver buckles, and Washington's dress sword with its steel scabbard. As important as the visual appeal of Washington's habiliment was its symbolic significance. Not only were the buttons decorated with spread eagles that represented American liberty, but the suit itself was made of Connecticut broadcloth, a gesture that linked Washington with the efforts to encourage domestic industry that extended back to the Townshend Acts controversy of the late 1760s.[67] The symbolism was subtle, but therein lay much of its appeal. Sharing his audience's concern about overzealous leaders who might prey upon the passions of the people for dictatorial ends, Washington maintained a perfect equipoise between spectacle and substance, reason and emotion, the heroic and the commonplace that allowed him to educe awe and reverence even as he inspired confidence in his character, judgment, and trustworthiness with power. "His great skill," as Paul Longmore has noted, "was that on important public occasions he successfully avoided the melodramatic without loss of effect. Repeatedly at such moments . . . he chose the right pose, the right gesture, the right words."[68]

Washington's ability to find the right words to complement his physical performance as president was fully evident on his regional tours. As had been the case with his official travels ever since the Revolution, he was greeted and feted by local dignitaries in town after town upon his route. As part of the festivities, which usually included a parade, a dinner, and illuminations, Washington was presented with a formal address of welcome and tribute. Sometimes the address was tendered as he rode into town on horseback. At other times, it was proffered in ceremonies at a town hall, church, college, Masonic lodge, or state legislature. Whenever possible, an advance copy of the address was given to one of Washington's aides so the president could present a brief, formal speech in response. If Washington did not receive an advance copy of the address, he would say no more than a few words on the spot and send a written reply the next day. Usually both the address and Washington's reply were published in the local press. All told, Washington received and answered at least forty-three addresses during his three presidential tours.[69]

The addresses presented to Washington followed a fairly routine pattern. They usually opened by welcoming him, praising him for his service to his country during the Revolution, and congratulating him on his unanimous election as president. Most affirmed the commitment to the new government of the group presenting the address, and almost all closed by wishing Washington good health and a long life. Imbued with tributes to Washington's "exalted merit," "eminent public services," and "extraordinary virtues," the addresses were so panegyrical that he feared, early in his presidency, that he might not be able to fulfill the expectations placed upon him.[70] Many apotheosized him in such terms as "the defender of liberty," "the guardian of his country," "the friend of mankind," and "the father of his country." Typical was the address he received in Newbern, North Carolina, where the citizens greeted him with "hearts impressed with the most lively emotions of Love, Esteem and Veneration." Extolling the president for having defended America "against the Arm of Despotism and Arbitrary Sway" in "a long and arduous War," the people of Newbern exclaimed: "Our Souls overflow with gratitude to the bountiful Dispenser of all good Gifts, that he has committed to your hands the reins of Government . . . during peace." Turning to a broader stage, the address declared "it is not America Alone" but the entire "Human Race" that benefited from Washington's noble deeds, for "the World shall learn from your example to what a stupendous height of Glory, a Nation may be elevated." The residents of Newbern concluded by offering "our most earnest Prayer to the throne of Heavenly Grace that the divine Benediction may accompany you here and hereafter."[71]

In keeping with eighteenth-century rhetorical conventions, Washington usually responded to the sentiments expressed in these ceremonial addresses by echoing portions of the language used in them. It was a highly stylized practice, and one that he had perfected during the Revolutionary War. Indeed, one of the most renowned statements in all of his public discourse comes from a speech he presented in response to an address from the New York Provincial Congress, on June 26, 1775, as he made his way north from Philadelphia to assume command of the continental troops outside Boston. The congress had concluded its address to Washington by stating its "fullest Assurances that whenever this important Contest shall be decided, . . . You will chearfully resign the important Deposit committed into Your Hands, and reassume the Character of our worthiest Citizen." Washington replied by saying, "When we assumed the Soldier, we did not lay aside the Citizen, & we shall most sincerely rejoice with you in that happy Hour, when the Establishment of American Liberty on the most firm, & solid Foundations, shall enable us to return to our private Stations in the bosom of a free, peaceful, & happy Country."[72] Here, prompted by the New York legislature, was the first expression of Washington's promise to resign his commission when the military conflict was over. No words of his were quoted more frequently during the war, and he underlined their significance by repeating the same pledge on other occasions.

Like the addresses he received on his tours as president, his replies were formulaic in structure and content. Yet they allowed him more opportunity for substantive expression than most students of the presidency have recognized. Rather than simply reiterating patriotic sentiments, as Tulis has claimed, Washington used his replies, within the rhetorical constraints imposed by the genre and eighteenth-century notions of appropriate presidential discourse, to reinforce attitudes and policies of which he approved.[73] He did this not by explicit exhortation, but by echoing the language of the addresses to him in such fashion as to praise his auditors for traits he wanted them to adopt: industry, virtue, love of country, and, above all, attachment to the Constitution. It was one of Washington's favorite rhetorical devices, and he employed it to great effect throughout his military and political careers, perhaps most notably in his first inaugural, when, under the guise of praising Congress, he admonished it to make sure that "no local prejudices, or attachments; no separate views, nor party animosities," would misdirect "the comprehensive and equal eye" that ought to control its proceedings.[74] Although transparent, it was an orthodox element of eighteenth-century public discourse, and it gave him considerably more rhetorical leeway than he would have had otherwise.

Washington was also adroit at coupling his echo of the address to him with language that amplified the sentiments voiced in the address so as to reinforce a point he wished to make. This strategy can be seen in the most memorable speech of his regional tours: his answer to an address from the Hebrew Congregation in Newport, Rhode Island, in August, 1790. A strong supporter of religious freedom, Washington used this occasion to reaffirm the inviolability of liberty of conscience. The government of the United States, he said in an echo of the congregation's address, "gives to bigotry no sanction, to persecution no assistance," and "requires only that they who live under its protection should demean themselves as good citizens." He then went well beyond the congregation's language by voicing his desire that "the children of the Stock of Abraham, who dwell in this land," would continue to enjoy "the good-will of the other inhabitants; while every one shall sit in safety under his own vine and fig-tree, and there shall be none to make him afraid."[75] There are no more eloquent statements of Washington's opposition to religious bigotry and intolerance than this passage with its powerful scriptural resonance.

Not only did Washington's speeches on his regional tours rehearse the values of union, patriotism, national honor, and civic virtue he believed essential to the survival of America's experiment in popular government, they also reinforced the public's sense of his character as a republican leader. Notwithstanding the "effusions of affection and personal regard" he received in stop after stop, he accepted them all with dignity and humility.[76] When responding to praise for his exploits in the Revolution or for his personal role in creating the Constitution, he consistently deflected attention from himself by attributing both of those momentous achievements to the blessings of divine providence and the exertions of the American people. If he had contributed in a special way to the establishment of American liberty, he insisted, it was as a result of doing "no more than what inclination prompted and duty enjoined."[77] Nor was this false modesty on Washington's part. The persona he projected in his replies to addresses—during his regional tours and throughout his administration—was part of his performance as president, but it was a persona that simultaneously reflected and reinforced his own personality, values, and sense of civic obligation.[78] The impact on his fellow citizens can be gauged by the comments of a Bostonian who exclaimed in June, 1789: "His replies to the various addresses of his fellow-citizens do the highest honor to his character. . . . Although the human mind is frequently intoxicated with exalted praises, our President has demonstrated that he is superior to its pernicious influence." According to this writer, Washington's magnanimity when he was "borne down with adulatory addresses" reflected "the best signs of virtue and moderation; and lead us to expect great happiness under his administration."[79]

From all signs, Washington's regional tours were highly successful. One newspaper reported that the president's presence in New England, "like the glorious luminary of Heaven, appears to have totally dissipated the fog of Anti-Federalism."[80] Certainly Washington was pleased with his journeys. After returning from the southern states, he noted that he had been able "to see with my own eyes the situation of the country . . . and to learn more accurately the disposition of the people than I could have done by any information." He was satisfied that "Tranquillity reigns among the people, with that disposition towards the general government which is likely to preserve it."[81] Although there is no way to gauge the exact impact of Washington's speeches during his regional tours, they were a centerpiece of the festivities at every stop and elicited much favorable commentary in the press. Notwithstanding the tendency of scholars to treat them lightly because of their ceremonial nature, they were of utmost importance to Washington and his audiences. As epideictic addresses, their purpose was not to advance specific policy proposals but to create a sense of communal identity and social cohesion by rehearsing shared values and aspirations. In this sense, they were crucial to Washington's efforts to foster confidence in the new government and to engender a truly American character.

They also confirm, in conjunction with Washington's other public addresses, his ability to employ public discourse as a powerful instrument of presidential leadership. Like other leaders of the founding generation, he placed great faith in the power of language to surmount what John Adams called "the difficulty of bringing millions to agree."[82] Knowing that in a republican government the ability to wield power effectively depends ultimately upon popular opinion, Washington used his speeches and writings with remarkable dexterity to help direct the nation through a series of crises that, with a lesser chief executive, might have imperiled its survival. Moreover, just as he gave shape and texture to the constitutional powers of the president by his actions in office, so he construed its rhetorical duties and opportunities in ways that continue to shape the practice of American politics and government. He certainly did not think of the presidency as a bully pulpit, and he will never be known as the "Great Communicator," but no president has understood better the nature of power, and few have been his equal in managing the rhetorical resources of the office.

NOTES

1. George W. Corner, ed., *The Autobiography of Benjamin Rush* (Princeton, N.J.: Princeton University Press, 1948), 249.

2. Although Lincoln has had a solid hold on the top spot since World War II, appreciation of Washington's achievements has risen in recent years and is reflected in an outpouring of books on his public career. These works include, in addition to those cited in subsequent notes, John R. Alden, *George Washington: A Biography* (Baton Rouge: Louisiana University Press, 1984); Barry Schwartz, *George Washington: The Making of an American Symbol* (New York: Free Press, 1987); John E. Ferling, *The First of Men: A Life of George Washington* (Knoxville: University of Tennessee Press, 1988); *David Humphreys' "Life of General Washington," with George Washington's "Remarks,"* ed. Rosemarie Zagarri (Athens: University of Georgia Press, 1991); Thomas A. Lewis, *For King and Country: George Washington, the Early Years* (New York: John Wiley and Sons, 1993); Richard Norton Smith, *Patriarch: George Washington and the New American Nation* (Boston: Houghton Mifflin, 1993); Richard Brookhiser, *Founding Father: Rediscovering George Washington* (New York: Free Press, 1996); Matthew Spalding and Patrick J. Garrity, *A Sacred Union of Citizens: George Washington's Farewell Address and the American Character* (Lanham, Md.: Rowman and Littlefield, 1996); Harrison Clark, *All Cloudless Glory: The Life of George Washington*, 2 vols. (Washington, D.C.: Regnery, 1996); Willard Sterne Randall, *George Washington: A Life* (New York: Henry Holt, 1997); John H. Rhodehamel, ed., *George Washington: Writings* (New York: Library of America, 1997); Stephen E. Lucas, ed., *The Quotable George Washington* (Madison, Wisc.: Madison House, 1999). For a succinct statement of the case for Washington as the nation's most important president, see Gordon S. Wood, "The Greatness of George Washington," *Virginia Quarterly Review* 68 (1992): 189–207.

3. Notebooks of Timothy Pickering, Pickering Papers, Massachusetts Historical Society, Boston; Thomas Jefferson to Walter Jones, Jan. 2, 1814, in *The Writings of Thomas Jefferson*, ed. Paul Leicester Ford, 20 vols. (New York: G. P. Putnam's Sons, 1892–99), 9:449.

4. Silas Deane to Elizabeth Deane [Sept. 10–11, 1774], in *Letters of Delegates to Congress, 1774–1789*, vol 1, ed. Paul H. Smith (Washington, D.C.: Library of Congress, 1976), 62; Ashbel Green, *Life of Ashbel Green* (New York: Robert Carter and Brothers, 1849), 266.

5. Jeffrey K. Tulis, "Revising the Rhetorical Presidency," in *Beyond the Rhetorical Presidency*, ed. Martin J. Medhurst (East Lansing: Michigan State University Press, 1996), 3.

6. James Thomas Flexner, *George Washington in the American Revolution* (Boston: Little, Brown, 1967), 534.

7. Washington to Elbridge Gerry, Dec. 25, 1777, in *The Writings of George Washington*, ed. John C. Fitzpatrick (Washington, D.C.: GPO, 1939), 10:201.

8. For the text of Washington's speech, see *The Papers of George Washington: Revolutionary War Series*, vol. 1, ed. Philander D. Chase (Charlottesville: University Press of Virginia, 1985), 1–3; Fitzpatrick, ed., *Writings of George Washington*, 3:292–93.

9. Jefferson to Washington, Apr. 16, 1784, in *The Papers of Thomas Jefferson*, vol. 7, ed. Julian P. Boyd (Princeton, N.J.: Princeton University Press, 1953), 106–107. Richard H. Kohn, "The Inside History of the Newburgh Conspiracy: America and the Coup d'Etat," *William and Mary Quarterly* 27 (1970): 187–220, provides a thorough discussion of the crisis that led to Washington's speech. The address itself is printed in Fitzpatrick, ed., *Writings of George Washington*, 26:222–27.

10. Marquis de Lafayette to George Washington, Sept. 8, 1783, in *The Letters of Lafayette to Washington, 1777–1799*, ed. Louis Gottschalk (New York: Helen Fahnestock Hubbard, 1944), 269. For the text of the circular letter, see Fitzpatrick, ed., *Writings of George Washington*, 26:483–96.

11. See "Address to Congress on Resigning His Commission," Dec. 23, 1783, in Fitzpatrick, ed., *Writings of George Washington*, 27:284–85.

12. Washington to Catherine Macaulay Graham, Jan. 9, 1790, in Fitzpatrick, ed., *Writings of George Washington*, 30:496.

13. The analysis that follows builds upon and extends points made in Stephen E. Lucas, "George Washington," in *American Orators before 1900: Critical Studies and Sources*, ed. Bernard K. Duffy and Halford R. Ryan (New York: Greenwood Press, 1987, 406–15, and Stephen E. Lucas and Susan Zaeske, "George Washington," in *U.S. Presidents as Orators*, ed. Halford Ryan (Westport, Conn.: Greenwood Press, 1995), 3–17.

14. Fitzpatrick, ed., *Writings of George Washington*, 27:285.

15. "First Inaugural Address," in Fitzpatrick, ed., *Writings of George Washington*, 30:291–96. For further discussion, see Stephen E. Lucas, "Genre Criticism and Historical Context: The Case of George Washington's First Inaugural Address," *Southern Speech Communication Journal* 51 (1986): 354–71.

16. *New York Daily Gazette*, May 14, 1789.

17. *Federal Gazette* (Philadelphia), May 9, 1789.

18. *Providence Gazette*, May 16, 1789.

19. Robert A. Ferguson, "The American Enlightenment," in *The Cambridge History of American Literature*, vol. 1, *1590–1820*, ed. Sacvan Bercovitch and Cyrus R. K. Patell (Cambridge: Cambridge University Press, 1995), 490.

20. Ibid., 352, 366.

21. "First Inaugural Address," in Fitzpatrick, ed., *Writings of George Washington*, 30:291–92.

22. Scholarly interest in the first inaugural has focused disproportionately not on the speech Washington delivered, but on the discarded seventy-three-page draft David Humphreys prepared for him sometime before early Jan., 1789. Washington rejected the draft, though not before copying it into his own hand, and turned to

James Madison for assistance in preparing a briefer, more suitable address. In the early nineteenth century, Jared Sparks discovered Washington's autograph of Humphreys's draft in the course of gathering materials for his edition of Washington's writings. After consulting with Madison, who deemed the draft "so strange a production," Sparks decided that it should not be published. He subsequently cut the draft into snippets and distributed them to friends and patrons eager for a genuine sample of Washington's handwriting. Although it is highly unlikely that the full text will ever be recovered, researchers have sought to reconstruct Humphreys's draft based on the fragments that have come to light. The most notable efforts include Fitzpatrick, ed., *Writings of George Washington,* 30:296–308; Nathaniel E. Stein, "The Discarded Inaugural Address of George Washington," *Manuscripts* 10 (1958): 2–17; Dorothy Twohig, ed., *The Papers of George Washington: Presidential Series,* vol. 2 (Charlottesville: University Press of Virginia, 1989), 152–73; and W. B. Allen, ed., *George Washington: A Collection* (Indianapolis: Liberty Classics, 1988), 440–59. Allen, however, errs in assuming that the draft was composed by Washington simply because the fragments are in his hand. Not only is such an assumption incompatible with the historical evidence, it is belied by the fact that Humphreys used several lengthy passages from the discarded draft in a Fourth of July oration he delivered just three months after Washington's inauguration. It is inconceivable that he would have done so had the draft been Washington's composition rather than his own. See David Humphreys, "An Oration on the Political Situation of the United States of America in the Year 1789," in *The Miscellaneous Works of David Humphreys,* ed. William K. Bottorff (1804; reprint, Gainesville, Fla.: Scholars' Facsimiles, 1968), 331–42.

23. While Washington's first inaugural established a prototype followed by all subsequent presidents, his second inaugural did not. In that speech of 135 words, by far the briefest of presidential inaugurals, Washington perfunctorily acknowledged his reelection and signified his commitment to the oath of office he was about to take. Although the unusual nature of the second inaugural has puzzled many scholars, it is explained when we understand that Washington wanted a simple ceremony without the pomp and extravagance of his first inauguration. In Washington's view, the political situation of March, 1793, did not require more than a few brief comments before being sworn into office for a second term, while that of April, 1789, had demanded a major speech to help develop confidence in the new government. The prototype for second inaugurals was not established until Thomas Jefferson's speech of March 4, 1805. See "Second Inaugural Address," Mar. 4, 1793, in Fitzpatrick, ed., *Writings of George Washington,* 32:374–75.

24. Address of the Legislature of New Jersey, Nov. 15, 1796, Washington Papers, Library of Congress, Washington, D.C. (hereafter Washington Papers).

25. Address of the Citizens of Northumberland County, Jan. 28, 1797, Washington Papers.

26. Felix Gilbert, *To the Farewell Address: Ideas of Early American Foreign Policy* (Princeton, N.J.: Princeton University Press, 1961), 100–101.

27. Washington to Madison, May 20, 1792, in Fitzpatrick, ed., *Writings of George Washington,* 32:46–47.

28. Fitzpatrick, ed., *Writings of George Washington*, 26:487, 35:218–19.

29. Victor Hugo Paltsits, *Washington's Farewell Address* (New York: New York Public Library, 1935), 67.

30. Address of the Legislature of Massachusetts, Feb. 11, 1797, Washington Papers.

31. Address of the Legislature of the State of Vermont, Oct. 27, 1796, and Address of the Citizens of Northumberland County, Jan. 28, 1797, Washington Papers.

32. *Daily Advertiser* (New York), Sept. 21, 1796, and *New-Jersey Journal*, Sept. 28, 1796, in Paltsits, *Farewell Address*, 340, 345; Address of the House of Representatives of Pennsylvania, Feb. 17, 1797, and Address of the Grand Lodge of Pennsylvania, Dec. 27, 1796, Washington Papers; and *Courier of New Hampshire*, Oct. 11, 1796, in Paltsits, *Farewell Address*, 338. I have found only one statement that refers to the Farewell Address as a testament, and that characterizes it as "a second new testament." See R. Troup to Rufus King, Nov. 16, 1796, in *Life and Correspondence of Rufus King*, ed. Charles R. King (New York: G. P. Putnam's Sons, 1895), 3:110.

33. "Farewell Address," in Fitzpatrick, ed., *Writings of George Washington*, 35:237.

34. Garry Wills, *Cincinnatus: George Washington and the Enlightenment* (Garden City, N.Y.: Doubleday, 1984), 88, mistakenly characterizes Washington's notes as being dictated to Madison. In fact, the notes were not communicated orally, but rather in a letter dated May 20, 1792 (in Fitzpatrick, ed., *Writings of George Washington*, 32:45–49).

35. Washington to Hamilton, May 15, 1796, in Fitzpatrick, ed., *Writings of George Washington*, 35:48–49.

36. Washington to Hamilton, Aug. 25, 1796, in Fitzpatrick, ed., *Writings of George Washington*, 35:190.

37. "Certification of David C. Claypoole," Feb.22, 1826, in Paltsits, *Farewell Address*, 291. Paltsits's definitive work provides a complete account of the process by which the Farewell Address was composed, complete with reprints of the drafts, correspondence, and related primary documents.

38. Madison to Washington, June 20, 1792, in *The Papers of James Madison*, vol. 14, ed. Robert A. Rutland and Thomas A. Mason (Charlottesville: University Press of Virginia, 1983), 320.

39. Washington to Hamilton, Aug. 25, 1796, 35:191.

40. Wills, *Cincinnatus*, 88.

41. Jean-Jacques Rousseau, *Du Contrat Social* 2.7, quoted in Wills, *Cincinnatus*, 162. As Abigail Adams stated of Washington, he "has so happy a faculty of appearing to accommodate & yet carrying his point, that if he was not really one of the best-intentioned men in the world he might be a very dangerous one" (to Mary Cranch, Jan. 5, 1790, in "New Letters of Abigail Adams, 1788–1801," ed. Stewart Mitchell, *Proceedings of the American Antiquarian Society* 55 [1947]: 147).

42. Washington to Catherine Macaulay Graham, Jan. 9, 1790, and to Madison, May 5, 1789, in Fitzpatrick, ed., *Writings of George Washington*, 30:496, 311. Madison made much the same point with respect to Congress, where, he wrote Jefferson, "We are in a wilderness without a single footstep to guide us" (June 30, 1789, in *The Papers of James Madison*, vol. 12, ed. Charles F. Hobson and Robert A. Rutland [Charlottes-

ville: University Press of Virginia, 1979], 268). See also, in general, Glenn A. Phelps, "George Washington: Precedent Setter," in *Inventing the American Presidency*, ed. Thomas E. Cronin (Lawrence: University Press of Kansas, 1989), 259–81; Glenn A. Phelps, "George Washington and the Founding of the Presidency," *Presidential Studies Quarterly* 17 (1987): 345–63.

43. Jeffrey K. Tulis, *The Rhetorical Presidency* (Princeton, N.J.: Princeton University Press, 1987), 55, erroneously characterizes Washington's first inaugural address as his initial Annual Message, which was presented on Jan. 8, 1790 (in Fitzpatrick, ed., *Writings of George Washington*, 30:491–94).

44. Elizabeth Smith to William Smith, Dec. 4, 1794, quoted in John Alexander Carroll and Mary Wells Ashworth, *George Washington: First in Peace* (New York: Charles Scribner's Sons, 1957), 220 n 38. For details about the ceremonial aspects of Washington's speech, see Green, *Life of Ashbel Green*, 266; diary of Moreau de Saint-Méry, in *George Washington as the French Knew Him: A Collection of Texts*, ed. and trans. Gilbert Chinard (1940; reprint, New York: Greenwood Press, 1969), 99–100; Carroll and Ashworth, *George Washington*, 219–21.

45. Washington to John Jay, Nov. 1, 1794, in Fitzpatrick, ed., *Writings of George Washington*, 34:18.

46. Randolph to Washington, Nov. 6, 1794, quoted in Carroll and Ashworth, *George Washington*, 216 n 14.

47. "Sixth Annual Address to Congress," Nov. 19, 1794, in Fitzpatrick, ed., *Writings of George Washington*, 34:28–37.

48. George Thacher to Mrs. Thacher, Nov. 17, 1794, quoted in Carroll and Ashworth, *George Washington*, 220 n 38.

49. Jefferson to Madison, Dec. 28, 1794, in Ford, ed., *Writings of Thomas Jefferson*, 6:517; James Madison to James Monroe, Dec. 4, 1794, in *The Papers of James Madison*, vol. 15, ed. Thomas A. Mason, Robert A. Rutland, and Jeanne K. Sisson (Charlottesville: University Press of Virginia, 1985), 406.

50. For more information on the Whiskey Rebellion and its aftermath, see Leland D. Baldwin, *Whiskey Rebels: The Story of a Frontier Uprising* (Pittsburgh: University of Pittsburgh Press, 1939); Jacob E. Cooke, "The Whiskey Rebellion: A Re-evaluation," *Pennsylvania History* 30 (1963): 316–46; Steven R. Boyd, ed., *The Whiskey Rebellion: Past and Present Perspectives* (Westport, Conn.: Greenwood Press, 1985); Thomas P. Slaughter, *The Whiskey Rebellion: Frontier Epilogue to the American Revolution* (New York: Oxford University Press, 1986).

51. "Seventh Annual Address," Dec. 8, 1795, in Fitzpatrick, ed., *Writings of George Washington*, 34:386–93.

52. *Gazette of the United States*, Dec. 7, 1796, quoted in Carroll and Ashworth, *George Washington*, 420.

53. "Eighth Annual Address to Congress," Dec. 7, 1796, in Fitzpatrick, ed., *Writings of George Washington*, 35:310–20.

54. See Washington to Tobias Lear, Oct. 7, 1791, in Fitzpatrick, ed., *Writings of George Washington*, 31:383–85; and Washington to Lear, Oct. 1, 1792, ibid., 32:172–73.

55. Washington did send special messages to Congress, but these were brief written documents that did not carry anything approaching the weight of his Annual

Messages. For the full corpus of his official presidential addresses, see *A Compilation of the Messages and Papers of the Presidents, 1789–1897*, vol. 1, ed. James D. Richardson (Washington, D.C.: GPO, 1897), 41–224.

56. Wayne Fields, *Union of Words: A History of Presidential Eloquence* (New York: Free Press, 1996), 177.

57. Tulis, *Rhetorical Presidency*, 69–93, provides a useful survey of presidential tours from the 1790s through the end of the nineteenth century, though he mistakenly states that Washington took only two tours.

58. Donald Jackson and Dorothy Twohig, eds., *The Diaries of George Washington* (Charlottesville: University Press of Virginia, 1976–79), 4:453.

59. *Gazette of the United States*, May 7, 1791, quoted in Douglas Southall Freeman, *George Washington: Patriot and President* (New York: Charles Scribner's Sons, 1954), 322 n 79.

60. Tulis, *Rhetorical Presidency*, 69.

61. Forrest McDonald, "Washington, Cato, and Honor: A Model for Revolutionary Leadership," in *American Models of Revolutionary Leadership: George Washington and Other Founders*, ed. Daniel J. Elazar and Ellis Katz (Lanham, Md.: University Press of America, 1992), 43–58; Albert Furtwangler, *American Silhouettes: Rhetorical Identities of the Founders* (New Haven, Conn.: Yale University Press, 1987), 64–84. See also Frederic M. Litto, "Addison's Cato in the Colonies," *William and Mary Quarterly* 23 (1966): 431–49.

62. W. W. Abbot, "An Uncommon Awareness of Self: The Papers of George Washington," *Prologue: Quarterly of the National Archives* 21 (1989): 7.

63. Paul K. Longmore, *The Invention of George Washington* (Berkeley: University of California Press, 1988), 11.

64. Comte de Moustier to Comte de Montmorin, June 5, 1789, in *The History of the Centennial Celebration of the Inauguration of George Washington as First President of the United States*, ed. Clarence Winthrop Bowen (New York: D. Appleton, 1892), 49.

65. Rush to Thomas Ruston, Oct. 29, 1775, in *Letters of Benjamin Rush*, ed. L. H. Butterfield (Princeton: Princeton University Press, 1951), 1:92.

66. Abigail Adams to John Adams, July 16, 1775, in *Adams Family Correspondence*, vol 1, ed. L.H. Butterfield (Cambridge: Harvard University Press, 1963), 246. Fifteen years later, Adams's opinion remained the same. Washington, she wrote after a levee at the president's residence, was "polite with dignity, affable without familiarity, distant without Haughtyness, Grave without Austerity, Modest, wise & Good" (to Mary Cranch, Jan. 5, 1790, in "New Letters of Abigail Adams," 147).

67. Freeman, *George Washington*, 188; James Thomas Flexner, *George Washington and the New Nation* (Boston: Little, Brown, 1969), 185; Clarence Winthrop Bowen, "The Inauguration of Washington," *Century Magazine* 37 (1889): 828.

68. Longmore, *Invention of George Washington*, 183.

69. This count of the addresses to and from Washington on his regional tours is based on the documents collected in the Washington Papers. For details on the planning, logistics, and progress of the tours, see Freeman, *George Washington*, 240–45, 274–76, 298–99, 305–22; Archibald Henderson, *Washington's Southern Tour, 1791* (Boston: Houghton Mifflin, 1923).

70. See, for example, his statement to Edward Rutledge, on May 5, 1789: "I greatly apprehend that my Countrymen will expect too much from me. I fear, if the issue of public measures should not corrispond with their sanguine expectations, they will turn the extravagant (and I may say undue) praises which they are heaping upon me at this moment, into equally extravagant (though I will fondly hope unmerited) censures. So much is expected, so many untoward circumstances may intervene, in such a new and critical situation, that I feel an insuperable diffidence in my own abilities" (in Fitzpatrick, ed., *Writings of George Washington*, 30:309).

71. Address of the Inhabitants of the Town of New-Berne (Apr. 21, 1799), in Henderson, *Washington's Southern Tour*, 86–87. This address, along with a representative selection of poems, songs, and newspaper accounts illustrating the adulation bestowed upon Washington during his regional tours, is also available in *A Great and Good Man: George Washington in the Eyes of His Contemporaries*, ed. John P. Kaminski and Jill Adair McCaughan (Madison, Wisc.: Madison House, 1989), 145–96.

72. Chase, *Papers of Washington*, 1:40–41.

73. Tulis, *Rhetorical Presidency*, 67.

74. Fitzpatrick, ed., *Writings of George Washington*, 30:294.

75. Both the Address of the Hebrew Congregation and Washington's reply are in Kaminski and McCaughan, eds., *Great and Good Man*, 179–81.

76. Washington to Alexander Martin, Nov. 14, 1791, in Fitzpatrick, ed., *Writings of George Washington*, 31:415–16.

77. Address to the Executive of the State of New Hampshire [Nov. 3, 1789], Washington Papers.

78. See Forrest McDonald, *The American Presidency: An Intellectual History* (Lawrence: University Press of Kansas, 1994), 217, on the reciprocal relationship between one's public persona and personal character in the eighteenth century.

79. *Virginia (Winchester) Gazette*, June 3, 1789. Washington's skill in answering the many adulatory addresses he received can be gleaned from the comments of Louis-Philippe, Comte de Ségur, who observed: "with great modesty, he strove to avoid the tributes which people were delighted to offer him; and yet no man ever knew better how to acknowledge them and to respond to them. He used to listen with kind attention to those who addressed him and the expression upon his face answered before his very words" (in Chinard, ed. and trans., *Washington as the French Knew Him*, 38).

80. *Gazette of the United States*, Oct. 28, 1789, quoted in Freeman, *George Washington*, 243.

81. Washington to Humphreys, July 20, 1791, in Fitzpatrick, ed., *Writings of George Washington*, 31:318.

82. Quoted in Ferguson, "American Enlightenment," 353.

CHAPTER 3

Classical Virtue and Presidential Fame

John Adams, Leadership,

and the Franco-American Crisis

James M. Farrell

N MARCH 5, 1770, a squad of British soldiers stationed in Boston fired their muskets at a threatening crowd of citizens, killing five people. By the end of the next day the soldiers and their captain had retained as their attorney John Adams, one of the most respected Whig lawyers in the town. Reflecting on what he considered his unselfish labor, Adams identified it as "one of the best pieces of service I ever rendered my country."[1] In 1809, he told Benjamin Rush, "my sense of equity and humanity impelled me, against a torrent of unpopularity, and the inclination of all my friends, to engage in Defense of Captain Preston and the soldiers."[2] Six years later, he explained to James Lloyd that "my head or my heart, and perhaps a conspiracy of both, compelled me to differ in opinion from all my friends, to set at defiance all their advice, their remonstrances, their raillery, their ridicule, their censures, and their sarcasms, without acquiring one symptom of pity from my enemies."[3]

In ensuring that desperate defendants had the benefit of legal counsel, Adams exercised his personal independence and followed a philosophy of republican virtue that demanded a sacrifice of private interest in the pursuit of the larger public good. As he once wrote to Mercy Warren, "Men must be ready, they must pride themselves, and be happy to sacrifice their private pleasures, passions and interests, nay their private friendships and dearest connections, when they stand in competition with the rights of society."[4] Although he was certain his defense of the soldiers was "perfectly conformable to law and justice," it nevertheless, in his mind, "brought upon me a load of indignation and unpopularity, which I knew would never be forgotten, nor entirely forgiven."[5]

Yet it was not the Boston Massacre trial, but instead his decision as president to send a second peace mission to France in 1799 that Adams considered "the most splendid diamond in my crown; or, if any one thinks this expression too monarchial, I will say the most brilliant feather in my cap." But the peace mission, like his service in the Boston Massacre trial, was not universally popular, a fact Adams reflected on for many years after his presidency. His efforts at peace were considered his "error, heresy, and great offence in the judgment, prejudices, predilections, and passions of a small party in every State."[6] For his trouble, Adams believed he was "turned out of office" and "degraded and disgraced by my country."[7]

Public recognition of his political and personal sacrifices was important to Adams, and to protect the reputation of his own presidency and assist future historians, he vowed to set the record straight. So important was the peace with France that fifteen years later the eighty-year-old former president vowed to "defend my missions to France, as long as I have an eye to direct my hand, or a finger to hold my pen. They were the most disinterested and meritorious actions of my life. I reflect upon them with so much satisfaction, that I desire no other inscription over my gravestone than: 'Here lies John Adams, who took upon himself the responsibility of the peace with France in the year 1800.'"[8]

To understand how John Adams defined the attributes and duties of presidential leadership, then, it is instructive to examine his extensive rhetorical effort to defend his missions to France. In this chapter, I will briefly outline the events of the Adams administration and examine them in light of what Adams himself wrote about the presidency. From time to time, in letters and essays, Adams offered reflections on the powers and privileges of the presidency, as well as on the "passions" and values that should properly motivate American presidents.

As I intend to show, Adams aspired to manifest specific attributes of classical republican character during his presidency. Writing later about his own administration, Adams sought to display the personal qualities he had exhibited in the performance of his duty, virtues he was anxious for the public and for we of later generations to recognize. This critical study of Adams's efforts to defend his presidency, and especially his actions toward France, reveals then, if not an objective historical account of John Adams in office, at least a self-portrait that dresses him in his ideal of presidential leadership. By writing his apologia, Adams hoped to construct a view of his presidency that would justify his actions, win public gratitude and esteem for his services, and earn him lasting fame.

In his memoirs, letters, political essays, and autobiographical notes, we find a former president clearly anxious about his historical reputation and concerned to commit to history a transparent record of his own motives, decisions, and actions. At the same time, we see a man despairing of ever being properly remembered and convinced that his leadership in preserving peace during his administration would be misunderstood, misrepresented, and mistakenly or mischievously forgotten. In that apologia, we recognize a self-portrait of Adams drawn within the lines of classical republican virtue, exercising independent executive leadership and sacrificing his political career and reputation for the public good.

THE PRESIDENCY OF JOHN ADAMS

"The whole of Adams's single term," wrote Stanley Elkins and Eric McKittrick, "was absorbed, to a degree unequaled in any other American presidency, with a single problem, a crisis in foreign relations."[9] Relations between the United States and revolutionary France suffered in the wake of the ratification of the Jay Treaty between America and Great Britain. With the two great European powers at war, France was sensitive to any favor shown to its enemy. The French Directory had refused to credential or even admit Charles Pinckney, the newly appointed American minister to France. In addition, the French fleet began to harass American ships, confiscate American property, and sequester American seamen. Upon taking office, Adams determined to send another mission to France, appointing John Marshall and Elbridge Gerry to join Pinckney, who remained in Europe. The new ministers were not only refused, they also were met with the demand of a bribe by the infamous unnamed French operatives X, Y, and Z. Doubting that the French could be that stupid, Republicans in Congress demanded proof. Adams quickly produced dispatches from Marshall, which he considered "proof as strong as Holy Writ." The result was devastating to the Republican challenge to Adams's policy. "The Jacobins were confounded," wrote Fisher Ames, "and the trimmers dropt off from the party like windfalls from an apple tree in September."[10]

When news of the French insult reached the public, the country began clamoring for war. Faced with that possibility, Adams called for strong defensive measures, and former president George Washington, who had settled into retirement at Mount Vernon, was appointed commander of the army. The vigorous defensive posture pleased the arch-Federalists, who looked for a clean break from France and an end to French influence in American politics. But war preparations caused great anxieties among the Jeffersonian Republicans, who saw the French as their revolutionary brethren and who distrusted what they considered to be the pro-British attitudes of Adams and Hamilton.

Yet, even as the country rallied around the president in his efforts to prepare the nation for a military conflict with France, Adams never entirely abandoned the possibility of reconciliation and peace, as long as both could be achieved in a manner consistent with American dignity and honor. He made it clear that with the proper assurances that an American representative would be received and afforded the regular diplomatic courtesies, he would consider appointing another minister to France. On February 18, 1799, against the advice of his Hamiltonian cabinet, and much to the surprise of leaders in both parties, Adams nominated William Vans Murray, to serve as minister plenipotentiary to France. Murray was already in Europe as American ambassador to Holland, but Adams assured the Senate "he shall not go to France without direct and unequivocal assurances from the French government, signified by their minister of foreign relations, that he shall be received in character, shall enjoy the privileges attached to his character by the law of nations, and that a minister of equal rank, title, and powers, shall be appointed to treat with him, to discuss and conclude all controversies between the two republics by a new treaty."[11] Adams later added Oliver Ellsworth and William Davie to the mission, which was viewed by the "thunderstruck" members of the Federalist Party as "inconsistent," and "a hasty measure." Federalist Theodore Sedgwick believed that "had the foulest heart & the ablest head in the world, been permitted to select the most embarrassing and ruinous measure, perhaps it would have been precisely the one which has been adopted."[12] One irate Federalist commercial trader even sent an anonymous death threat. "Assassination shall be your lot," he wrote, signing himself "a ruined merchant, alas! with ten children!! made beggars by the French."[13] But Adams saw no advantage to war and felt he owed nothing to the Hamiltonian Federalists. "For what end or object should the war have been continued?" he asked. "*Cui bono?* What profit? What loss? Losses enough. Taxes enough."[14]

His decision to send a second mission not only resurrected the possibility of peace with France, it also deflated efforts by Hamilton and other arch-Federalists to recruit and equip a large standing army. Throughout the crisis with France, Adams had always stressed the need for a strong naval defense and encouraged the building of ships and recruiting of sailors to protect American commercial vessels. "I thought brigantines, sloops, schooners, and frigates, well armed and manned and officered, the most economical, the most certain and effectual defence."[15] Still, he "was never happy with the idea of an expanded army," and only reluctantly he went along with the Federalist Congress, which authorized the president to "increase the regular military establishment with twelve regiments of infantry of 700 men each and with six troupes of light dragoons." In addition, he was authorized to create a "provisional army" of 50,000 men and to call 80,000 militiamen to active duty.[16] "That army was as unpopular as if it had been a ferocious wild beast let loose upon the nation to devour it," Adams wrote. "In newspapers, in pamphlets, and in common conversation they were called cannibals."[17]

The army was not only unpopular, it was "far greater in size than anything Adams had asked for, or wanted, or thought was necessary."[18] And, until there was a war to fight, the army would remain "in total idleness and inaction," and consequently might occupy their time "in pillage and plunder, in debauching wives and seducing daughters."[19]

What was worse, for Adams, the day-to-day operation of the army would be under the command of Alexander Hamilton. As Stephen Kurtz explained, "the key to the situation was the army, and from Adams' point of view it made far more sense to destroy it himself than to sit back while the Republicans took full credit for doing so after 1800."[20] By dispatching the peace mission, Adams could also "deal as mortal a stroke to Hamilton's army as any act he could think of."[21]

Adams, then, chose peace. "If I had possessed the hands of Midas, and could have changed trees and rocks into gold, or could I by stamping on the ground, have called up legions of infantry and cavalry, for what purpose should I have continued the war?" he asked. "The end of war is peace; and peace was offered me."[22] So, despite Federalist objections, the ministers departed for France in November, 1799.

By the time the American delegation arrived in Paris in March, 1800, a variety of new developments had contributed significantly to a change in French attitudes and in prospects for a successful negotiation. Not least among these events was the rise to power of Napoleon Bonaparte in the coup d'état of November 9, 1799. The American navy had also experienced considerable success in protecting American shipping, thus foiling French efforts to interrupt American commerce. The American ministers were received with appropriate ceremony and seriousness, and, after eight months of difficult negotiations, the Convention of 1800 was signed in Paris on October 3.

The resulting agreement was, from the American perspective, a specimen of diplomatic mediocrity and, like the Jay Treaty before it, met with less than enthusiastic support in Congress. Still, although the Convention failed to settle claims for damage done to American shipping, the agreement nevertheless allowed American merchants to resume a lucrative trading relationship with France, ended the abuses of French privateering, and enabled America to "wash its hands of a connection that had brought disruptions of every variety, internationally and domestically, from 1789 onwards."[23]

With his great work accomplished, and failing in his bid for reelection, President Adams looked forward to retirement, "far removed from all the intrigues and out of reach of all the great and little passions that agitate the world."[24] Accepting the conditional ratification of the Senate, he told that body, "I shall take no further measures relative to this business, and leave the convention with all the documents in the office of State, that my successor may proceed with them according to his wisdom."[25] As he prepared to leave Washington, he wrote to a friend, summarizing the accomplishments of his administration: "after the 3rd of March I am to be a private citizen and your brother farmer. I shall leave the State with its coffers full, and the fair prospects of a peace with all the world smiling in its face, its commerce flourishing, its navy glorious, its agriculture uncommonly productive and lucrative. O, my country! May peace be within thy walls, and prosperity within thy palaces."[26]

ADAMS AND THE PRESIDENCY

It is useful to begin our examination of John Adams's presidential leadership during the crisis with France by developing some idea of how Adams himself understood the role of the executive. Reflecting on the office of the president in a letter to George Washington, Adams remarked that the presidency, "by its legal authority, defined in the constitution, has no equal in the world."[27] The "constitutional dignity, authority, and power" of the president was remarkable, he wrote on another occasion: "The power of sending and receiving ambassadors, of raising and commanding armies and navies, of nominating and appointing and commissioning all officers, of managing the treasures, the internal and external affairs of the nation; nay, the whole executive power, coextensive with the legislative power, is vested in him, and he has the right, and his is the duty, to take care that the laws be faithfully executed."[28]

Moreover, he believed, "the executive ought to be the reservoir of wisdom," and with the prudent use of his legislative veto "prevent laws from being passed without mature deliberation, and to preserve stability in the administration of government."[29] He further explained to Roger Sherman: "The president has the power of suspending a law; of giving the two houses an opportunity to pause, to think, to collect themselves, to reconsider a rash step of a majority." The veto authority, therefore, preserved the balance of power necessary for stability in government. "Longitude, and the philosopher's stone, have not been sought with more earnestness by philosophers than a guardian of the laws has been studied by legislators from Plato to Montesquieu; but every project has been found to be no better than committing the lamb to the custody of the wolf, except that one which is called a *balance of power.*"[30]

But for Adams, his "dogma of balance," went farther than merely exercising an executive check on legislative excesses. "I am for a balance between the legislative and executive powers," he wrote to Benjamin Rush, "and I am for enabling the executive to be at all times capable of maintaining the balance between the Senate and House, or in other words, between the aristocratical and democratical interest."[31] With such political theory in mind, Peter Shaw argues that Adams saw the presidency "not so much as a strong office as an independent one. A man of integrity stood above contending factions in the Senate and House of Representatives, and above parties as well. He represented the dignity of government and the interests of all the people."[32] As Adams himself argued, "The people, then, ought to consider the President's office as the indispensable guardian of their rights. . . . The people cannot be too careful in the choice of their Presidents; but when they have chosen them, they ought to expect that they will act their own independent judgments, and not be wheedled nor intimidated by factious combinations of senators, representatives, heads of departments, or military officers."[33]

Thus, "the executive figure so dear to John Adams," according to Bruce Miroff, "was the purest exemplar of his classical politics of meritorious leadership." As Miroff explains:

> When Adams spoke of the executive's motives, he adopted a different tone from that he employed to describe aristocratic or democratic motives. Ambition and avarice typically drove the few and the many; in the best of institutional contexts, their desire for fame might come to play a significant role. About the executive, however, Adams seemed to assume that either disinterestedness or the love of fame would be uppermost. Standing apart from the passions of the aristocratic and democratic parties, the executive as mediator was supposed to "calm and restrain the ardor of both." . . . the executive would become a rallying point for the "honest and virtuous of all sides." He was to be a figure marked not by energy but by impartiality and integrity.[34]

Such noble executive service, however, inevitably "entailed sacrifice whenever personal goals clashed with public needs."[35] And, such leaders were rare, even in a republic. "There are a few," Adams wrote, who "aim at approbation as well as attention; at esteem as well as consideration; and at admiration and gratitude, as well as congratu-

lation. This last description of persons is the tribe out of which proceed your patriots and heroes, and most of the great benefactors to
mankind."[36]

CLASSICAL REPUBLICAN VIRTUES

Still, as Miroff has shown, "the classical republican visionary in John
Adams directed his theoretical and practical efforts to establishing a
symbol-rich republic in which political merit would receive its due."[37]
And to the chief executive of the nation was left the greatest portion
of fame. "Fame has been divided into three species," Adams wrote in
his "Discourses on Davila." "Glory, which attends the great actions of
lawgivers and heroes, and the management of the great commands
and first offices of state. Reputation, which is cherished by every gentleman. And Credit, which is supported by merchants and tradesmen."[38]
Adams, however, lamented the fact that genuine talent and true excellence would not likely be recognized by the public or by historians.
"The real merit of public men is rarely fully known and impartially
considered," he wrote.[39] He later became convinced that his own services would be forgotten or distorted. "Mausoleums, statues, and monuments will never be erected to me," he wrote to Benjamin Rush in 1809.
"Panegyrical romances will never be written, nor flattering orations
spoken, to transmit me to posterity in brilliant colors."[40]

Yet, for Adams, fame remained a powerful motive and drove him
always to conduct himself with an eye toward posterity and the historical record. It was a natural attitude, especially for those in "the first
offices of state," for "Nature has ordained it, as a constant incentive to
activity and industry, that to acquire the attention and complacency,
the approbation and admiration of their fellows, men might be urged
to constant exertions of beneficence."[41] As Douglass Adair has explained, "The desire for fame is thus a dynamic element in the historical process; it rejects the static complacent urge in the human heart to
merely *be* and invites a strenuous effort to *become*—to become a person
and force in history larger than the ordinary. The love of fame encour-
ages a man to make history, to leave the mark of his deeds and his
ideals on the world." And, observed Adair, with Adams we have a historical figure whose "passion for fame . . . can be charted with more
exactitude than that of any of his major contemporaries."[42]

Among the qualities of meritorious presidential leadership that Adams would no doubt agree ought to earn lasting fame and be properly recognized in a republic were those attributes of character, and instances of political skill, which manifested the virtue and excellence of the political leader: moral conduct, patriotic eloquence, prudent deliberation, independent and courageous action. This political creed was of ancient heritage. It was in his classical reading, and especially in the life and works of Cicero, that he found the model of the virtuous citizen. In *De Officiis,* Adams read Cicero's prescription for the good public servant and found a light to guide his path through the challenges of his administration. As early as his college days at Harvard, he noted in his diary that the cardinal virtues of "Temperance, Prudence, Justice, and Fortitude," were the "Duties of the Law of human Nature," and were ever "productive of the Happiness and Perfection" of humanity.[43] It was from Cicero that Adams first understood the principle that: "all that is morally right rises from some one of four sources: it is concerned either (1) with the full perception and intelligent development of the true [prudence]; or (2) with the conservation of organized society, with rendering to every man his due, and with the faithful discharge of obligations assumed [justice]; or (3) with the greatness and strength of a noble and invincible spirit [fortitude]; or (4) with the orderliness and moderation of everything that is said and done, where in consist temperance and self-control."[44]

Taking these prescriptions to heart, Adams reflected in his inaugural address on the service of George Washington. Adams praised his predecessor for exhibiting "a long course of great actions regulated by prudence, justice, temperance, and fortitude," which has "merited the gratitude of his fellow citizens . . . and secured immortal glory with posterity."[45] His classical reading told Adams that these cardinal virtues were the essence of strong political leadership. As he praised Washington he also recognized these virtues as a code of conduct for his own administration. "This example has been recommended to the imitation of his successors," he said of the retiring first president, "by both Houses of Congress, and by the voice of the legislatures and the people throughout the nation."[46]

From Cicero Adams could also find support for his emphasis on independence and impartiality in office. "Those who propose to take charge of the affairs of government," Cicero advised, "should not fail to remember two of Plato's rules: first, to keep the good of the people so clearly in view that regardless of their own interests they will make their every action conform to that; second, to care for the welfare of the whole body politic and not in serving the interest of some one party to betray the rest." In words almost identical to those Adams himself had written in his *Defence* and in his letter to Benjamin Rush, Cicero warned that leaders who attend to "the interests of a part of the citizens and neglect another part," corrupt politics. "The result," wrote the Roman, "is that some are found to be loyal supporters of the democratic, others of the aristocratic party, and few of the nation as a whole."[47]

Adams likewise found support from his ancient hero for his specific policy decisions regarding the peace mission. "Most people think that the achievements of war are more important than those of peace," wrote Cicero, "but this opinion needs to be corrected. . . . if we will face the facts, we shall find that there have been many instances of achievement in peace more important and no less renowned than in war."[48]

Furthermore, as Cicero taught, and Adams himself came to realize, those in offices of great responsibility "run the risk of losing their lives, others their reputation and the good-will of their fellow citizens. It is our duty, then to be more ready to endanger our own than the public welfare and to hazard honour and glory more readily than other advantages."[49] Writing to former Federalist Congressman James Lloyd in 1815, Adams reflected upon events during his presidency when "Washington, Hamilton, and Pinckney were assembled at Philadelphia to advise in the selection of officers for the army. The history of the formation of this triumvirate would be as curious as that of Pompey, Caesar, and Crassus, or that of Antony, Octavius and Lepidus, and the effects of it have been and may be, for anything I know, as prosperous or adverse to mankind. One thing I know, that Cicero was not sacrificed to the vengeance of Antony by the unfeeling selfishness of the latter triumvirate more egregiously than John Adams was to the unbridled and unbounded ambition of Alexander Hamilton in the American triumvirate."[50]

The themes of Adams's comparison echo an earlier letter to Benjamin Rush, when Adams considered that

> I will not die wholly unlamented. Cicero was libeled, slandered, insulted by all parties—by Caesar's party, Catiline's crew, Clodius' myrmidons, aye, and by Pompey and the Senate too. He was persecuted and tormented by

turns by all parties and all factions, and that for his most virtuous and glorious actions. In his anguish at times and in the consciousness of his own merit and integrity, he was driven to those assertions of his own actions which have been denominated vanity. Instead of reproaching them with vanity I think them the most infallible demonstration of his innocence and purity. He declares that all honors are indifferent to him because he knows that it is not in the power of his country to reward him in any proportion to his services. Pushed and injured and provoked as I am, I blush not to imitate the Roman and to say to these snarlers against me that if, to avoid misrepresentations of my words, I had omitted to speak and write, they would never have been wealthy and powerful as they are. This country would never have been independent.[51]

It is not surprising to find Adams making these reflections at a time when he was also engaged in composing a history of his administration in a series of letters to the *Boston Patriot,* letters that Joseph Ellis called "his final spasm of unbridled self-vindication," and which Adams feared would add substance to the charge that he, like Cicero, was vain.[52] Although Adams knew that Cicero "could not hire so many scribblers to defend him as his enemies did to reproach him,"[53] the former president hoped that by recording his version of events he might defend his conduct "against the charges and insinuations of conceited Blockheads."[54] As he explained to Skelton Jones, "the causes of my retirement are to be found in the writings of Freneau, Marke, Ned Church, Andrew Brown, Paine, Callender, Hamilton, Cobbett, and John Ward Fenno and many others, but more especially in the circular letters of members of Congress from the southern and middle States. Without a complete collection of all these libels, no faithful history of the last twenty years can ever be written, nor any adequate account given of the causes of my retirement from public life."[55]

The chief "blockhead" by a length, however, was Alexander Hamilton, who sought to ruin Adams's chances for a second term by alienating arch-Federalists from the president. His scandalous pamphlet entitled *The Public Conduct and Character of John Adams, Esquire, President of the United States,* focused on the policies Adams adopted during the quasi-war with France and condemned the president's decision to send a second peace mission to Paris. In the view of Charles Francis Adams, the pamphlet was "intended to destroy Mr. Adams's chance of reelection at all hazards."[56]

There was great enmity between Hamilton and the second president. Adams considered his nemesis to be "the most restless, impatient, artful, indefatigable and unprincipled intriguer in the United States, if not the world."[57] According to Adams, Hamilton had a "disturbed imagination," that "was always haunted by that hideous monster or phantom, so often called a *crisis*."[58] Moreover, Hamilton was frustrated by Adams's independence. "I have not a doubt," Adams wrote, "that one of his principal vexations was, that neither himself nor his privy counsellors could have influence enough with me to persuade or intimidate me to disgrace myself in the eyes of the people of America and the world."[59]

Along with the "pharisaical, jesuitical, machiavelian intrigue and influence of the leading federalists,"[60] it was "the insidious and dark intrigues as well as open remonstrances of Mr. Hamilton," that led Adams to the necessity of a public defense of his administration. "On April 10th, 1809, I commenced in the Boston Patriot a series of letters in vindication of my missions to France," he wrote to James Lloyd. In those letters "you will see the history of the rise and progress of the negotiations with France, which led to that happy conclusion."[61] As it turns out, Adams's correspondence with Lloyd forms a second text of self-defense, which Adams promises will "remain in my letterbook, to enable my children to apologize for my memory."[62]

SELF-DEFENSE OF A PRUDENT PRESIDENT

Adams explained his purposes as he addressed the editors of the *Patriot:* "If you will allow me a little room in your Patriot, I may hereafter produce proofs to the satisfaction of the public, that this measure [the second peace mission] was neither odious nor ridiculous."[63] Specifically, Adams aimed to show anyone willing to read his public correspondence that the embassy to France was the sort of public service that reflected his independent and upright character, as well as his political skill, and deserved to be remembered with gratitude by his fellow citizens.

Yet, as he wrote, he must have been convinced that his motives for writing a public defense would be misunderstood. A year earlier, another Ciceronian comparison enabled him to express his frustration. To his son, John Quincy Adams, he lamented: "When poor Cicero found himself almost the only Roman left Surrounded by Clodius, Cataline, Caesar, and Pompey, all alike ambitious and selfish, the two last with Legions at their heels Sufficient to overawe every independent Soul by four and twenty per Cent. . . . he had no consolation but in his own Vanity as most men call it, But his own Consciousness of Merit as I deem it."[64]

The next day, he continued the theme in a letter to Benjamin Rush: "What other people call Vanity in Cicero, I denominate Naivete. The superiority of his Virtue and Talents excited Jealousy and Envy among the Citizens in general, and Clodius, Cataline, Sallust, & Caesar and Pompey too. . . . He blazoned forth his own Virtues, Talents, and great services . . . bidding open Defiance to every citizen to contradict him if he could. . . . Do you call this Vanity? It was self Defense, Independence, Intrepidity, or in one word Naivete."[65]

Now it was Adams himself, of course, who was engaged in an effort of "self-Defense," who "blazoned forth his own Virtues, Talents, and great services," exhibiting his own "Consciousness of Merit," as well as his "Independence" and "Intrepidity." Indeed, what we find in Adams's defense of his administration is a self-portrait largely informed by the classical republican virtues of Cicero. Specifically, we see Adams represent his presidency as an administration governed altogether by the cardinal virtue of prudence.

Robert Hariman defines prudence as "the capacity for effective political response to contingent events. It arises in deliberation, requires implicit understanding of the possible, the probable, and the appropriate within a specific community."[66] Hariman and Francis Beer further explain that "prudence is a form of reasoning that at some point has to be realized in action," which means that "the most important skill for the prudent leader is deliberation."[67]

We can recognize Adams's emphasis on prudence, first in his characterizations of Hamilton. Adams describes his adversary as prone to "erroneous conceptions" which led him often into "imprudent measures."[68] In general, the Hamiltonian "faction was dizzy. Their brains turned round. They knew not, they saw not the precipice on which they stood."[69] In contrast, Adams notes, "the soundest statesmen of the ruling [Federalist] party in both houses approved of my missions to France."[70] One supporter expressed to Adams that "to judge of the conduct of the American government, both in their naval and other preparations for war, and in their political and diplomatic negotiations upon that occasion, a man must go to Europe, where it was considered as the greatest demonstration of genius, firmness, and wisdom."[71]

Hariman and Beer maintain that there are three modes of prudence, "three different mentalities" that together define "political intelligence." Normative prudence is reasoning about the ends of policy. It is "ethical reasoning in a political context" a "form of reasoning that manages the incommensurability of goods." Calculative prudence is reasoning about means and involves "making valid predictions with a potentially large number of variables." In calculative prudence, the emphasis is on "developing foresight." Finally, performative prudence encompasses the "aesthetic dimension of politics," focuses on the "effective performance of one's role," and "becomes a capacity for managing appearances for political effect."[72]

In his apologia, Adams made it clear that his decision to send the mission to France was thoughtful, right, and just. It was a choice that exhibited his "normative prudence." "The institution of an embassy to France, in 1799," he wrote, "was made upon principle, and in conformity to a system of foreign affairs, formed upon long deliberation, established in my mind, and amply opened, explained, and supported in Congress."[73]

Adams further explained that his decision was a "point of honor in which my moral character was involved as well as the public faith of the nation."[74] In such decisions, he concluded, "the ministers are responsible for nothing, the President for everything." Therefore, the president "is bound by his honor and his conscience, by his oath to the Constitution, as well as his responsibility to the public opinion of the nation, to act his own mature and unbiased judgment, though unfortunately, it may be in direct contradiction to the advice of all his ministers."[75] And, in this situation, "if, with all this information, I had refused to institute a negotiation, or had not persevered in it after it was instituted, I should have been degraded in my own estimation as a man of honor, I should have disgraced the nation I represented, in their own opinion and in the judgment of all Europe."[76] In these reflections on his decision, Adams emphasizes his "honor," and represents what Hariman and Beer call the "suitably competent and ethical personality," that best characterizes the normative dimension of prudence in "the model political leader."[77]

Adams also reasoned about the means of achieving peace. In his self-defense, he spent considerable effort recollecting his deliberative efforts. His decision to send the mission, he said, was made "upon mature reflection," and had "engrossed my attention for a long time." It was a decision in which he tried to "take every thing into consideration, and determine nothing suddenly." He made "deliberate inquiries concerning characters, and maturely consider[ed] the qualities and qualifications of candidates, before anything was finally determined."[78]

Adams also measured the situation in France, as well as the multitude of other political circumstances, that formed the context for his decision. "I considered, moreover, that France was an undulating ocean in a violent storm," he wrote. "Party had exterminated party, and constitution had succeeded constitution, as billow rolls and roars, froths and foams after billow in the Gulf Stream."[79] In addition, "The gulf of national bankruptcy yawned. The monsters, paper money, tender law, and regulation of prices, all stalked in horrors before me."[80]

Neither was he intimidated by opposition from the arch-Federalists: "I did not think that the rumbling noise of party calumny ought to discourage me from consulting men whom I knew to be attached to the interest of the nation, and whose experience, genius, learning, and travels had eminently qualified them to give advice." Therefore, Adams resolved to "ask Mr. Jefferson what he thought of another trip to Paris."[81] The final judgment regarding his deliberative skills, Adams left to posterity: "And now, let the world judge who 'consulted much,' who 'pondered much,' who 'resolved slowly,' and who 'resolved surely.'"[82] Here, indeed, is Adams's exhibition of his own calculative prudence, his ability to deal with "the problem of radical contingency," and his effort to "acquire sufficient knowledge to act in a complex environment."[83]

But Adams was also concerned with appearance and performance. He aimed to show posterity his success in dealing persuasively, and in a timely fashion, with his cabinet and the public. With his numerous replies to the private addresses he received from around the nation, as well as in his various official messages to Congress, the president was able to "animate this nation to war" when it was necessary and then respond to "the popular clamor of peace" at the appropriate time.[84] Once the decision to send the mission was settled, Adams "directed the instructions to be prepared, the heads of the departments were assembled, and the instructions deliberately considered, paragraph by paragraph, and unanimously approved by me and by them."[85] As he considered a delay in the mission to France, he set off to Trenton (where the government had retreated from a yellow fever epidemic) to meet his cabinet "face to face, to confer with them coolly on the subject, and convince them, or be convinced by them, if I could."[86]

Even with Hamilton, who visited Adams "to remonstrate against the mission to France," the president observed the greatest decorum. "I received him with great civility, as I always had done," he remembered, "and treated him throughout with great mildness and civility." But despite the public display, Adams in private was astonished at "the total ignorance he had betrayed of every thing in Europe, in France, England, and elsewhere."[87] His "civility" to Hamilton, then, is a mark of his "propriety," as Cicero understood it; his understanding that his conduct "manifestly embraces temperance and self-control, together with a certain deportment such as becomes a gentleman."[88]

In these subtle revelations, Adams depicts his own understanding of "the linkage between the concepts of prudence and decorum," and his ability to engage in "the social conventions that make action intelligible." Hariman and Beer maintain that Cicero is the "major representative of this mentality," so it is not surprising to find Adams displaying a "sensitivity to the uniqueness of a given situation and to the problem of how one ought to conduct oneself in it."[89]

At another level, the entirety of Adams's apologia reflects on his ability to manage appearances vis-à-vis France. The correspondence with Lloyd and his letters to the *Boston Patriot* ultimately put on display his diplomatic talent for "reaching the right conclusion in the right way and at the right time."[90] "Ranks, titles, and etiquettes, and every species of punctilios, even down to the visits of cards, are of infinitely more importance in Europe than in America," Adams once wrote, "therefore Congress cannot be too tender of disgracing their ministers abroad in any of these things."[91] Indeed, from his long diplomatic service Adams understood, as Hariman and Beer maintain, that "diplomatic performance is thoroughly prudential."[92] His *Patriot* letters reveal his gift for managing the demands of diplomatic propriety, interpreting French "gestures," and deciding upon action that would satisfy the conventions of foreign negotiation as he sought to "listen to every proposal and embrace the first opportunity to restore peace, whenever it could be done consistently with the honor and interest of the country."[93]

"In general," write Hariman and Beer, "a prudent actor is one who balances incommensurable goods, discerns probable courses of action, and interacts with others in an appropriate and timely manner."[94] In his address to posterity in defense of his administration, John Adams aimed to exhibit his own presidency as one occupied by that consummate "prudent actor." Guided by the classical virtues and motivated by his desire for fame, Adams risked his political career to achieve peace with France. Looking back on his administration, he was certain he had done the right thing, whether or not we, as his posterity, would be prepared to recognize his prudence. "I had complete and perfect success," he wrote to James Lloyd, "and left my country at peace with all the world, upon terms consistent with the honor and interest of the United States."[95]

NOTES

1. L. H. Butterfield, ed., *Diary and Autobiography of John Adams* (Cambridge, Mass.: Belknap Press, 1961), 2:79.

2. Adams to Rush, Apr. 12, 1809, in *The Works of John Adams, Second President of the United States: with A Life of the Author, Notes and Illustrations,* ed. Charles Francis Adams, 10 vols. (Boston: Little, Brown, 1853), 9:616–17.

3. Adams to Lloyd, Apr. 24, 1815, in Adams, ed., *Works of John Adams,* 10:162. Elsewhere I have speculated on the motives that led Adams to take on this unpopular legal task. See James M. Farrell, "*Pro Militibus Oratio:* John Adams's Imitation of Cicero in the Boston Massacre Trial," *Rhetorica* 9, no. 3 (summer, 1991): 233–49.

4. Adams to Warren, Apr. 16, 1776, in *Papers of John Adams,* vol. 4, ed. Robert S. Taylor (Cambridge, Mass.: Harvard University Press, 1979), 124. See the excellent discussion of Adams's classical republican philosophy in Bruce Miroff, *Icons of Democracy: American Leaders as Heroes, Aristocrats, Dissenters, & Democrats* (New York: Basic Books, 1993), 50–82.

5. Adams to Rush, Apr. 12, 1809, in Adams, ed., *Works of John Adams,* 9:617.

6. Adams to Lloyd, Feb. 6, 1815, ibid., 10:115.

7. Adams to Lloyd, Mar. 31, 1815, ibid., 10:154.

8. Adams to Lloyd, Jan. 1815, ibid., 10:113.

9. Stanley Elkins and Eric McKittrick, *The Age of Federalism* (New York: Oxford, 1993): 529. Elsewhere I have outlined in some detail my views on Adams's presidential rhetoric. See James M. Farrell, "John Adams," in *Presidents as Orators: A Bio-Critical Source Book,* ed. Halford Ryan, (Westport, Conn.: Greenwood Press, 1994), 18–27.

10. Page Smith, *John Adams,* vol. 2 (Garden City, N.Y.: Doubleday, 1962), 959.

11. "Message to the Senate; nominating an Envoy to France," Feb. 18, 1799, in Adams, ed., *Works of John Adams*, 9:162. For a detailed study of the French crisis, see Alexander DeConde, *The Quasi-War: The Politics and Diplomacy of the Undeclared War with France 1797–1801* (New York: Charles Scribner's Sons, 1966); See also Elkins and McKittrick, *Age of Federalism*, 529–662; and John C. Miller, *The Federalist Era, 1789–1801* (New York: Harper, 1960), 205–50.

12. Elkins and McKittrick, *Age of Federalism*, 619.

13. Smith, *John Adams*, 2:1001.

14. Adams to Lloyd, Feb. 6, 1815, 10:114.

15. Adams to Lloyd, Feb. 21, 1815, in Adams, ed., *Works of John Adams*, 10:127.

16. DeConde, *Quasi-War*, 96.

17. Adams to Lloyd, Feb. 18, 1815, in Adams, ed., *Works of John Adams*, 10:118.

18. Elkins and McKittrick, *Age of Federalism*, 593.

19. Adams to Lloyd, Feb. 21, 1815, 10:130.

20. Stephen G. Kurtz, *The Presidency of John Adams: the Collapse of Federalism, 1795–1800* (Philadelphia: University of Pennsylvania Press, 1957), 366.

21. Elkins and McKittrick, *Age of Federalism*, 618.

22. Adams to Lloyd, Feb. 21, 1815, 10:130.

23. Elkins and McKittrick, *Age of Federalism*, 664.

24. Adams to Elias Boudinot, Jan. 26, 1801, in Adams, ed., *Works of John Adams*, 9:94.

25. "Message to the Senate on the Convention with France," Mar. 2, 1801, ibid., 9:167.

26. Adams to F. A. Vanderkemp, Dec. 28, 1800, ibid., 9:577. Adams here quotes Psalm 122.7: "Peace be within thy walls, and prosperity within thy palaces" (KJV).

27. Adams to Washington, May 17, 1789, in Adams, ed., *Works of John Adams*, 8:493.

28. Adams to Roger Sherman, July 18, 1789, ibid., 6:430.

29. Adams to Elbridge Gerry, Nov. 4, 1779, ibid., 9:506; John Adams to Roger Sherman, July 17, 1789, ibid., 6: 427–28.

30. Adams to Sherman, July 18, 1789, 6:431

31. Adams to Rush, Apr. 19, 1790, in Adams, ed., *Works of John Adams*, 9:566. For more on this point, see "John Adams and the Dogma of Balance," in Elkins and McKittrick, *Age of Federalism*, 529–79. See also "The Relevance and Irrelevance of John Adams," in Gordon Wood, *The Creation of the American Republic, 1776–1787* (New York: Norton, 1969), 567–92.

32. Peter Shaw, *The Character of John Adams*, (Chapel Hill: University of North Carolina Press, 1976): 247.

33. "To the Printers of the Boston Patriot," in Adams, ed., *Works of John Adams*, 9:302.

34. Miroff, *Icons of Democracy*, 76–77.

35. Ibid., 53.

36. Adams, ed., *Works of John Adams*, 6:248.

37. Miroff, *Icons of Democracy*, 63.

38. Adams, ed., *Works of John Adams,* 6:241.

39. Ibid., 6:158.

40. Adams to Rush, Mar. 23, 1809, in *The Spur of Fame: Dialogues of John Adams and Benjamin Rush, 1805–1813,* ed. John A. Schutz and Douglass Adair (San Marino, Calif.: Huntington Library, 1966), 139.

41. Adams, ed., *Works of John Adams,* 6:245.

42. Douglass Adair, *Fame and the Founding Fathers: Essays by Douglass Adair,* ed. Trevor Colbourn (New York: Norton, 1974), 11, 20. Elsewhere, I have written at length on John Adams's desire for fame. See James M. Farrell, "John Adams's *Autobiography*: The Ciceronian Paradigm and the Quest for Fame," *New England Quarterly* 62, no. 4 (Dec., 1989): 505–28.

43. L. H. Butterfield, ed., *Earliest Diary of John Adams* (Cambridge, Mass.: Harvard University Press, 1966), 54.

44. Cicero, *De Officiis,* trans. Walter Miller (Cambridge, Mass.: Harvard University Press, 1975), I.15. In several studies I have documented the influence of Cicero's career and writing on the life and work of John Adams. See: "Letters and Political Judgment: John Adams and Cicero's Style," *Studies in Eighteenth-Century Culture* 24 (1994): 137–53; "New England's Cicero: John Adams and the Rhetoric of Conspiracy," *Proceedings of the Massachusetts Historical Society* 104 (1992): 55–72; "'Syren Tully' and the Young John Adams," *Classical Journal* 87 (1992): 373–90.

45. Adams, ed., *Works of John Adams,* 9:108.

46. Ibid., 9:108–109.

47. Cicero, *De Officiis,* I.85. See also Adams, ed., *Works of John Adams,* 6:533; Adams to Rush, Apr. 19, 1790, 9:566; Wood, *Creation of the American Republic,* 574–80.

48. Cicero, *De Officiis* I.74.

49. Ibid., I.83.

50. Adams to Lloyd, Feb. 11, 1815, in Adams, ed., *Works of John Adams,* 10:118; See also: Adams to Rush, Dec. 4, 1805, in Schutz and Adair, *Spur of Fame,* 44–45.

51. Adams to Rush, Mar. 23, 1809.

52. Joseph Ellis, *Passionate Sage: The Character and Legacy of John Adams* (New York: Norton, 1993), Useful in understanding Adams's thinking at this time in his life is Peter Shaw's *Character of John Adams,* especially 270–99.

53. Adams to Rush, Jan. 18, 1808, Adams Papers Microfilm Series, reel 405, Massachusetts Historical Society, Boston.

54. Adams to Nicholas Boylston, Nov. 3, 1819, quoted in Ellis, *Passionate Sage,* 77.

55. Adams to Jones, Mar. 11, 1809, in Adams, ed., *Works of John Adams,* 9:612. Given the present moral climate in Washington, it is perhaps appropriate to note here that Adams could assert in his old age that "among all the errors, follies, failings, vices, and crimes, which have been so plentifully imputed to me, I cannot recollect a single insinuation against me of any amorous intrigue, or irregular or immoral connection with a woman, single or married, myself a bachelor or a married man" (Adams to Rush, Aug. 28, 1811, in Adams, ed., *Works of John Adams,* 9:637).

56. Charles Francis Adams, "Preliminary Note," in Adams, ed., *Works of John Adams,* 9:239. See Harold C. Syrett, ed., *The Papers of Alexander Hamilton,* vol. 25 (New York: Columbia University Press, 1977), 169–234.

57. Adams to Lloyd, Feb. 17, 1815, in Adams, ed., *Works of John Adams,* 10:124.

58. "To the Printers of the Boston Patriot," ibid., 9:281, 289–90.

59. "To the Patriot," ibid., 9:292.

60. Adams to Joseph Lyman, Apr. 20, 1809, ibid., 9:620.

61. Adams to Lloyd, Mar. 30, 1815, ibid., 10:148, 151.

62. Ibid., 10:151.

63. "To the Patriot," 9:241.

64. Adams to John Quincy Adams, Jan. 17, 1808, Adams Papers, reel 405.

65. Adams to Rush, Jan. 18, 1808, ibid.

66. Robert Hariman, "Prudence/Performance" *Rhetoric Society Quarterly* 21, no. 2 (spring, 1991): 26.

67. Robert Hariman and Francis Beer, "What Would Be Prudent? Forms of Reasoning in World Politics," *Rhetoric and Public Affairs* 1, no. 3 (fall, 1998): 303.

68. "To the Printers," in Adams, ed. *Works of John Adams,* 9:277, 290.

69. Adams to Lloyd, Feb. 6, 1815, 10:115.

70. Adams to Lloyd, Feb. 18, 1815, 10:118.

71. "To the Patriot," 9:267.

72. Hariman and Beer, "What Would Be Prudent?" 304–10.

73. "To the Patriot," in Adams, ed. *Works of John Adams,* 9:242.

74. Ibid., 9:295.

75. Ibid., 9:270.

76. Ibid., 9:246.

77. Hariman and Beers, "What Would Be Prudent?" 306.

78. "To the Patriot," in Adams, ed. *Works of John Adams,* 9:308, 283.

79. Ibid., 9:247.

80. Adams to Lloyd, Feb. 14, 1815, in Adams, ed. *Works of John Adams,* 10:123.

81. "To the Patriot," ibid., 9:285.

82. Ibid., 9:294.

83. Hariman and Beers, "What Would Be Prudent?" 306–307.

84. "To the Patriot," in Adams, ed. *Works of John Adams,* 9:243, 279.

85. Ibid., 9:255.

86. Ibid., 9:252.

87. Ibid., 9:254–55.

88. Cicero, *De Officiis,* I.96.

89. Hariman and Beer, "What Would Be Prudent?" 308–309.

90. Ibid., 309. It is interesting that perhaps the single most troubling problem for Adams in the French crisis was the "timing" of the second mission. This difficulty is made evident by a study of the "Official" correspondence of his administration. See Adams, ed., *Works of John Adams,* 8:624–9:39.

91. Adams to Secretary Livingston, Nov. 8, 1782, in Adams, ed., *Works of John Adams,* 8:3.

92. Hariman and Beer, "What Would Be Prudent?" 309.

93. "To the Patriot," in Adams, ed. *Works of John Adams*, 9:243. At the same time, one might argue that Adams's inability to use his rhetorical skills to mold a national consensus on the peace with France was ultimately responsible for his failure to win a second term and for the lasting damage done by his opponents to his reputation. In short, Adams was unable to master the "imaginative use of the materials and techniques of artistic appeal . . . which requires effective use of a culture's conventions of political display" (Hariman, "Prudence/Performance," 30, 32).

94. Hariman and Beer, "What Would Be Prudent?" 310.

95. Adams to Lloyd, Mar. 31, 1815, in Adams, ed. *Works of John Adams*, 10:153.

CHAPTER 4

Jefferson vs. Napoleon

The Limits of Rhetoric

Lawrence S. Kaplan

ISTORIANS AND BIOGRAPHERS of every generation have observed the many inconsistencies in Thomas Jefferson's behavior as a public man.[1] Most notable have been his shifts from a strict to a loose constructionist of the Constitution, from limiting the powers of the president to expanding them when in office, from an ardent advocate of an agrarian republic to a supporter of manufactures and commerce. Many of these apparent paradoxes can be unraveled by examination of their contexts, but some remain conundrums for future historians to ponder.

But there is one attribute that all his enemies and many of his friends have accepted as constant: a Francophilia that began with the American Revolution, blossomed during his years as minister plenipotentiary to Paris, solidified with his embrace of the French Revolution, and was activated by the Anglo-French conflict through the Napoleonic years. Only in his old age did he begin to recognize the errors of his judgments, and even then, as he told Albert Gallatin in 1815, he trusted that the French "will finally establish for themselves a government of rational and well-tempered liberty."[2] The consistency of his Francophilia earned him the amused condescension of his old friend and former adversary, John Adams, as well as the raillery of Patrick Henry—who accused Jefferson of being among those gentlemen "abjuring their native victuals" in favor of French cuisine—and the contempt of Alexander Hamilton for his "womanish attachment to France and his womanish resentment against Great Britain."[3] Of all his contemporaries, the youngest, thirteen-year-old poet William Cullen Bryant, arguably outdid his elders in 1808 when he identified President Jefferson as "Napoleon's slave" and "willing vassal of imperious France."[4]

Napoleon Bonaparte's successful manipulation of the president was a major theme of Henry Adams's influential interpretation of Jefferson's presidency, which expressed in more measured language the outrage of Federalists over his relations with France during the Napoleonic Wars. In the Adams canon, Jefferson the president was less the partisan of France than the dupe of Napoleon, in essence a pathetic figure who tried and failed to outwit the wily emperor. Granting that Jefferson was an honest man, Adams claimed that "in putting on the outward appearance of a Talleyrand, he resembled an amateur playing Talma and Garrick," the stars respectively of the Paris and London theaters.[5] Jeffersonians have tried with vigor if not with success to counter Adams, and none was more outspoken than Claude Bowers in the 1920s or more judicious than Dumas Malone in the next generation. Jefferson's high hopes were to play off the two superpowers—Britain and France—against each other. If he did not succeed, Malone believed that "it may now appear that he was slower than he should have been in recognizing how ruthless the rulers of the contending nations actually were."[6]

Critics have always noted a paradox in Jefferson's visceral aversion to Bonaparte, long before he became emperor, and at the same time a willingness to support Napoleon against his British enemy. There are explanations even if they are not definitive. The most credible ones have little to do with a putative incurable Francophilia; his love of France existed on a private and cultural level after he came to grips with the failure of its revolution. Rather, it lay in two key elements in the triangular relationship of the United States with France and Britain. First, Napoleon, "a cold-blooded, calculating, unprincipled Usurper, without a virtue,"[7] was nevertheless only one man, whereas Britain's Parliament would endure no matter who was its leader at any given moment. France without the charismatic figure of Napoleon was a lesser challenge to America. Second, Britain's naval power was a standing threat to the United States in a way that Napoleon's armies were not.

There is still another consideration that underlies the major thesis of this chapter: namely, that Jefferson's concerns with both superpowers lay in preventing their standing in the path of America's westward expansion as an "empire of liberty" was being created. As minister to France and as secretary of state before Bonaparte appeared on the scene, Jefferson was disturbed by French and British exploration of the West. He would have preferred dealing with Spain until the nation was strong enough to remove Spanish sovereignty from the Mississippi Valley and the Floridas. He hoped that through cajolery, bullying, or appeal to self-interest Spain would cede the territory surrounding New Orleans east of the Mississippi in return for an American guarantee west of the river. "In fine," he observed in 1790, "for a narrow slip of barren, detached and expensive country, Spain secures the rest of her territory, and makes an Ally, where she might have a dangerous enemy."[8]

But Spain was always a sideshow, as much a victim of American pressures as of the international politics of Britain and France. The wars of the French Revolution in the 1790s gave proof that Spain was essentially a pawn in the games of the great powers. Its very weakness bothered the United States. Arguably, Jefferson, early in his presidency, was just as worried about aggressive and impatient westerners seizing New Orleans on their own and separating themselves from the Union. But his eye was primarily on France and Britain. The ambitions of those nations, Britain in particular, drove Jefferson to urge George Rogers Clark in the 1770s and John Ledyard in the 1780s to mount expeditions to counter them. Historian Stephen Ambrose observed that even after Louisiana was secured, "it was not the French who got Jefferson to start another project for an exploring expedition across the West—the retrocession had nothing to do with it—but the British."[9] The Briton in this case was a Scot, Alexander Mackenzie, a Montreal fur trader who had crossed the continent to the Pacific Coast in the 1780s but found the route unsuitable for commercial profit. His account of the journey, published in London in 1801, induced Jefferson to challenge a potential British effort to take over the west. Meriwether Lewis was recruited for this task before Louisiana was retroceded.

The arrival of Bonaparte on the French scene only aggravated worries that the Directory had stoked by speculations in 1797 that a now-hostile France was conspiring with the Spanish to block navigation on the Mississippi. Jefferson gloomily predicted that there would be "new neighbors in Louisiana (probably the present French armies when disbanded)" who would expose America to a "combination of enemies on that side where we are most vulnerable."[10] When the Directory was shoved aside in Bonaparte's coup d'état of November 9, 1799, it merely confirmed the vice president's assessment of increased danger to an expanding American empire. He saw in this man on horseback another Caesar and made a connection between Bonaparte and Hamilton.

It is clear that in assuming the presidency in 1801 Jefferson recognized that the nation confronted two enemies, both hostile to American interests. Of the two, France was potentially more useful in keeping Europe at bay. It had no navy to fear and none of the special animus that characterized Anglo-American relations. But to exploit the French card required considerable finesse. The French dictator had to be enticed, cajoled, and—if necessary and possible—even intimidated into serving America's interests. War against either party was not the means of eliciting this service. When his fears of France as a neighbor in Louisiana first surfaced in 1797, Jefferson noted that "war is not the best engine for us to resort to, nature has given us one in our commerce [that], if properly managed, will be a better instrument for obliging the interested nations of Europe to treat us with justice."[11]

However, as Jefferson assumed office in 1801, "commerce" was not the best instrument for dealing with Bonaparte's Consulate. By 1799 the emphasis was on "political connections with none," a sentiment that echoed Washington's Farewell Address and prefigured his first inaugural address. Small wonder that the Convention of Mortefontaine in September, 1800, which terminated the French alliance, evoked no protest from the president-elect or from his supporters in Congress and the press when news of the convention reached Philadelphia. If Jefferson called it a "bungling" treaty in a letter to Madison, it was because there were so many loose ends, including a failure to win compensation for France's depredations against American shipping.[12] This was not his primary sentiment, however.

A week after disparaging Adams's successful peacemaking, he noted in another letter to Madison that "the French treaty will be violently opposed by the federalists; the giving up the vessels is the article they cannot swallow."[13] Jefferson, in fact, had little trouble swallowing this concession. He had more difficulty with the positions of his American friends in France who praised France's proposal of a new league of armed neutrals that favored liberal maritime regulations, which the United States had advocated for a generation. But neutral rights in the abstract had lost their luster, if only because they had failed to curb British sea power. The new president pointedly agreed with George Logan, a devoted Quaker peace seeker, that the United States ought to join no confederacies, even when they pursued laudable goals of freeing the seas for neutral trade: "It ought to be the very first object of our pursuits to have nothing to do with the European interests and politics."[14]

These words were written a little more than two weeks after Jefferson's inaugural address, and they reflected the major sentiments of that notable speech. The merging of Anglophiles and Francophiles to identify the common bond minimized partisan differences. The passions of the political arena, which churned out extravagant charges against the presidential candidates, particularly against Jefferson himself, were characterized simply as "a difference of opinion." His intention was to soothe those passions and yoke them to a common effort. What could be more accommodating than his asking the nation "to bear in mind this sacred principle, that though the will of the majority is in all cases to prevail, that will to be rightful must be reasonable; that the minority possess their equal rights, which equal law must protect."

It was in this setting that he stated: "every difference of opinion is not a difference of principle. We have called by different names brethren of the same principle. We are all Republicans. We are all Federalists."[15] This mingling of the two parties appropriately has received the attention of historians, who have looked for meanings behind the words. Was this a genuine abandonment of partisanship? Or was it a means of lowering the temper of political life while the new administration tried to pursue its Republican objectives? The latter objective was the judgment of Henry Adams. He felt that Jefferson belittled the revolution that his own success had achieved and was convinced that "in no party sense was it true that all were Republicans and all were Federalists. He asserted that Jefferson himself was far from meaning what he seemed to say." While he certainly wanted to calm his adversaries, "he had no idea of harmony or affection . . . and in representing that he was in any sense a Federalist, he did himself wrong."[16]

A more recent historian, Joseph Ellis, seconded this judgment by noting that in the handwritten version of Jefferson's inaugural address, as opposed to the printed version, "the key words were not capitalized." No one would disagree with the idea of a republican form of government undergirded by a federal bond, but Ellis judged Jefferson's sentiments to be "more a political platitude than an ideological concession."[17] Yet the new president managed to convince his old adversary, Hamilton, that he "will not lend himself to dangerous innovations, but in essential points will tread in the steps of his predecessors."[18]

All too often the president's stance on foreign relations was missing in many of the analyses of his message. Ellis omitted it altogether. Adams, whose primary concern in his massive history was with Jefferson's incapacity to cope with the Pitts and Napoleons of Europe, observed that his conception of a proper foreign policy, "omitted from the Inaugural Address, was to be found in his private correspondence and in the speeches of Gallatin and Madison as leaders of the opposition."[19]

There is no doubt that Jefferson's private correspondence, as noted elsewhere in this essay, clearly displayed his distaste for both Britain and France at this time as well as his firm belief that in abstaining from entanglement in the affairs of the Old World the United States could profit from the conflict between the titans. But foreign affairs were not absent from his first inaugural address. His rephrasing of Washington's sentiments in 1796 in asking for "peace, commerce, and honest friendship with all nations, entangling alliances with none," underscored his acceptance of the Convention of Mortefontaine, which terminated the Franco-American alliance.[20] Jefferson wished to make sure that his audience recognized the potential hostility of both nations to the interests of the United States.

Henry Adams buried this passage in the long paragraph in which it was contained. He joined Federalist critics in mocking the mixed metaphors in the extended sentence that expresses the same idea in a more flowery rhetoric: "During the throes and convulsions of the ancient world, during the agonizing spasms of infuriated man, seeking through blood and slaughter his long-lost liberty, it was not wonderful that the agitation of the billows should reach even this distant and peaceful shore." If he made light of "spasms" transformed into "billows" it may have been because his primary complaint was against the last portion of this paragraph when "We are all Republicans, we are all Federalists."[21] Dumas Malone, the most authoritative of Jefferson's biographers in the twentieth century, praised "this poetical sentence," for the very reason Adams had denigrated it: namely, that it represented President Jefferson's honorable effort to minimize differences between the parties. Where Adams saw some deception, Malone found an effort to restore harmony in "one of his most moving passages."[22]

Rhetorician Wayne Fields noted the power of the presidency to shape political culture: "where rhetorical eloquence in all circumstances can be measured by the extent to which the disparate entities of speaker, argument, and audience are brought into a mutually affirming harmony, presidential eloquence must similarly coalesce the America of the moment, an executive's own person, and the presidential office."[23] Such a dynamic seemed to have been at work in Jefferson's first inaugural address. William Raymond Smith's analysis of the speech judged that Jefferson successfully "attempted to demonstrate through the rhetorical questions concluding the paragraph ["We are all Republicans . . .], a republican government could tolerate even those opposed to republicanism."[24]

Jefferson's concerns about the threats from the Old World, as expressed in his inaugural address, were quickly justified. Even before Jefferson entered the new White House, Bonaparte had taken an action that was certain to place France above Britain as America's enemy. This was the secret Treaty of San Il de Fonso, signed on October 1, 1800, one day after the Franco-American Treaty of 1778 was terminated at Mortefontaine. Bonaparte may have failed to bring the United States into his proposed anti-British league, but he was able to keep secret the retrocession of Louisiana to France. Certainly, a credible reason for secrecy was a clause in the treaty that gave the Duchy of Parma to Spain in exchange for returning Louisiana to France after almost forty years in Spanish possession. Bonaparte, after all, had yet to obtain Parma and would not be in a position to validate his offer until Austria ceded the territory in the Treaty of Campo Formio. But an equal, if not more persuasive, factor in Bonaparte's concealment was his recognition that if Jefferson won the presidency from Adams the new president would be as unhappy with the new neighbor as any Anglophilic Federalist, and perhaps even more so. A disillusioned friend of the French Revolution could become a vindictive adversary.

Within three months of his accession to the presidency, Jefferson heard rumors of the Louisiana cession, and he recognized "the inauspicious circumstance" it presented to the United States.[25] The possibility of the rumors becoming true did not stop him from reducing the size of the federal government, most notably its military and naval establishments. His posture was prefigured in the inaugural address: namely, to limit connections with the Old World but maintain cordial ties as best he could with those nations. He kept Federalist Rufus King as minister to Britain to assure that nation of America's wish for continuing accommodation; and he did not rush to judgment with respect to Louisiana. Not until King was able to present more positive evidence of France's reacquisition of Louisiana did the president act. He had little choice, pressed as he was by charges of weakness from Federalist opponents and by demands for aggressive action by western democrats worried about closure of the Mississippi once again.

But his actions did not replicate a Federalist-style rearmament or include a public condemnation of France, or constitute a genuine effort at collusion with France's enemy, Britain. His answer was to use persuasion, combining an appeal to Bonaparte's rationality with an implied threat of consequences if the French did not yield to America's needs. He appealed to the dictator's cupidity by a willingness to pay for control of New Orleans. A display of belligerence would not work. The Consulate had not yet ratified the Treaty of Mortefontaine, and the United States lacked the means to employ force against France. Besides, the First Consul gave an opening for diplomacy simply by his silence on the question of the Louisiana cession. He never admitted it until the territory was sold to the United States.

For his part, Jefferson was no less willing than Bonaparte to avoid recognition of the Louisiana retrocession. As long as he could, the president accepted the fiction that New Orleans was still Spanish. If he did not recognize the existence of a transfer, he would not have to take action until France was actually in possession of the territory. As he wrote in July, 1801, to his young protégé, Gov. William C. Claiborne of the Mississippi Territory, it was important to keep an "amiable and even affectionate" relationship with the Spanish neighbor. "We consider her possession of the adjacent country as most favorable to her interests, & should see, with extreme pain any other nation substituted for them."[26] That France was the "other nation" was never in doubt. But since he had no solution for the moment beyond delay, public silence was his interim answer. He was playing for time.

Silence over Louisiana was evident in his first Annual Message in December, 1801. He seemed to be in denial—or pretended to be—as rumors flew around Washington. His task in his address to the nation at the end of his first year in office was twofold: to calm his countrymen by displaying the advantages that the new peace in Europe gave the United States and to announce for the benefit of both the Congress and Bonaparte America's appreciation for the "cessation of irregularities which had affected the commerce of neutral nations and of the irritations and injuries produced by them." Given the space devoted to the reduction of offices he "deemed unnecessary," it was hardly surprising that he not only avoided a suggestion of a military challenge to France but went out of his way to emphasize in his first paragraph the "hope that wrongs committed on unoffending friends . . . will be considered as founding just claims of retribution for the past and new assurance for the future."[27] The Louisiana cession did not appear in this address.

Conceivably, Jefferson's seeming optimism about the consequences of France's new order in Europe calmed Bonaparte's concerns about American reaction to Spain's surrender of Louisiana. The First Consul could indulge his hopes that Jefferson's friendship with French ideologues might soften the political, if not visceral, rejection that France's return to Louisiana would elicit. He had already won over such figures as Constantin-François de Volney and Destutt de Tracy, who accepted seats in Bonaparte's senate, and especially the Marquis de Lafayette, who assured Jefferson in June, 1801, of the dictator's goodwill even as he fully recognized the meaning of the illegal overthrow of the Directory.[28] Why could he not manipulate President Jefferson, a fellow traveler of the liberal French intelligentsia? It was significant that Bonaparte offered Jefferson nomination to the Class of Moral and Political Science of the National Institute in November, 1801. Jefferson's acceptance of the honor appeared to bestow a presidential blessing upon the Consulate.

Bonaparte could take comfort in learning that Jefferson's messages to Congress in the spring of 1802 continued to ignore the Louisiana retrocession. Not until his second Annual Message to Congress on December 15 did he even mention the subject, and this in a brief paragraph noting that "the cession of the Spanish Province of Louisiana to France . . . will, if carried into effect, make a change in the aspect of our foreign relations which will doubtless have just weight in any deliberations of the Legislature connected with that subject." The language conveying this information obviously was designed to calm concerned Federalists and westerners as well as the French government. The thrust of his message seemed to be in the opening paragraph, where he observed: "another year has come around, and finds us still blessed with peace and friendship abroad."[29]

That the president had Louisiana high among his priorities was not evident in his public rhetoric or in his formal communications to the Consulate. But in his private communications he made it clear that if France prized America's friendship, it would have to do more than grant the same commercial favors Spain had accorded the United States; New Orleans at the very least would have to be surrendered—by purchase or grant. The alternative would be loss of this territory the moment the perennial troubles of Europe, temporarily quieted by the Treaty of Amiens, distracted the belligerents' attention from the New World. An alliance with Britain might be the consequence of France's failure to concede. Jefferson warned Bonaparte that "the day France takes possession of New Orleans . . . seals the union of two nations, who in conjunction, can maintain exclusion possession of the ocean. From that moment we must marry ourselves to the British fleet and nation."[30]

The president wrote these often-quoted words in a letter to Robert R. Livingston, the American minister to France, in April, 1802, at the very time he was avoiding any mention of Louisiana in his messages to Congress. His expectation was that these comments would have an impact upon the bearer of the letter, Pierre Samuel Du Pont de Nemour, a distinguished Physiocrat and friend of Jefferson, who was returning to France for what he thought would be only a brief stay. Jefferson saw an opportunity to exploit the economist's contacts with Bonaparte by exaggerating America's response to France's occupation of Louisiana. His newfound Anglophilia was a tactic rather than a genuine revaluation of Britain's relationship with the United States. Jefferson underscored his intentions in a special note to Du Pont asking him to impress upon his countrymen the importance of ceding to the United States all French territory in America, not just New Orleans.[31]

The unofficial emissary accepted the assignment and obtained results that exceeded the president's expectations. Jefferson's objective was the free navigation of the Mississippi. New Orleans and its surrounding territory, not the Missouri Valley, were his objectives. The unexpected suspension of the right of deposit in New Orleans by the Spanish intendant in October, 1802, left no doubt about the locus of Jefferson's attention even though he mistakenly attributed the Spanish official's action to French intervention. Therefore, Bonaparte's parting with all that he received from Spain—and not just New Orleans— was serendipitous; it was the apparent vindication not only of the administration's diplomatic tactics, but also of the effect of private persuasion upon public actions. That Du Pont's warnings were irrelevant in the face of Bonaparte's decision to abandon his plans for an American empire—at least temporarily—in the wake of his army's defeat in Haiti and in anticipation of renewed war with Britain was immaterial. Jefferson and his colleagues believed that their arguments had persuaded the dictator to serve America's interests.

Shortly after the Louisiana problem had been solved so successfully, Jefferson's emissary in Paris, James Monroe, unwittingly gave the president an opportunity to express fully his motives in cultivating foreign friendships. While in France, he noticed that Jefferson's correspondence with influential Frenchmen had produced a good effect during his mission. He then recommended to Jefferson that he continue to nourish his relations with literary and philosophic personages, especially those connected with the National Institute. Monroe was convinced that this body was the most powerful institution in France outside the executive circle itself.[32]

If Jefferson's reply to these observations was somewhat didactic in tone, it was not because he thought Monroe had misunderstood or overestimated the role of the intellectual in Napoleonic France. He merely regarded the advice as gratuitous, since he had examined long before and put into operation just such a project with reference to British as well as French intellectuals. He pointed out that he had consciously made use of his relations with Lafayette and Du Pont when he was minister to France. More recently, he had been writing freely to men of distinction "on subjects of literature, and to a certain degree, on politics, respecting however their personal opinions, and their situation so as not to compromise them were a letter intercepted." Most of his suggestions, he underscored, were of the kind "that would do us good if known to their governments, and as probably, as not are communicated to them." He took pride in his ability to make "private friendships instrumental to the public good by inspiring a confidence which is denied to public and official communications."[33] It was no coincidence that both Destutt and Du Pont had been elected members of the American Philosophical Society in 1798 during his presidency of that organization.

It was hardly surprising that Jefferson would make a causal connection between his use of Du Pont in a back-channel mission and the securing of Louisiana, particularly in a letter written in the first week of January, 1804, soon after the territory fell into American hands. Nor was it surprising that a triumphal note crept into his third Annual Message to Congress in which he contrasted the "extraordinary agitation produced in the public mind by the suspension of our right of deposit at the port of New Orleans" with the actions of "the enlightened Government of France," which "saw with just discernment the importance to both nations of such liberal arrangements as might best and permanently promote the peace, friendship, and interests of both." Such was the gloss Jefferson put on the acquisition of Louisiana as he urged the Senate to give its "constitutional sanction" to the purchase. His concerns, though, were less with congressional approval than with the impression he could make in applauding France for its wise decision.[34] It should be noted that he was well aware of renewed warfare in Europe. He noted that "while we regret the miseries in which we see others involved, let us bow with gratitude to that kind Providence" which permits the United States to escape from this calamity. Strict neutrality should be America's response. Once again, Jefferson expressed his gratitude for the separation by a "wide ocean from the nations of Europe and from the political interests which entangle them together, with productions and wants which render our commerce and friendship useful to them and to us."[35]

Diplomacy seemingly had worked wonders and could do even more in the future. New lands had been won, and new prosperity might follow from the European wars. Congress and the nation in 1804 paid tribute to the president's shrewdness. Although opponents questioned the constitutionality of the acquisition, the prize was too great to be sacrificed for the sake of principles. Consequently, Jefferson should have been able to look forward to a second term freer from the anxieties of his first. That was not to be. The two great belligerents, frustrated in their ability to strike at each other after Austerlitz and Trafalgar, waged a war of attrition through abuse of America's neutral rights. Instead of manipulating France and Britain, the United States was their victim; instead of winning national approval of his economic policies, Jefferson left office with a sense of failure and rejection.

It is understandable that Jefferson, flush with success over Louisiana, should expect his statecraft to win new successes, particularly after Britain and France went to war again in 1803. After all, he perceived that it was the European conflict that permitted him to extract Louisiana from Bonaparte (Emperor Napoleon after 1804). Since the boundaries of that territory were so fluid, he assumed the French would honor his claim of Spanish West Florida as part of the purchase. They did not. Charles-Maurice de Talleyrand, Napoleon's foreign minister, left it up to Americans to deal with Spain over the matter. But that was not the path Jefferson wished to follow, assuming as he did that Napoleon's control of Spain would bring Florida into the American fold. As early as August, 1803, the president asserted that "the ancient boundary of Louisiana" extended eastward to the Perdido River, between Mobile and Pensacola.[36] Congress's passage of the Mobile Act of 1804, with its assumption that the territory west of the Perdido was part of Louisiana and therefore part of the United States, was just the first step in a process that would end in the United States controlling all of Florida. West Florida was not explicitly annexed by this act, but since Jefferson was empowered to erect a separate customs district in the territory, it was a distinction without a difference.

In the early years of his second term, the president remained under the spell of his success with France over Louisiana. He reasoned that if he could manipulate a great power, he should be able to do even more with a lesser power. Resisting advice to seize territory by force, he continued to expect France to pressure its Spanish satellite to provide the solution without bloodshed. This strategy should yield results, he felt, especially since the United States had many unresolved claims against France, including claims for damages to American commerce by Spanish vessels operating under French orders. France failed to respond, even as Jefferson applied the tactics that won Louisiana: a warning of rapprochement with Britain, a $2 million offer to Spain for the territory east of the Perdido, and even a threat of military action.

The outside world from which he would have America detached, yet advantaged, no longer served American interests. Instead of the renewed war in Europe conferring opportunities for Jefferson to seize, it limited his options and forced him into positions that turned the nation as well as the European belligerents against him. Britain, without Continental allies after Napoleon's victories at Austerlitz, Jena, and Friedland between 1805 and 1807, had no ground forces to engage the enemy; and Napoleon, having lost his navies at Trafalgar in 1805, had to give up hope of invading Britain. But both powers could wage an economic war of attrition by violating the neutral rights of the United States.

Jefferson's fifth Annual Message to Congress on December 3, 1805, the day after Austerlitz and six weeks after Trafalgar, reflected the president's plight. "Since our last meeting," he lamented, "the aspect of our foreign relations has considerably changed. Our coasts have been infested." Private armed vessels, along with public ships, "have captured in the very entrance of our harbors, as well as on the high seas, not only the vessels of our friends coming to trade with us, but our own also." The unnamed offenders were obviously British. Their actions were a source of anguish and anger, but not a call to arms. By contrast, the nation named as an adversary in this address and in a special message the next day was Spain. Not only had "our negotiations for a settlement of difference have not had a satisfactory issue," but "inroads have been recently made into the Territory of Orleans and the Mississippi, our citizens have been seized, and their property plundered in the very parts of the former which had been actually delivered up by Spain, and this by the regular officers and soldiers of that Government." The president then learned that some of the injuries "are of a nature to be met by force only, and all of them may lead to it."[37]

France too was mentioned in the president's addresses, but in a different context. That country "was prompt and decided in her declarations that our demands on Spain for French spoliations carried into Spanish ports were included in the settlement between the United States and France. She took at once the ground that she had acquired no right from Spain, and had meant to deliver us none eastward of the Iberville, her silence as to the western boundary leaving us to infer her opinion might be against Spain in that quarter." He added that information from Paris made it clear that France had no "suspicion of the hostile attitude Spain had taken . . . ; on the contrary, we have reason to believe that she was disposed to effect a settlement on a plan analagous to what our ministers had proposed, and so comprehensive as to remove as far as possible the grounds for future collision and controversy on the eastern as well as the western side of the Mississippi."[38]

Even as Napoleon matched British seizures of American vessels with his paper blockade of the British Isles in the Berlin and Milan Decrees of 1806 and 1807, Jefferson's rhetoric for the benefit of Congress and presumably of the imperial court as well was far more considerate of France than of Britain. In a communication to Congress on February 19, 1807, he enclosed a letter from the French minister of marine assuring the minister plenipotentiary "that the imperial decree [Berlin Decree] lately passed was not to affect our commerce, which would still be governed by the rules of the treaty established between the two countries."[39] The failure of the Monroe-Pinckney mission to London and the continuing violations of American neutrality and even sovereignty in the Chesapeake affair in 1807 made Britain the focus of presidential wrath in his seventh Annual Message. French depredations are touched on opaquely, but with an optimism not found in his references to Britain. And when Jefferson transmitted the Milan Decree in March, 1808, he did so dispassionately, noting that "these decrees and orders, taken together, want little of amounting to a declaration that every neutral vessel found on the high seas, whatsoever be her cargo and whatsoever foreign port be that of her departure or destination, shall be deemed lawful prize." Instead of castigating the emperor for these illegal acts, however, Jefferson cited them to prove "more and more the expediency of retaining our vessels, our seamen, and property within our own harbors until the dangers to which they are exposed can be removed or lessened."[40] In brief, the Embargo Act then in force in essence removed Americans from the dangers Napoleon's edicts evoked.

Although the embargo, which prohibited American commerce with the outside world, had other objectives, Jefferson was well aware of the service it provided France. As master of continental Europe in 1808, Napoleon was not dependent on American products, as Jefferson assumed the island kingdom to be. Although the embargo was literally aimed equally at both belligerents, it should have been obvious to Napoleon that the United States was serving the interests of France's Continental System, a system that would isolate Britain and bring it to its knees by depriving it of vital supplies. The reward for President Jefferson would be France's delivery of Spanish Florida to the United States. Since

Napoleon's older brother Joseph had been installed as king of Spain, such a concession seemed within the French emperor's power. While continuing to sequester American ships and property that had found their way to French ports despite the embargo, Napoleon hinted in a letter from the French foreign minister to the U.S. minister in Paris, John Armstrong, that if "America should be disposed to enter into a treaty of alliance and make common cause, with me, I should not be unwilling to intervene with the court of Spain to obtain the cession of these same Floridas in favor of the Americans."[41] Conceivably, these suggestions might have borne fruit even without an alliance if Britain had invaded Florida.

But how serious was Napoleon in dealing with Jefferson, or with any Americans? His concerns were with the war with Britain and with his global ambitions. America was just another pawn to be given, as Bradford Perkins noted, a "carrot or stick"—whichever would be most effective at any given moment.[42] Jefferson's effort to have the embargo substitute for a declaration of war with Britain or an alliance with France was never good enough for Napoleon. He wanted the United States in the position of one of his European satellites, and had he prevailed over Britain that would have been the case. In the meantime, seizing American ships that had traded with Britain was part of his continuing commercial war. There never was a time in the course of the ill-fated embargo when America had to be granted control of the Floridas.

The shrewd diplomatic moves that had succeeded in 1803 were employed again, notably careful public rhetoric to appease or woo the French accompanied by private warnings. Jefferson's French friends, whom he regarded as influential intellectuals, were summoned once again to service. Regrettably, they had little influence over Napoleon. When they were no longer useful to him, he ridiculed their pretensions and drove many out of the country without losing the support of most of them. There was a belief among liberals that Napoleon's crimes, bad as they were, were preferable to the return of the Bourbons. At least he had equalized taxes, extended education, and introduced reforms they hoped in the long run would negate his tyranny. At the same time that Lafayette lamented the fate of friends driven into exile, he told Jefferson that "these jolts and bars" would not disturb the liberal impulses that the United States had given to France.[43] The emperor's greatest power over them was their intrinsic patriotism.

Whenever they became too disturbed about the shortcomings of the imperial government, they had only to look across the Channel and see the alternative of British conquest.

That Napoleon commanded the loyalty of these men even as he victimized them under ordinary circumstances would not have had a particularly adverse effect on the United States. It would have meant merely that his idea of using private friendships to serve public purposes did not always succeed. Jefferson might have dismissed their views as a temporary setback in the progress toward a republican future. But at a time in his second administration when he needed a clear understanding of the emperor's' purposes, the liberals' silence bore some responsibility for the president's failure to understand the extent of Napoleon's duplicity. On the problem of Napoleon's harassment of American commerce, Lafayette was convinced that the emperor was simply misinformed: "I every day hope his great powers of sagacity and calculation will at last discover that in his plan to bring Great Britain he has taken the wrong end."[44]

In fact, Napoleon calculated that Jefferson was as gullible as his intellectual French friends, and acted accordingly. It seemed that he was correct in his disparagement of Jefferson. At no time in any of his addresses during the embargo in 1808 did the president chastise Napoleon for his behavior. Nor did he ever give up his hope of using the European conflict to win the Floridas or expand the western boundaries of Louisiana. In the summer of 1808 he was pleased to learn of Napoleon's troubles with Spain and told the secretary of the navy that the moment might be favorable for us to take possession of "our territory held by Spain, and so much more as may make a proper reprisal for her spoliations."[45] Moreover, as he left office relieved of "a drudgery to which I am no longer equal," he could still speculate that if Napoleon succeeds in Spain, "he will look immediately to the Spanish colonies, and think our neutrality cheaply purchased by a repeal of the legal parts of his decrees, with perhaps the Floridas thrown into the bargain."[46]

It is tempting to view Jefferson as a prisoner of his illusions and write him off, as Henry Adams did, as an amateur on the world stage, with the president as an actor in provincial Washington out of his depth in the company of a Talma in Paris or a Garrick in London. Yet it may be as much a mistake to ridicule Jefferson for his pretensions as it would have been to denigrate Franklin for his efforts to manipulate the French and British in Paris twenty-five years earlier. President Jefferson withdrew to Monticello depressed over the fate of the embargo. Circumstances beyond his control blocked him in 1808, just as they helped him in 1803. There were limits to how far rhetorical persuasion could be carried at this juncture. But naivete was not one of them. He was as cold-blooded and realistic as Franklin about the nature of the nation's adversaries and the choices he made to serve the national interest. As he wrote to his friend Thomas Leiper in 1807, "the English being equally tyrannical at sea as he is on land that tyranny bearing on us in every point of either honor or interest, I say 'down with England' and as for what Bonaparte is then to do with us, let us trust to the chapter of accidents."[47] If France ultimately should prevail, the Atlantic Ocean could prevent Napoleon from attacking the United States, if some other obstacle in the "chapter of accidents" did not stop him first.

When Henry Adams patronizingly claimed that Jefferson was too "honest" to play "a game safely in the face of men like Godoy, Talleyrand, and Napoleon,"[48] he was not quite on the mark. The American president was much more than a provincial Garrick. He had reason to believe that his careful use of rhetoric would win advantages for America. And it did in Louisiana. If he failed to gain the Floridas or to extract his country from the ravages of the Napoleonic Wars, it was not his naivete that was at fault. External forces as well as hubris accounted for his failure, as they did in the case of France's Talma at Waterloo in 1815.

NOTES

1. The wide variety of views on Jefferson, as seen over the years, is well presented in Merrill D. Peterson, *The Jefferson Image in the American Mind* (New York: Oxford University Press, 1960); the most nuanced recent interpretation is Joseph J. Ellis, *American Sphinx: The Character of Thomas Jefferson* (New York: Alfred A. Knopf, 1997).

2. Jefferson to Gallatin, Oct. 16, 1815, in *The Writings of Thomas Jefferson*, 20 vols., ed. Andrew A. Lipscomb and Albert E. Bergh (Washington, D.C.: Thomas Jefferson Memorial Association of the United States, 1904), 14:359.

3. Henry S. Randall, *The Life of Thomas Jefferson*, 3 vols. (New York: Derby and Jackson, 1858), 3:508; Hamilton to Edward Carrington, 20 May 1792, in *The Papers of Alexander Hamilton*, 26 vols., ed. Harold C. Syrett and Jacob E. Cooke (New York: Columbia University Press, 1961–79), 11:439.

4. William Cullen Bryant, "The Embargo, or Sketches of the Times: A Satire," in *William Cullen Bryant: Representative Selections*, ed. Tremaine McDowell (New York: 1935), 431ff.

5. Henry Adams, *History of the United States during the Administrations of Thomas Jefferson and James Madison*, 9 vols. (New York: Charles Scribner's Sons, 1889–91), 3:115.

6. Dumas Malone, *Jefferson and His Time: Jefferson the President: Second Term, 1805–1809*, 6 vols. (Boston: Little, Brown, 1974), 5:xix.

7. Jefferson to Adams, July 5, 1814, in *The Adams-Jefferson Letters*, 2 vols., ed. Lester J. Cappon (Chapel Hill: University of North Carolina Press, 1959), 431.

8. Secretary of State to William Carmichael, enclosing "Outline of Policy on the Mississippi Question, Aug. 2, 1790, in *The Papers of Thomas Jefferson*, 27 vols., ed. Julian P. Boyd (Princeton, N.J.: Princeton University Press, 1965), 17:116.

9. Stephen E. Ambrose, *Undaunted Courage: Meriwether Lewis, Thomas Jefferson, and the Opening of the American West* (New York: Simon and Schuster, 1996), 73.

10. Jefferson to Charles Pinckney, May 28, 1797, in Lipscomb and Bergh, *Writings of Thomas Jefferson*, 9:389–90.

11. Ibid.

12. Jefferson to Madison, Dec. 19, 1800, ibid., 10:185.

13. Jefferson to Madison, Dec. 26, 1800, ibid., 10:187.

14. Jefferson to George Logan, Mar. 21, 1801, in *The Writings of Thomas Jefferson*, 20 vols., ed. Paul Leicester Ford (New York: G. P. Putnam's Sons, 1892–99), 8:23.

15. Jefferson, first inaugural address, Mar. 4, 1801, in *A Compilation of the Messages and Papers of the Presidents, 1789–1897*, 10 vols., ed. James D. Richardson (Washington, D.C.: GPO, 1897), 1:310.

16. Adams, *History*, 1:200–201.

17. Ellis, *American Sphinx*, 182.

18. Quoted in ibid., 182.

19. Adams, *History*, 1:212.

20. Jefferson, first inaugural address, 1:311.

21. Ibid, 310; Adams, *History*, 1:200–201.

22. Dumas Malone, *Jefferson and His Time: Jefferson the President: First Term, 1801–1805*, 6 vols. (Boston: Little, Brown, 1948–81), 4:19.

23. Wayne Fields, *Union of Words: A History of Presidential Eloquence* (New York: Free Press, 1996), 11.

24. William Raymond Smith, *The Rhetoric of American Politics: A Study of Documents* (Westport, Conn.: Greenwood Publishing Corporation, 1969), 137.

25. Quoted in Malone, *Jefferson the President, First Term*, 4:248.

26. Jefferson to Claiborne, July 13, 1801, in *The Works of Thomas Jefferson*, 12 vols., ed. Paul L. Ford (New York: G. P. Putnam's Sons, 1904–1905), 9:275.

27. First Annual Message, Dec. 8, 1801, in Richardson, ed., *Messages and Papers*, 1:316, 324.

28. Lafayette to Jefferson, Feb. 10, 1800, in *The Letters of Lafayette and Jefferson*, ed. Gilbert Chinard (Baltimore: Johns Hopkins University Press, 1929), 210; Lafayette to Jefferson, June 21, 1801, ibid., 213.

29. Second Annual Message, Dec. 15, 1802, in Richardson, ed., *Messages and Papers*, 1:331–32.

30. Jefferson to Livingston, Apr. 18, 1802, in Lipscomb and Bergh, eds., *Writings of Thomas Jefferson*, 10:313.

31. Jefferson to Du Pont, Apr. 25, 1802, ibid., 10:316–19.

32. Monroe to Jefferson, Sept. 20, 1802, Jefferson Papers, reel 29, Library of Congress, Washington, D.C. (hereafter Jefferson Papers).

33. Jefferson to Monroe, Jan. 8, 1804, in Ford, ed., *Works of Thomas Jefferson*, 10:60–61.

34. Third Annual Message, Oct. 17, 1803, in Richardson, ed., *Messages and Papers*, 1:346.

35. Ibid., p.346.

36. Jefferson to Breckenridge, Aug. 12, 1803, in Lipscomb and Bergh, eds., *Writings of Thomas Jefferson*, 10:408.

37. Fifth Annual Message, Dec. 3, 1805, in Richardson, ed., *Messages and Papers*, 1:371–73.

38. Special Messages to the Senate and House of Representatives, Dec. 6, 1805, ibid., 1:377–78.

39. Jefferson to the Senate and House of Representatives, Feb. 19, 1807, ibid., 1:409.

40. Jefferson to the Senate and House of Representatives, Mar. 17, 1808, ibid., 1:432.

41. Adams, *History*, 4:293.

42. Bradford Perkins, *Prologue to War: England and the United States: 1805–1812* (Berkeley: University of California Press, 1961), 68–69.

43. Lafayette to Jefferson, Feb. 20, 1807, in Chinard, ed., *Letters of Lafayette and Jefferson*, 253

44. Lafayette to Jefferson, Nov. 18, 1809, ibid., 294.

45. Quoted in Joseph I. Shulim, "Thomas Jefferson Views Napoleon," *Virginia Magazine of History and Biography* 60 (Apr., 1952): 295.

46. Jefferson to Monroe, Jan. 28, 1809, in Lipscomb and Bergh, eds., *Writings of Thomas Jefferson*, 12:241–42.

47. Jefferson to Leiper, Aug. 21, 1807, in Ford, ed., *Works of Thomas Jefferson*, 10:483–84.

48. Adams, *History*, 3:115.

CHAPTER 5

Politics as Performance Art

The Body English of Theodore Roosevelt

H. W. Brands

THEODORE ROOSEVELT was the one of the most effective communicators ever to occupy the White House, and one of the least impressive speakers. His high-pitched voice lacked timbre, melodiousness, and carrying power. He had an odd, almost violent way of clipping his words, snapping his teeth as though biting ten-penny nails. His gestures were abrupt and equally violent; from a distance he appeared to be practicing karate. Roosevelt disdained William Jennings Bryan and despised Woodrow Wilson. He had political reasons for his opinions of both men, but he was not above envy, and, in an age of political oratory, he knew he lacked the riveting imagery and delivery of Bryan and the soaring eloquence of Wilson.

But Roosevelt had something Bryan and Wilson lacked, and it was this that transfixed the American public for two decades beginning in the late 1890s, allowing Roosevelt to revolutionize the art of presidential communication. Roosevelt had a compelling persona as a man of action. (This despite the fact that he was a genuine intellectual, the author of more books than any other president—possibly of more books than all the other presidents combined.) Very early Roosevelt learned the value of this persona, and in an age when machine power was replacing muscle power, when office work was supplanting farm and ranch work, when the open range was being fenced, when meat came from the icebox instead of the forest or stream, when the frontier was vanishing, he represented himself as an icon of that romantic era. Not in words but by action, he spoke a language that resonated with millions of American men and women and made him the political phenomenon of his day.

He hit upon this form of physical rhetoric by accident. In the summer of 1884 he left New York, the city of his youth and the state of some of his early political triumphs, for the Badlands of the Dakota Territory. Personal considerations figured in the move: the previous February his darling bride had died in childbirth, and his mother died the same day. He left New York in part to escape his grief, to avoid the scenes he associated with the loved ones so untimely taken.

But politics entered as well. The 1884 Republican national convention, held in Chicago, nominated James G. Blaine for president. Those who said Blaine had a checkered past were occasionally accused of libeling an innocent board game. Roosevelt, in high dudgeon, had backed Blaine's opponent—and in doing so backed himself into a corner, for when Blaine won the nomination Roosevelt had to choose between loyalty to party and loyalty to avowed principle. He made his escape, literally, by hopping a westbound train from Chicago and disappearing into Dakota. And, deciding that Medora, Dakota Territory, was not remote enough, he embarked on a hunting trip that took him into the wilds of Wyoming, leagues beyond the nearest railroad track or telegraph office.

As it turned out, he changed his mind and went on the record for Blaine before November—to the everlasting dismay of his mugwump friends. But this western strategy was already paying off. In the New York Assembly in the early 1880s, Roosevelt had acquired a reputation as a dandy, dressed to the nines and rather effete. Dakota knocked the dandy out of him—about the tenth time a bronco he was trying to break bucked him off—and though he was always well dressed by the standards of the Upper Missouri, he was just one in a crowd along the Lower Hudson.

More tellingly, his western years won him the reputation of being a cowboy. Actually, he called himself a ranchman, an owner rather than mere laborer, but he did not argue the point with those disposed to class him as one of that dying breed that won the West. It was not simply a pose. Roosevelt *was* a ranchman: he identified with the interests of his Dakota neighbors; he represented those interests in politics when he returned to politics; and he took great pride in his western connection.

But if it was not a pose, it *was* beneficial to his career. And he knew it. As the tide of populism rose on the western plains and in the mountains, the Republican Party was desperate for anyone who could keep the radicals at bay. Roosevelt was just the man. In election after election he was dispatched to the West to hold the line, and with each tour of duty he increased his claim on the party's perquisites. He received his share, the most important being appointment to the federal Civil Service Commission.

But overseeing job tests and the appointment of postmasters was too tame to claim him forever. In 1895 he accepted an appointment that struck many as a decided step down: to police commissioner of New York City (this at a time, moreover, when New York did not even include the outer boroughs).

He took the job for two reasons. First, for all his reputation as a man of the West, if his career was going to go anywhere, he needed a political base in his home state of New York. New York City was as good a place to start as any. Second, he understood that a police commissioner could make an impression on the public at large.

Roosevelt certainly did make an impression. He habitually prowled the midnight streets in disguise, searching for criminals and especially for that subspecies simultaneously employed as policemen. The New York papers—whose correspondents he invited along on his rambles—loved it. "A Bagdad Night," headlined the *Commercial Advertiser:* "Roosevelt in the Role of Haroun Alraschid."[1] The *New York World,* establishing what would become a pattern in coverage of Roosevelt, could not decide whether he was to be taken entirely seriously, but neither could the paper let this remarkable character go unreported. "We have a real police commissioner," the *World* explained. "His teeth are big and white, his eyes are small and piercing, his voice is rasping. He makes our policemen feel as the little froggies did when the stork came to rule them. His heart is full of reform, and a policeman, in full uniform, with helmet, revolver and night club, is no more to him than a plain, every day human being."[2]

It was during this time on the beat that something else took hold in the press about Roosevelt: the instantly identifiable cartoon figure. Editorial cartoonists, always on the lookout for something distinctive and easy to draw, settled on Roosevelt's flashing teeth and his thick eyeglasses. One cartoonist carried the caricature to the extreme in a picture of a pitiful, boozy copper being terrified into eternal sobriety and straight shooting by an imagined oversized specter of Roosevelt—which in fact was nothing more than an optician's shingle featuring a pair of absurdly large eyeglasses above a dentist's sign showing an enormous pair of dentures.

Needless to say, there was much of a joke in this caricature, as in all caricatures. But it worked because it captured an important aspect of the man. The frightened patrolman would have had nothing to fear from the teeth and the glasses had he not fully expected the rambunctious police commissioner—the man who had shot grizzly bears in their dens, broken wild horses, and captured outlaws in the Wild West—to be close behind.

In 1898, Roosevelt added a critical new element to his political persona. Upon the outbreak of war with Spain—a war he had been fomenting for many months—he resigned a responsible, important, and safe position in the Navy Department in favor of dirty and dangerous service in the trenches. He did so largely for reasons having to do with his own emotional history; but he knew his American history well enough to recognize that Americans have never been able to resist a military hero—especially one well covered by the press.

The Spanish-American War was the first war of the era of modern mass communications. The American yellow press had invested a great deal of money making this war happen, and William Randolph Hearst, Joseph Pulitzer, and the rest were determined for their investment to pay off. Theodore Roosevelt was the perfect candidate for war hero. He already had a colorful reputation, and the volunteer regiment he was putting together was more colorful still. The "Rough Riders"—a name devised by some newsman in San Antonio, where the 1st Volunteer Cavalry trained, after "Teddy's Texas Tarantulas" was discovered to take up too much space—mixed equal parts of the myth of the West with the ideal of the citizen soldier. Cowboys from the territories formed the bulk of the regiment, and when the War Department authorized additional saddles, polo players from the East jumped at the chance to fill them. "You would be amused to see three Knickerbocker club men cooking and washing dishes for one of the New Mexico companies," Roosevelt wrote fellow Harvard alum Henry Cabot Lodge. He went on to describe his men: "It is as typical an American regiment as ever marched or fought. I suppose about 95 per cent of the men are of native birth, but we have a few from everywhere, including a score of Indians and about as many men of Mexican origin as from New Mexico; then there are some fifty Easterners—almost all graduates of Harvard, Yale, Princeton, etc.—and almost as many Southerners; the rest are men of the plains and Rocky Mountains. Three fourths of our men have at one time or another been cowboys or else are small stockmen; certainly two thirds have fathers who fought on one side or the other in the Civil War."[3]

The correspondents covering the war loved the Rough Riders almost as much as Roosevelt did, and they loved Roosevelt most of all. He cultivated and flattered them; best of all, when it came to heroism, he was the real thing. Richard Harding Davis followed the Rough Riders from Florida to Cuba and from the landing at Daiquiri to the battle in front of Santiago. Roosevelt distinguished himself in that battle with conspicuous bravery, leading his men in an initial assault on Kettle Hill and then joining the main attack on San Juan Hill. Davis explained: "Roosevelt, mounted high on horseback, and charging the rifle pits at a gallop and quite alone, made you feel that you would like to cheer. He wore on his sombrero a blue polka-dot handkerchief, a la Havelock, which, as he advanced, floated out straight behind his head like a guidon. Afterward, the men of his regiment who followed this flag, adopted a polka-dot handkerchief as the badge of the Rough Riders."[4]

The image of the colonel of the Rough Riders perfectly complemented that of Roosevelt as cowboy and crusading police chief, and the new composite persona rocketed Roosevelt to national fame. The first step was the governorship of New York. The Republican boss of New York, Thomas Platt, had serious doubts regarding Roosevelt's regularity, but some misappropriation of funds involving the Erie Canal had damaged the incumbent, Frank Black, leaving Platt to consider an alternative. Chauncey Depew, a GOP old-timer, explained the advantages of a Roosevelt candidacy.

If you nominate Governor Black and I am addressing a large audience—and I certainly will—the heckler in the audience will arise and interrupt me, saying, "Chauncey, we agree with what you say about the Grand Old Party and all that, but how about the Canal steal?" I have to explain that the amount stolen was only a million, and that would be fatal.

If Colonel Roosevelt is nominated, I can say to the heckler with indignation and enthusiasm: "I am mighty glad you asked that question. We have nominated for governor a man who has demonstrated in public office and on the battlefield that he is a fighter for the right, and always victorious. If he is selected, you know and we all know from his demonstrated characteristics, courage and ability, that every thief will be caught and punished, and every dollar that can be found restored to the public treasury." Then I will follow the colonel leading his Rough Riders up San Juan Hill and ask the band to play the "Star-Spangled Banner."[5]

Platt bowed to Depew's advice, and the campaign went as Depew predicted. Roosevelt included a bugler and several Rough Riders in his campaign entourage. "You have heard the trumpet that sounded to bring you here," he explained to audiences. "I have heard it tear the tropic dawn, when it summoned us to fight at Santiago."[6] His comrades in arms testified on his behalf—although not always according to script. "My friends and fellow citizens," said one grizzled veteran, "my colonel was a great soldier. He will make a great governor. He always put us boys in battle where we would be killed if there was a chance, and that is what he will do with you."[7]

Roosevelt won all the same—and proceeded to confirm Platt's fears that he would not listen to Republican reason. After William McKinley's vice president, Garret Hobart, unexpectedly died, Platt conceived the clever device of getting Roosevelt off the New York stage by pushing him onto the national stage. Another Republican boss, Mark Hanna of Ohio, who happened to be McKinley's manager, tried to block the move on grounds that Platt should not be allowed to foist his own problems off on the country. When Hanna's opposition failed, he flew into a rage. Someone innocently asked what was the matter. "Matter!" he famously exploded. "Matter! Why, everybody's gone crazy! What is the matter with all of *you?* Here is this convention going headlong for Roosevelt for vice president. Don't any of you realize that there's only one life between that madman and the presidency?"[8]

When an assassin ended that one life, the "madman" became president. America had never seen his like. The youngest president in history, the first president of the post–Civil War generation, the first president to take office in the twentieth century, Roosevelt at once set about overturning conventional wisdom regarding the office and its occupant.

The most noticeable thing about the man was his energy. Henry Adams called him "pure act."[9] He roared through his day at a velocity that alarmed those accustomed to the more sedate pace of the century just ended. He wore out stenographers dictating letters, and he wore out clerks reading his messages to Congress. (His first message, drafted before McKinley was cold in his grave, weighed in at twenty thousand words. "It might have been shorter," his inherited navy secretary, John D. Long, observed diplomatically.[10]) He wore out visiting diplomats with scrambles through Rock Creek park. He wore out his own generals with long rides on horseback. He wore out sparring partners in the martial arts—and occasionally injured himself. Once, while boxing, he damaged one of his eyes in a manner that led to eventual blindness on that side. He broke an arm fighting singlesticks with Leonard Wood, his friend and superior officer from the Rough Riders. He hunted, although not as much as before, partly because the reporters who insisted on accompanying him tended to scare off the game, or get themselves nearly shot. His "tennis cabinet" discussed events great and small between vigorous volleys.

What did all the athletics, the outdoorsmanship, and the martial airs and arts get Roosevelt? In the first place, a great deal of publicity, most of it favorable. Roosevelt possessed an enormous ego; he simply loved the limelight. But more than that, he appreciated the possibilities for presidential leadership that accrued to a chief executive who was the chief focus of national attention. In an age of mass journalism, a president who was good copy could lift himself above the bosses who controlled the party organizations and, through the party organizations, the leadership and agenda of Congress. Other presidents had hoped to accomplish this; for Roosevelt, who entered office as the foe of the bosses, it was a necessity. Roosevelt would govern as the president of the people, or he would not be able to govern at all.

Roosevelt knew news. He studied the newspaper business and cultivated its practitioners. He understood the weekly news cycle, how he had Sunday's journalists to himself, if he wanted them, and therefore Monday's headlines. He invited reporters to the White House and to

Sagamore Hill, where he seductively apprised them of administration plans, making them almost coconspirators with him. He rigidly enforced a distinction between what he said as Theodore Roosevelt, that is, privately, and what he said as the president of the United States, that is, publicly. Those who ignored the distinction were cast into the Ananias Club of transgressors of his trust. In a later era of more aggressive journalism and more potential sources of information, such a policy would never have stood up. Nonetheless, it worked well in Roosevelt's era.

Yet what made it work was the fact that Roosevelt himself was such a compelling story. What editor could resist the tale of the Louisiana bear hunt on which he spared the pitiful creature that then became the inspiration for the Teddy bear? Or the ninety-mile horseback ride in one day (undertaken to inspire army officers, who were required to demonstrate the ability to ride ninety miles in *three* days) that ended in a blizzard of sleet, with Edith waiting at the door of the White House, and mint juleps for all survivors?

Beyond providing a platform—the "bully pulpit"—his persona as the Rough Riding man of action afforded credibility to some of his more ambitious policies. In 1902 he shocked the corporate world by declaring war on J. P. Morgan's latest brainchild, the Northern Securities railroad trust. Antitrust was not supposed to be a Republican policy; and Morgan took the first train to Washington to straighten out "that damned cowboy"—another of Mark Hanna's terms of endearment for Roosevelt. "If we have done something wrong," Morgan declared, "send your man to my man and they can fix it up." Roosevelt replied coolly, "That can't be done."[11]

Morgan was a formidable opponent (the photographer Edward Steichen once remarked that looking into Morgan's eyes was like staring into the headlight of an onrushing express train: you had to blink or turn away lest you be run over and crushed). For Roosevelt to take on Morgan—who might easily send the stock and money markets into a dizzying downward spiral—required considerable nerve, especially just four months after assuming office, and long before being elected in his own right. Roosevelt had plenty of nerve—but as important as *having* the nerve was being *perceived* to have it. The hero of Santiago surely did.

Later that same year—1902—Roosevelt felt obliged to intervene in a coal strike. The work stoppage threatened to starve the northeast of fuel as winter approached; severe social hardship impended. The coal bosses were acting obnoxious. Their leader, George Baer, asserted that the rights of workingmen would be safeguarded not by "labor agitators" but "the Christian men to whom God in His infinite wisdom has given the control of the property interests of the country."[12]

At the time of the strike, Roosevelt was nursing an injury—this one not the result of an athletic mishap, but of a streetcar accident. Yet even from his wheelchair he was tempted to take on the managers. "If it wasn't for the high office I held," he said of one, "I would have taken him by the seat of the breeches and nape of the neck and chucked him out of that window."[13]

Yet it was not the threat of getting physical that caught the operators' attention; it was his threat of getting martial. Roosevelt let slip that he was readying the army to take over the coal mines if the owners did not come to reasonable terms with the union. Nothing like that had ever been done, certainly not in peacetime. Roosevelt himself was unsure he possessed the constitutional authority. "I do not know whether I would have had any precedents, save perhaps those of General Butler at New Orleans," he conceded afterward. "But in my judgment it would have been imperative to act, precedent or no precedent—and I was in readiness."[14]

Again, the critical point was the perception. The operators had to believe he would do what he threatened to do. And if the country's reigning military hero said the army was essential to the safety and welfare of the nation in this critical hour, how could they credibly contradict him? After he provided some face-saving cover, they caved in.

The wonderful thing about being perceived as a man of action was that it lent authority even to what might have been bluffs. Would Roosevelt really have taken over the mines? No one ever knew. Roosevelt could speak softly (not that he always did) precisely because he was known to carry a big stick and understand how to use it.

The communicative credibility that came to the man of action—especially of military action—served Roosevelt particularly well in foreign affairs. For all his warmongering as assistant navy secretary, for all his talk about war being the health of the nation, when he actually had the opportunity to thrust the nation into war—that is, as commander in chief—he never did. He cleaned up and concluded the war he inherited in the Philippines, but otherwise he let the threat of force suffice. Two instances illustrate.

At the end of 1902, Germany and Britain imposed a blockade on Venezuela for nonpayment of debts. Although Roosevelt credited Britain's promise that the blockade was temporary and indicated no permanent designs on South America or the Caribbean, he was less certain about Germany. Kaiser Wilhelm was known to be ambitious and to believe that Germany deserved a larger empire than it possessed. Roosevelt determined to let the kaiser know that he—Roosevelt—would brook no tampering with the Monroe Doctrine. He ordered Adm. George Dewey to assemble the battle fleet off Puerto Rico, for maneuvers—or any other eventuality. He discreetly—and by means diplomatic historians still debate today—signaled to the kaiser that the fleet was there, that it placed Germany's squadron at a distinct disadvantage, and that American honor and German good sense dictated a German withdrawal. The kaiser lifted the blockade and consented to arbitration.

The second illustration is more flamboyant. For some time a variety of irritations had vexed U.S. relations with Japan; these included Korea, the Philippines, Hawaii, racism, and immigration. Underlying all was the simple fact that Japan's rapidly growing strength was upsetting the status quo in the Pacific and forcing the United States to pay attention. Roosevelt did so during the Russo-Japanese War, to the point of mediating the treaty that ended the conflict (and won him the Nobel Peace Prize). But that simply annoyed the Japanese even more, for they thought they should have received a better deal at the peace table. Roosevelt worried that Japan's leaders might attempt something rash, perhaps from a miscalculation of American determination.

To forestall this, he arranged a remarkable show of force. He ordered the American battleship fleet on a round-the-world cruise. Nothing on such a scale had ever been attempted; nothing at all like it had ever been carried off. Roosevelt's critics charged that it would provoke Japan, leave American shores defenseless, and cost too much. Congress refused to advance the funds necessary for the voyage. Roosevelt replied that the voyage threatened no country; but if Japan chose to pick a fight, the ships would be in fighting trim and under a full head of steam. As for congressional reluctance to fund the voyage, he adopted the audacious expedient of sending the ships to the far Pacific with only the funds on hand and dared Congress to leave them there. Congress declined his dare.

The voyage proved a political and public relations coup for Roosevelt. The fleet impressed all who saw it during its many port calls around the globe. Whether it delayed the showdown with Japan is impossible to know. Suffice it to say that that showdown did not occur for another thirty years. The fleet arrived home just before Roosevelt left office in early 1909. He went out in the style Americans had come to expect of him: The mighty guns of the great fleet boomed out their salute to the departing commander in chief. The event, observed one journalist, marked "the apotheosis of Roosevelt," the "one supreme, magnificent moment" of his career.[15]

Roosevelt's contribution to the art of presidential communication hardly ended with his departure from office. Indeed, because he remained a national presence for another decade, and a potential president again, he exerted a strong influence on his successors—often to their chagrin. And he remained a national presence and viable candidate precisely because of his persona as a man of action.

Shortly after the Great White Fleet came home, he handed the keys to the White House to William Howard Taft and headed off to Africa to hunt big game. ("Let every lion do his duty," was the toast on Wall Street.) As in everything Roosevelt did, his African safari mixed art with artlessness. He genuinely wanted Taft, his anointed successor, to have the opportunity to start his presidency without reporters constantly asking Roosevelt's opinion of how his heir was doing. And where better to dodge such questions than in the wilds of Africa?

At the same time, though, his African safari could only whet the interest of Americans for when he *did* return. He was a far more galvanizing story than the tepid Taft; after a year or so incommunicado, there would be all the more demand to hear about him when he resurfaced. Which was precisely what happened. Roosevelt's return in 1910 produced an explosion of enthusiasm. New Yorkers turned out by the hundreds of thousands; a cavalry unit of Rough Riders and a military band accompanied his car up Broadway. The hero was home from his latest triumph.

Under the circumstances, it would have required greater gifts of self-denial than Roosevelt possessed not to have reentered politics. He was told constantly that only he could retrieve the Republic from the clutches of the bosses into which it had fallen since his departure from the presidency. The people would respond to him and to no other.

When Roosevelt inevitably agreed, he did so in characteristic fashion. "By George, this is bully!" he declared. "It is great to be back in the thick of the fight again." On his way to a convention of New York

Republicans, where party reactionaries were intending to put up a fight against his progressive wing, he predicted: "We are going to beat them to a frazzle. Do not forget the word, frazzle. I came back from Africa with some trophies, and when we get back from Saratoga we shall have some trophies." (The old guard avoided being frazzled, but its members were demoralized. Several were sitting on the porch of their hotel when a little girl came up inquiring for Teddy Roosevelt. "Oh, hell! What's the use?" one lamented. "Even the babies cry for Roosevelt. He is the whole three rings, ringmaster and elephant. Maybe he will let us into the show if we carry water for the elephant.")[16]

One thing led to another, and Roosevelt announced his challenge to Taft for the Republican nomination. To no one's surprise, he employed a boxing metaphor: "My hat is in the ring."[17] The bout was bloody, and low blows were thrown. The most dramatic moment came when Roosevelt, having lost the Republican nomination to Taft and thereupon bolted the GOP for the Progressives, was shot in Milwaukee. "It takes more than that to kill a Bull Moose," he said. "The bullet is in me now, so that I cannot make a very long speech." He unbuttoned his coat and showed the bloodstained shirt to the crowd, which gasped in shock and appreciation. Forty minutes later he was still on his feet, still talking. "My friends are a little more nervous than I am," he said, gesturing to those at the edge of the stage who were trying to get him to stop and go to a hospital. "Don't you waste any sympathy on me. I have had an A-1 time in life and I am having it now."[18]

He lost, of course. But the fact that he finished second—ahead of Taft—taught two lessons to those willing to learn. First, the bosses no longer controlled politics, at least not in the national presence of a compelling persona like Roosevelt. The bosses had denied Roosevelt the Republican nomination, but they could not deny him a place in the race. The 1912 presidential race did not signal the end of boss rule, but it signaled that the end was coming.

Second, Roosevelt's Bull Moose campaign—coming after a decade and a half of Roosevelt's presence at the center of national politics—suggested that the old style of presidential communication was doomed. Taft was a perfectly acceptable candidate by pre-Rooseveltian standards; his campaign was certainly more exciting than the front-porch campaigns of William McKinley. But Roosevelt, with his bugles, his Rough Riders, his lions and elephants (these last in voters' imaginations if not actually on the stump with him), even his attempted assassination—Roosevelt put on a show. Future candidates would be well advised to put on a show, too.

Nor was the show over. Having fractured the Republican Party without creating a credible alternative, Roosevelt once more entered the political wilderness. What could be more fitting, then, than to enter the physical wilderness as well? From youth he had admired the great explorers of Africa: Speke, Livingstone, and the others who had mapped the blank spaces on the Dark Continent. Now he emulated them, undertaking a voyage of discovery down the unknown and romantically named Rio da Duvida—the River of Doubt—into the uncharted interior of the Brazilian Amazon.

He nearly died. He badly injured himself rescuing one of the canoes from a cataract, and infection and fever set in. For days he was delirious, mumbling verses from Coleridge's "Xanadu." He might have given up the ghost, but his son Kermit explained that he was going to bring his father out dead or alive, and, frankly, alive would be easier.

Roosevelt never quite recovered. Some unidentified parasite plagued him for the rest of his days. But he battled to the end. When war broke out in Europe in 1914, he badgered the Wilson administration to prepare American forces for battle. Wilson tried to ignore him, but the colonel—the title he preferred above all others—would not be stilled. And, as on many occasions past, his reputation as a war hero lent particular credibility to his words. By the time Wilson grudgingly agreed that intervention was necessary, Roosevelt had regained nearly all the ground he had lost when bolting the Republican Party in 1912.

Had Roosevelt lived, he almost certainly would have been elected president again in 1920. When asked if the Republicans would nominate the colonel by acclamation, a Republican insider responded: Acclamation, hell, by assault. And, in light of Warren Harding's thrashing of James Cox, the Republican nomination was tantamount to election (although a Roosevelt on each ticket—Franklin Roosevelt was Cox's running mate—would have been interesting).

But Roosevelt died in January, 1919. Millions mourned his passing. Those most mournful may have been the political cartoonists, who understood perhaps better than any others how he had changed the art of political communication. One of them contributed the epitaph that endured in the minds of many. It was, of course, a cartoon. It showed Roosevelt riding off into the sunset, waving one last farewell as he went.

NOTES

1. *Commercial Advertiser*, June 7, 1895.

2. *New York World*, May 17, 1895.

3. Roosevelt to Lodge, May 19 and 25, 1898, in *Selections from the Correspondence of Theodore Roosevelt and Henry Cabot Lodge, 1884–1918*, ed. by Henry Cabot Lodge and Charles F. Redmond (New York: Da Capo, 1971).

4. Richard Harding Davis, *The Cuban and Porto Rican Campaigns* (New York: Charles Scribner's Sons, 1898), 217.

5. Chauncey M. Depew, *My Memories of Eighty Years* (New York: Charles Scribner's Sons, 1922), 161–62.

6. "Roosevelt's Trip," *New York Daily Tribune*, Oct. 19, 1898, 1.

7. Depew, *My Memories*, 162.

8. Arthur Wallace Dunn, *From Harrison to Harding*, 2 vols. (New York: G. P. Putnam's Sons, 1922), 1:335.

9. Henry Adams, *The Education of Henry Adams* (Boston: Houghton Mifflin, 1961), 417.

10. Lewis L. Gould, *The Presidency of Theodore Roosevelt* (Lawrence: University Press of Kansas, 1991), 19.

11. Joseph Bucklin Bishop, *Theodore Roosevelt and His Time Shown in His Own Letters* (New York: Charles Scribner's Sons, 1920), 211–12.

12. Mark Sullivan, *Our Times*, 6 vols. (New York: Charles Scribner's Sons, 1927–36), 2:426.

13. Frederick S. Wood, *Roosevelt As We Knew Him* (Philadelphia: John C. Winston, 1927), 109.

14. Roosevelt to W. M. Crane, Oct. 22, 1902, in *The Letters of Theodore Roosevelt*, 8 vols., ed. by Elting Morison and John M. Blum (Cambridge, Mass.: Harvard University Press, 1951–54).

15. "Brilliant End of World Cruise," *New York Times*, Feb. 23, 1909, 1.

16. "Leaders See Roosevelt," *New York Tribune*, Sept. 27, 1910, 2.

17. Henry F. Pringle, *Theodore Roosevelt* (New York: Harcourt, Brace, 1931), 556.

18. *The Works of Theodore Roosevelt*, Memorial ed., 20 vols. (New York: Charles Scribner's Sons, 1923–26), 19:441–52.

CHAPTER 6

Presidential Leadership and National Identity

Woodrow Wilson

and the Meaning of America

James R. Andrews

ARMISTICE DAY, 1921. Six shining black horses, their hoofs muffled, pulled the caissons carrying the coffin of the Unknown Soldier down Pennsylvania Avenue. Leading the mourners was the president of the United States, Warren G. Harding, walking alongside General of the Armies John J. Pershing, erstwhile commander of the American Expeditionary Force in Europe and now the chief of staff. In the solemn cortege that followed marched legislators, cabinet ministers, Supreme Court justices, generals, admirals, and foreign dignitaries. Farther back, behind a contingent of Medal of Honor recipients, a small carriage carried a mourner who could not walk in the procession, indeed, one whose inclusion was something of an afterthought. Murmurs came from the heretofore silent crowd as spectators recognized President Wilson. Some began to call his name and then cheers went up as the former commander in chief and Mrs. Wilson proceeded along the line of march to the White House, where former servants from the presidential mansion rushed out to greet him, and cheers grew to an ovation. After tipping his tall silk hat to the crowd and receiving a bow from President Harding, Mr. Wilson headed back in his carriage to his house on S Street where thousands more crowded in to greet him.[1]

It must have seemed ironic to such an astute observer as Ida Tarbell that a man whose polices had seemingly been so soundly rejected by the electorate could elicit such admiration and affection. She saw in the tribute some not easily defined longing to associate with what she called "their nobler phase." In an article for *Colliers* she described what she saw as a questioning hope that Wilson, at least, had not lost the vision and idealism that the country had embraced not so long before. He was "The Man They Cannot Forget."[2]

Wilson was difficult to forget, for one thing, because he had articulated a vision of America that reinterpreted old principles and values in a unique way in stirring times and with profound effect on the century that followed. At the very end of his life—barely two weeks before he died—in a conversation with Raymond Fosdick, he persisted in his determined belief that "The world is *run* by its ideals."[3] Wilson was convinced that leadership was, in part, the articulation of the nation's ideals. In a speech given on the one hundredth anniversary of Lincoln's birth, Wilson sought to explain the power of this "Man of the People."

A great nation is not led by a man who simply repeats the talk of the street corners or the opinions of the newspapers. A nation is led by a man who hears more than those things, or who, hearing those things, understands them better, unites them, and gives to them a common meaning. He speaks not the rumors of the street, but a new principle for a new age. He is a man in whose ears the voices of the nation do not sound like the accidental and discordant notes that come from the voice of a mob, but concurrent and concordant like the united voices of a chorus, whose many meanings, spoken by melodious tongues unite in his understanding in a single meaning and reveal to him a single vision, so that he can speak what no other man knows: the common meaning of the common voice. Such is the man who leads a great, free, democratic nation.[4]

Jeffery Tulis calls this type of speech Wilson's "visionary" speech. Such a speech "would articulate a picture of the future and impel a populace toward it. Rather than appealing to and invigorating established principles, this forward-looking speech taps the public's feelings and articulates it wishes. At its best it creates, rather than explains, principles."[5] I agree that such speeches can be inspirational and moralistic and that Wilson was convinced that a genuinely democratic leader could translate inchoate ideas and aspirations into a meaningful message. I would not say, however, based on readings of dozens of Wilson's "visionary" speeches, that he does not attempt to create new principles, even though Wilson himself speaks of "a new principle for a new age." His aim seems clearly to recreate, to reinterpret and refurbish old principles—or at least to bestow the legitimacy of historical precedent on the principles he offers as guides to action. This is not to deny Wilson's innovative and sometimes divergent constitutional and political views or to contradict Tulis's contention that Wilson significantly altered aspects of the presidency. Rather, as David Zarefsky has put it so neatly: "Rhetors challenge us to return to the best of our traditions. What we really return to is a changed understanding of those traditions, changed because of the rhetor's efforts."[6]

Wilson, then, saw as a virtual sine qua non of leadership the ability to project a unified vision of and for the people. One way of describing the American experience from its beginnings to the present day is as a struggle to discover and articulate an identity, to understand and to come to some general agreement of what it is to be "American," what it is that makes an "American nation." As students of nationalism clearly recognize, a specified territory formed into a political unit does not necessarily become a "nation." A "nation," much as a "class," does not spring full blown from a divine head; it does not automatically grow from a prescribed set of circumstances. As Drew Gilpin Faust emphasized in a recent study of the ideological contradictions and paradoxes upon which southern nationalism was founded—and upon which it ultimately foundered—nationalism "is not a substance available to a people in a certain premeasured amount; it is rather a dynamic of ideas and social realities that can, under the proper circumstances, unite and legitimate a people in what they regard as reasoned public action."[7] Distinguished Civil War historian Carl Degler has also observed that "nationalism . . . is not a commodity or a thing, it is created;" it may be seen "as a process, in the course of which flesh and blood leaders and followers creatively mold and integrate idea, events, and power to bring a nation into being."[8]

For Wilson, it was clearly the president's responsibility, indeed a measure of his fitness to hold office, to grasp the "meaning" of America and to use the rhetorical power of the presidency to fix that meaning in the minds of an American community. To try to understand just how Wilson went about performing this act of rhetorical leadership, I have examined an extensive sample of Wilson's ceremonial speeches from his academic period through his presidency. I have chosen to study Wilson's epideictic rhetoric precisely because the function of such rhetoric is to construct moral community. In Aristotle's famous classification this genre functioned to praise good and condemn evil in ways relevant to the present.[9] Chaim Perelman has described the function of epideictic as uniting diverse elements by projecting a unified vision of community.[10] More recently, scholars such as Celeste Condit and Bonnie Dow have explored the community-building functions of epideictic.[11]

In the twentieth century, as presidents from Theodore Roosevelt and Wilson began to speak more directly to and for the people, they increasingly took up the task of forging community out of the disparate segments of the American population. Woodrow Wilson, in short, sought to imbue the abstraction "American" with meaning. In doing so, he stressed the need for unity and expanded and refined our notions of uniqueness. To understand Wilson's efforts we must view them within at least two contextual frames: the Americanization movement and the First World War.

Briefly, one major activity stemming from Progressivism was the determination to "Americanize" immigrants. To Protestant, white, male, Anglo-Saxons who saw themselves as the direct descendants—spiritually, morally, politically, and, in some cases actually—of the Puritan vanguard, the swarm of immigrants that began arriving in the nineteenth century from Ireland and then from southern and eastern Europe seemed alarmingly foreign. Their geographic concentration in the cities exacerbated urban-rural tensions, their religion suggested to some an alien allegiance, and their tendency toward ethnic solidarity aroused deep suspicion about their true loyalties. Reactions sometimes took the dark and ugly path of violence and intimidation. The revived Ku Klux Klan, for example, attempted to "discipline" and control foreigners as well as African Americans. Similarly, fear of the effects of immigrant labor on the job market led the American Federation of Labor to support the restriction of immigration.

But Progressives were worried about the effects on self-government when, as they saw it, masses of people untutored in the ways of democracy and more prone to accept authoritarian dictates than civic responsibility were infused into the political system. One alarming symptom of the ill effects on good government of this inundation was the apparent success of the big-city "bosses" in corralling immigrant votes by providing them with services that met their immediate needs. The Progressive answer was to remake the immigrants into Americans. In large cities, settlement workers like Jane Addams and Lillian Wald spearheaded efforts to teach newcomers the ways of American culture through civics lessons and English-language instruction. To become real Americans, an immigrant guidebook advised new arrivals in 1891, "Forget your customs, and your ideals." Israel Zangwell provided the rhetorical epitome in his 1908 hit play *The Melting Pot* when David, a Russian Jewish immigrant exclaimed: "America is God's Crucible, the great Melting Pot where all the races of Europe are melting and reforming! Here you stand, good folk, I think, when I see them at Ellis Island, here you stand in your fifty groups with your fifty languages and histories, and your fifty blood hatreds and rivalries, but you won't be long like that, brothers, for these are the fires of God you've come to—these are the fires of God! A fig for your feuds and vendettas! German and Frenchmen, Irishman and Englishman, Jews and Russians—into the Crucible with you all! God is making the American."[12]

How to make an "American Nation" out of a plethora of nationalities is as much a rhetorical challenge as anything else. As Benedict Anderson has argued, a nation "is imagined as a *community*, because, regardless of the actual inequality and exploitation that may prevail in each, the nation is always conceived as a deep, horizontal comradeship."[13] How is such comradeship promoted? Wilson, in an early address commemorating Washington's inauguration, averred that gaining independence by driving out the British army was easier "than it will be to assimilate a heterogeneous horde of immigrants. . . . Minds cast in every mold of race, minds inheriting every bias of environment, warped by the histories of a score of different nations, warmed or chilled, closed or expanded by almost every climate of the globe." But it could be done by those willing "to stand face to face with our ideals, to renew our enthusiasms, to reckon again our duties, to take fresh views of our aims and fresh courage for their pursuit." The task, as Wilson saw it, was "to weld our people together in a patriotism as pure, a wisdom as elevated, a virtue as sound as those of the greater generation whom today we hold in special and grateful remembrance."[14] Such was to be the role Wilson envisioned for a democratic leader who could speak for and to the people.

The second principal contextual feature is, of course, the events surrounding America's reaction to and entry into the war and the peace negotiations and their aftermath. Wilson's determined effort to avoid the European conflict was thwarted by the direction of world events. As America was drawn into the maelstrom, Wilson's angst became apparent. Matters "lying outside our own life as a nation and over which we had no control" Wilson asserted in his second inaugural, had "despite our wish to keep free of them . . . drawn us more and more irresistibly into their own current and influence. It has been impossible to avoid them."[15] Obviously, Wilson's reluctance to be drawn into the European war, his determination to brook no opposition once the war was declared, and his intense campaign for ratification of the treaty he had brokered would color his rhetorical efforts to define what was essentially American.

These two contextual forces—Americanization and America's role in the First World War—influenced Wilson's rhetorical choices, but the ceremonial venue gave him the opportunity to talk in terms of foundational principles that glossed over political motivations and also lodged themselves in the American psyche as "ideals" for which to strive.

From the study of Wilson's ceremonial discourse, two intertwining themes arise around which the images and meanings of America cluster: unity and uniqueness. I believe that these themes have particular importance in the discourse of the United States because, although sometimes and in some ways contested, they helped to define what it meant to be American in the twentieth century.

Unity is a critical concept in promoting the "comradeship" that defines a nation. For America, being the "united" states had always been an issue of large import—from the initial attempts of colonials at united protest through the constitutional debates, the sectional quarrels, and the defining moment of American nationhood, the Civil War. As the twentieth century dawned, unity for Americans involved reinforcing a national as opposed to a sectional purpose, reconciling competing economic interests that threatened the notion of a classless society, and amalgamating diverse cultural practices into a homogeneous American culture.

Woodrow Wilson spoke frequently at events commemorating the Civil War. He spoke to the veterans—North and South—of Gettysburg, to the Grand Army of the Republic (GAR), to the Daughters of the Confederacy. He traveled to North Carolina to give an address in honor of Robert E. Lee's birthday and to Chicago to celebrate the centenary of Lincoln's birth. He remembered the epic struggle in numerous Memorial Day speeches. The Civil War, of course, was closer to Wilson and his contemporaries than the Second World War is to us. Wilson told one audience that his "earliest recollection is of standing at my father's gateway in Augusta, Georgia, when I was four years old, and hearing someone pass and say that Mr. Lincoln was elected and there was to be war."[16] His message remained consistent: the war had ended the sectionalism that prevented the country from becoming a real nation and allowed a true unity to develop. On July 4, 1919, the president delivered a speech at Gettysburg to a gathering that itself spoke to the national unity that had emerged when the smoke of battle cleared: a grand encampment of GAR and Confederate veterans on the fiftieth anniversary of the battle. In describing what the fifty years since the guns were stilled meant, Wilson asserted:

> They have meant peace and union and vigour, and the maturity and might of a great nation. How wholesome and healing the peace has been! We have found one another again as brothers and comrades in arms, enemies no longer, generous friends rather, our battles long past, the quarrel forgotten-except that we shall not forget the splendid valour, the manly devotion of the men then arrayed against one another, now grasping hands and smiling into each other's eyes. How complete the union has become and how dear to all of us, how unquestioned, how benign and majestic, as State after State has been added to this great family of free men! How handsome the vigour, the maturity, the might of the great Nation we love with undivided hearts; how full of large and confident promise that a life will be wrought out that will crown its strength with gracious justice and a happy welfare that will touch all alike with deep contentment! We are debtors to those fifty crowded years; they have made us heirs to a mighty heritage.[17]

The great accomplishment of the Civil War, Wilson suggests, was to make unity and thus nationhood possible. (In all his speeches, Wilson's allusion to slavery are only in passing. Slavery was divisive and never could have been eliminated without war; the implication is that the great good that came from the demise of slavery was the eradication of a barrier to unity.)

The war set the stage for the emergence of a unified America. In Wilson's mind it became a trope for the further development of the nation—a nation for whom he, the president spoke:

> I have been chosen the leader of the Nation. I cannot justify the choice by any qualities of my own, but so it has come about, and here I stand. Whom do I command? The ghostly hosts who fought upon these battlefields long ago and are gone? These gallant gentlemen stricken in years whose fighting days are over, their glory won? What are the orders for them and who rallies them? I have in my mind another host, whom these set free of civil strife in order that they might work out in days of peace and settled order the life of a great Nation. That host is the people themselves, the great and the small, without class or difference of kind or race or origin; and undivided in interest, if we have the vision to guide and direct them and order their lives aright in what we do.[18]

It was, Wilson firmly believed, "the business of every leader of government . . . to hear what the nation is saying and to know what the nation is enduring. It is not his business to judge for the nation but to judge through the nation as its spokesman and voice."[19] His was the vision, by right and duty, to guide the people. But who, exactly, were the people he guided? What made the American people a people?

The Americanization movement reflected a feeling that homogeneity was a prerequisite of true unity and thus true nationhood. Jefferson Davis, in his inaugural address, asserted as much in justification of secession. "To increase the power, develop the resources, and promote the happiness of a confederacy," Davis argued, "it is requisite that there should be so much of homogeneity that the welfare of every portion shall be the aim of the whole."[20] Wilson's vision of an American reflected a tension that has persisted into our own time. The one-out-of-many emblem that symbolized the need for colonial unity also may be seen as a continuing challenge. Pride in the fact that America has drawn to its shores the oppressed and tempest-tossed mingled with the uneasy feeling that aliens, rather than becoming more American would upset American values and practices so as to be more compatible with foreign ways. As Denise M. Bostdorff has pointed out, Wilson himself was not free of the theory that the Anglo-Saxon "race" had an inherent and superior capacity for self-government. She directs attention, for example, to Wilson's observation in *History of the American People* that certain southern and eastern Europeans "of the lower classes" had "neither skill, nor energy, nor an initiative intelligence" to govern themselves.[21] That was why the melting pot was such a convenient trope. The crucible burned away all the impurities and the good essences melded. As President Wilson put it in memorializing the heroes of Veracruz: "Notice how truly these men were of our blood. I mean of our American blood, which is not drawn from any one country, which is not drawn from any one stock, which is not drawn from any one language of the modern world; but free men everywhere have sent their sons and their brothers and their daughters to this country in order to make that great compounded Nation which consists of all the sturdy elements and of all the best elements of the whole globe."[22] While the melting pot is no longer a popular metaphor, the goal of a blended society has not been completely abandoned. In any case, it certainly undergirded Wilson's vision and maintained rhetorical respectability well into the twentieth century.

Of course, if fusion was to take place, vestiges of Old World culture had to be purged. In paying tribute to naval hero John Barry, Wilson described the Irish-born commodore as "an Irishman; but his heart crossed the Atlantic with him. . . . Some Americans need hyphens in their names, because only part of them has come over; but when the whole man has come over, heart and thought and all, the hyphen drops of its own weight out of his name. This man was not an Irish-American; he was an Irishman who became an American."[23]

After the war in Europe broke out, the issue of being American became more acute. As the president told a newly naturalized group of citizens in 1915: "I certainly would not be one even to suggest that a man cease to love the home of his birth and the nation of his origin—these things are very sacred and ought not to be put out of our hearts—but it was one thing to love the place where you were born and it is another to dedicate yourselves to the place to which you go. You cannot dedicate yourself to America unless you become in every respect and with every purpose of your will thorough Americans."[24]

This particular speech, given in the wake of the sinking of the *Lusitania*, showed Wilson's concern for the possibility that American neutrality could be threatened by exploiting national filial ties. He warned the new citizens that "You cannot become thorough Americans if you think of yourselves in groups. . . . A man who thinks of himself as belonging to a particular national group in America has not yet become an American, and the man who goes among you to trade upon your nationality is no worthy son to live under the stars and stripes." Arousing such ethnic loyalties was, for Wilson, a cardinal sin against unity: "It was but an historical accident no doubt that this country was called the 'United States,'" he said, "yet I am very thankful that it has the word 'United' in its title, and the man who seeks to divide man from man, group from group, interest from interest in this great Union is striking at its very heart."[25]

In June, 1916, with the war in Europe ending its second year, Woodrow Wilson was nominated for reelection, supported by the slogan, "He kept us out of war." The president's efforts to maintain neutrality made him sharply critical of Americans who appeared to him to have divided loyalties. Indeed, up to that point, the emotionally charged concept of loyalty had seemed directly at issue. However, "Certain men," he told an Americanization conference in Washington in July of that year, "born in other lands, have in recent months thought more of those lands than they have of the honor and interest of the government under which they are now living." The fact that those men had drawn "apart in spirit and organization from the rest of us," the president found "absolutely incompatible with the fundamental idea of loyalty." He maintained that "whether it hurts me or whether it benefits me, I am obliged to be loyal," and advised his audience that "this is the sort of loyalty that which ought to be inculcated into these newcomers, they are not to be loyal only so long as they are pleased, but that, once having entered into this sacred relationship, they are bound to be loyal whether they are pleased or not."[26] The relationship had become "sacred," and as America ultimately plunged into the war, the need for unity and the demands of loyalty became fierce.

In promoting unity, Wilson also envisioned America within the context of the economic struggles of the late nineteenth and early twentieth century: "the people great and small, without regard to class." In a 1911 speech in New York on "The Rights of the Jews," dealing specifically with the U.S.-Russian trade agreements, Wilson voiced a principle that was for him a guide to his domestic policy and his articulation of principle as it should be practiced: "America is not a mere body of traders; it is a body of free men. Our greatness is built upon our freedom—is moral, not material. We have a great ardor for gain; but we have a deep passion for the rights of man. Principles lie back of our action. America would be inconceivable without them. These principles are not incompatible with great material prosperity. On the contrary, unless we are deeply mistaken, they are indispensable to it. We are not willing to have prosperity, however, if our fellow-citizens must suffer contempt for it, or lose the rights that belong to every American in order that we may enjoy it."[27]

More than a year later, in his first inaugural address, Wilson argued that Americans, in their haste to succeed, had sometimes been "crude and heartless and unfeeling," they had been "heedless and in a hurry." Through him, however, America had been "vouchsafed a vision" that would reconcile "every process of our national life again with the standards we so proudly set up at the beginning." Wilson saw those standards of "justice and fair play" as a necessary ingredient to national unity. Indeed, they served in part to define Americans and distinguish them from others.[28]

Americans, of course, had always seen themselves as different from others—and not necessarily because of the supposed amalgamation that had produced a new being. That idea, after all, was a creature of the late nineteenth and early twentieth centuries. Americans thought of themselves as exceptional from the beginning, whether as models of a true Christian polity, or exemplars of self-government. (We are of course, talking here about perceptions, quite apart from scholarly debates over the real nature and extent of such supposed exceptionalism.) Throughout our history, our uniqueness has been coupled with our sense of mission.

Now there is the obvious implication, given what I have already discussed, that Americans were unique because they blended together so many different groups. That, however, was not really central to what defined America in such a way as to set it apart from the rest of the world. At times Wilson spoke of Americans as "apostles of liberty and self government,"[29] much in the way Americans had explained their singular role in the past. Daniel Webster, for example, in an address commemorating the battle of Bunker Hill, had extolled America's special contribution to the world in the form of self-government, and generations of Americans, Jefferson and Lincoln among them, had pointed to the American "experiment." Wilson routinely reiterated this sentiment. He saw America as "the nation God has builded by our hands,"[30] and carried on the image of this country as a beacon of hope, a haven for the oppressed: "We opened our gates to all the world and said 'Let all men who wish to be free come to us and they will be welcome,'" he told a July 4 audience in 1914. "We said," he continued, "'This independence of ours is not a selfish thing for our own exclusive private use.' It is for everybody for whom we can find the means of extending it."[31] However, as the war in Europe increasingly occupied his thoughts, Wilson saw the need to extend the vision. He hinted at this in a 1915 Memorial Day speech: "America, I have said, was reborn by the struggle of the Civil War, but America is reborn everyday of her life by the purposes we form, the conceptions we entertain, the hopes that we cherish. We live in our visions. We live in the things we see. We live, and hope abounds in us as we live, in the things that we purpose. Let us go away from this place renewed in our devotion to daily duty and to those ideals which keep a nation young, keep it noble, keep it rich in enterprise and achievement; make it to lead the nations of the world in those things that make for hope and for the benefit of mankind."[32]

Wilson had always seen a special mission for America; in his first year as president of Princeton University, for example he proclaimed: "in our stroke for independence we struck a blow for all the world."[33] In 1914, on the eve of the European conflict, he had been content to hope that the world would "turn to America for those moral inspirations which lie at the basis of all freedom."[34] A year later the mission became a bit more assertive in a speech in which the president declared that democracy was no longer an experiment: "I hope we shall never forget that we created this Nation, not to serve ourselves, but to serve mankind."[35] The nature of such service became less ambiguous as war clouds darkened. By the time the president had been inaugurated in March, 1917, he felt compelled to state as the first principle of "a liberated mankind. . . . That all nations are equally interested in the peace of the world and in the political stability of free people, *and equally responsible for their maintenance* [emphasis added]."[36] That phrase significantly altered the vision; it was a rhetorical move that placed on the United States the responsibility not to serve as a shining example, but to maintain peace and political stability. A month later the president asked for a declaration of war to make the world safe for democracy.[37]

In the speeches that followed, Wilson's revision fully justified American involvement in the war. Less frequently did he assert the defense of the nation's rights and more stridently did he insist on America's mission. In his 1917 Memorial Day address, the president reflected: "In one sense this great struggle into which we have now entered is an American struggle because it is in defense of American honor and American rights, but it is something even greater than that; it is a world struggle. It is a struggle of men who love liberty everywhere, and in this cause America will show herself greater than ever because she will rise to a greater thing. . . . in the providence of God America will once more have the opportunity to show the world that she was born to serve mankind."[38]

In transforming the notion of service, Wilson consistently linked the service America was doing in the war with the nation's most cherished symbols. On Thanksgiving Day 1917, the president proclaimed: "We have been given the opportunity to serve mankind as we once served ourselves in the great day of our Declaration of Independence, by taking up arms against a tyranny that threatened to master and debase men everywhere."[39] As the war ended, Wilson saw the effort not as a victory of force, but as "a symbol of self sacrifice."[40]

Wilson's rhetorical restructuring had transformed the long-held vision of America as a shining example of liberty for the world to emulate to its embodiment as the self-sacrificing defender of liberty. Democracy was, indeed, no longer an experiment in America—it was now constructed as a moving force in history, and America was its agent in the world.

Wilson's ceremonial discourse appears to me to point to the conclusion that he indeed saw it as a fundamental role of the president to provide a vision of America—to interpret America to itself.[41] In doing so, Wilson espoused a national view that applauded, as the result of the Civil War, the death of sectionalism, making a true nation possible,[42] and portrayed the people as a distillation of what was best in all the races of the world. Loyalty for Americans, then, was tested by one's ability to rise above one's national origin and pledge allegiance, instead, to this new land of new people. This blending of many into one was an updated feature of traditional American exceptionalism. Moreover, as events moved America closer to war, Wilson offered a new vision of America as a nation destined to serve the world and to accept responsibility for peace and political stability among nations.

With the return to normalcy that followed his crushing defeat in 1920, it may have seemed that Wilson's vision was dead. His last public words, delivered in a halting, broken Armistice Day address over that amazing new medium, the radio, Wilson asserted: "The only way we can worthily give proof of our appreciation of Armistice Day is by resolving to put self-interest away and once more formulate and act upon the highest ideals and purposes of international policy. Thus, and only thus, can we return to the true traditions of America."[43] Three months later Wilson was dead.

But, for good or ill, Wilson's vision was not as easily laid to rest—it had a profound impact on the twentieth century, as Woodrow Wilson firmly believed a president's vision should. The questions of the role of government in protecting the weak against the strong—or the poor against the rich, of reconciling the pull of smaller, self-defined communities with a loyalty to a larger society, of articulating a moral agenda for the world and taking responsibility for implementing it, have been affected by Wilson's vision and, still with us today, influence how we think about confronting such issues—how, in short, we define what it means to be American and to fulfill America's mission.

NOTES

1. See George Creel, *Rebel at Large: Recollections of Fifty Crowed Years* (New York: G. P. Putnam, 1947), 230–31; Gene Smith, *When the Cheering Stopped: The Last Years of Woodrow Wilson* (New York: William Morrow, 1967), 200–204; August Heckscher, *Woodrow Wilson* (New York: Scribners, 1991), 657–58.

2. Ida Tarbell, "The Man They Cannot Forget," *Colliers*, Feb. 18, 1922.

3. Smith, *When the Cheering Stopped*, 234.

4. Woodrow Wilson, *College and State: Educational, Literary and Political Papers (1875–1913)*, 2 vols., ed. Ray Stannard Baker and William E. Dodd (New York: Harper, 1925), 2:94–95.

5. Jeffrey K. Tulis, *The Rhetorical Presidency* (Princeton, N.J.: Princeton University Press, 1987), 135.

6. David Zarefsky, *The Roots of American Community* (Boston: Allyn and Bacon, 1996), 10.

7. Drew Gilpin Faust, *The Creation of Confederate Nationalism: Ideology and Identity in the Civil War South* (Baton Rouge: Louisiana State University Press, 1988), 6.

8. Carl Degler, "One Among Many: The United States and National Unification," in *Lincoln the War President*, ed. Gabor S. Boritt (New York: Oxford U Press, 1992), 97–98.

9. Aristotle, *The Rhetoric*, trans. Rhys Roberts (New York: Random House, 1954), 31–34, 56–57.

10. Chaim Perelman and Lucie Olbrects-Tyteca, *The New Rhetoric: A Treatise on Argumentation*, trans. John Wilkinson and Purcell Weaver (University of Notre Dame Press, 1969), 51.

11. Celeste Michelle Condit, "The Functions of Epideictic: The Boston Massacre Orations as Exemplar," *Communication Quarterly* 33, no. 4 (fall, 1985): 284–99; Bonnie J. Dow, "The Function of Epideictic and Deliberative Strategies in Presidential Crisis Rhetoric," *Western Journal of Speech Communication* 53, no. 3 (summer, 1989): 294–310. See also, Lawrence W. Rosenfield, "The Practical Celebration of Epideictic," in *Rhetoric in Transition: Studies in the Nature and Uses of Rhetoric*, ed. Eugene White (University Park, Pa.: Pennsylvania State University Press, 1980), 131–56.

12. Harold Evans, *The American Century* (New York: Alfred A. Knopf, 1998), 90–91.

13. Benedict Anderson, *Imagined Communities*, rev. ed. (London: Verso, 1983), 7.

14. Wilson, "Make Haste Slowly," in Baker and Dodd, eds., *College and State*, 1:185–86.

15. Wilson, second inaugural address, in *War and Peace: Presidential Addresses, Messages, and Public Papers*, 2 vols., ed. Ray Stannard Baker and William E. Dodd (New York: Harper, 1927), 1:1.

16. Wilson, "Abraham Lincoln: A Man of the People," in Baker and Dodd, eds., *College and State*, 2:83.

17. Wilson, "Hard Tasks Ahead of the Nation," in *The New Democracy: Presidential Addresses, Messages, and Other Papers (1913–1917)*, 2 vols., ed. Ray Stannard Baker and William E. Dodd (New York: Harper, 1926), 1:41.

18. Ibid., 1:43

19. John Wells Davidson, ed., *A Crossroads of Freedom: The 1912 Campaign Speeches of Woodrow Wilson* (New Haven, Conn.: Yale University Press, 1956), 93.

20. Lynda Lasswell Crist and Mary Seaton Dix, eds., *The Papers of Jefferson Davis*, 8 vols. (Baton Rouge: Louisiana State University Press, 1971–94), 7:49.

21. Denise M. Bostdorff, "Response to James Andrews' 'Presidential Leadership and National Identity'" (paper presented at the Fifth Annual Conference on Presidential Rhetoric, Mar., 1999), 3–4.

22. Wilson, "The Heroes of Vera Cruz," in Baker and Dodd, eds., *New Democracy*, 1:104.

23. Wilson, "Men Who Think of Themselves Not True Americans," ibid., 1:109.

24. Wilson, "Too Proud to Fight," ibid., 1:319.

25. Ibid., 1:319–20

26. Wilson, "Loyalty Means Self-Sacrifice," ibid., 2:251.

27. Wilson, "The Rights of the Jews," in Baker and Dodd, eds., *College and State*, 2:320.

28. Wilson, "First Inaugural Address," in Baker and Dodd, eds., *New Democracy*, 1:3.

29. Wilson, "The Ideals of America," in Baker and Dodd, eds., *College and State,* 1:429.

30. Wilson, "Hard Tasks," 1:44.

31. Wilson, "Be Worthy of the Men of 1776," in Baker and Dodd, eds., *New Democracy,* 1:142.

32. Wilson, "Meaning of the Civil War," ibid., 1:337.

33. Wilson, "Ideals of America," 1:420.

34. Wilson, "Be Worthy," ibid., 1:147.

35. Wilson, "Democracy No Longer an Experiment," in Baker and Dodd, eds., *New Democracy,* 1:371.

36. Wilson "Second Inaugural Address," in Baker and Dodd, eds., *War and Peace,* 1:3.

37. Denise Bostdorff properly calls attention to the fact that the conception of an active American mission in the world did not originate with Wilson, but was evident in the debates over "imperialism" at the end of the nineteenth century. I certainly agree with her; the point that I wish to make is that Wilson's notion of an active America, while not original perhaps, was qualitatively different from, for example, the "March of the Flag" idea of mission (Bostdorff, "Response to James Andrews," 6–8).

38. Wilson, "America Was Born to Serve Mankind," in Baker and Dodd, eds., *War and Peace,* 1:53.

39. Wilson, "Thanksgiving Day Proclamation," ibid., 1:111.

40. Wilson, "Address at the Lord Mayor's Luncheon," ibid., 1:349.

41. Ronald Carpenter has convincingly argued that the precursors of Wilson's views as president can be discerned in his academic writings in *History as Rhetoric: Style, Narrative, and Persuasion* (Columbia: University of South Carolina Press, 1995). See esp. chap. 6, which discusses Wilson as a writer of a persuasive American history textbook. See also Carpenter's "On American History Textbooks and Integration in the South: Woodrow Wilson and the Rhetoric of *Division and Reunion 1829–1880," Southern Speech Communication Journal* 51, no. 1 (fall, 1985): 1-23.

42. Wilson and his party, of course, did not abandon the cherished doctrine of states rights and local control. It has been argued that the major difference between the New Freedom and Theodore Roosevelt's New Nationalism lay with Wilson's efforts to portray government intervention in economic matters as leveling the playing field for the unprotected as opposed to TR's clear belief in the efficacy of more direct federal control and direction of the economy. See, for example, John Milton Cooper Jr., *The Warrior and the Priest: Woodrow Wilson and Theodore Roosevelt* (Cambridge, Mass.: Harvard University Press, 1983), esp. chap. 14, "The New Nationalism versus the New Freedom," 206–28.

43. Wilson, "High Significance of Armistice Day," in Baker and Dodd, eds., *War and Peace,* 2:541.

CHAPTER 7

FDR at Gettysburg

The New Deal and the Rhetoric
of Presidential Leadership

Thomas W. Benson

I N 1934 and again in 1938, Pres. Franklin Delano Roosevelt pre-sented commemorative speeches on the battlefield at Gettysburg, Pennsylvania. Roosevelt, who is perhaps second only to Abraham Lincoln as a canonically eloquent president, redefined the literature of American oratory in a long series of speeches from which passages are still immediately recognizable.[1] His best known speeches were im-portant policy addresses or occurred at—and defined—dramatic mo-ments in American history in campaign speeches, inaugural addresses, fireside chats, and the declaration of war. Roosevelt's eloquence is memorable not only for its literary brilliance and homely accessibility, but also for its energetic instrumentality and its sense of dramatic ac-tion and personality.

Roosevelt's Gettysburg speeches seem to offer an ideal opportunity to hear the resonance between the Great Emancipator and the great New Dealer. But for an American admirer of both Roosevelt and Lincoln, FDR's two speeches at Gettysburg strike one at first as a disappointment, even an embarrassment. They are also something of a mystery. Why are they as they are? How did they come to be? And how are we to understand them? These speeches, which have been largely forgotten, have much to teach us—as texts and as public actions—about the rhetoric of public memory. An examination of the production, the circumstances, the texts, and the reception of these two speeches reveals how even a single, simple act of public memorializing may, under the lens of rhetorical criticism, disclose itself also as a site of silent contestation, revision, and forgetting. The speeches may also teach us something about our own sentimental evasions. Because I argue that it is worthwhile to begin with the theory in the text and only then refract it through our own theories and myths, I shall turn immediately to the speeches, placing them before us in their fullness, their detail, their partly forgotten and in some ways startling circumstances, and their sometimes uncomfortable reminders of a former time. If we are to appreciate rather than merely mythologize these speeches, we must first subject them to the refining fire of a critical analysis suspicious but not dismissive of the impulses and practices of political power.

"THE SELFISHNESS OF SECTIONALISM HAS NO PLACE IN OUR NATIONAL LIFE," ADDRESS AT GETTYSBURG, MAY 30, 1934

ROOSEVELT SPOKE AT GETTYSBURG ON MEMORIAL DAY IN 1934.[2] THE BRIEF SPEECH IS WORTH READING IN ITS ENTIRETY.

Governor Pinchot, Mr. Chairman, my friends:

1. What a glorious day this is! I rejoice in it and I rejoice in this splendid celebration of it.

2. On these hills of Gettysburg two brave armies of Americans once met in contest. Not far from here, in a valley likewise consecrated to American valor, a ragged Continental Army survived a bitter winter to keep alive the expiring hope of a new Nation; and near to this battlefield and that valley stands that invincible city where the Declaration of Independence was born

and the Constitution of the United States was written by the fathers. Surely, all this is holy ground.

3. It was in Philadelphia, too, that Washington spoke his solemn, tender, wise words of farewell—a farewell not alone to his generation, but to the generation of those who laid down their lives here and to our generation and to the America of tomorrow. Perhaps if our fathers and grandfathers had truly heeded those words we should have had no family quarrel, no battle of Gettysburg, no Appomattox.

4. As a Virginian, President Washington had a natural pride in Virginia; but as an American, in his stately phrase, "the name of American, which belongs to you, in your national capacity, must always exalt the just pride of patriotism, more than any appellation derived from local discrimination."

5. Recognizing the strength of local and State and sectional prejudices and how strong they might grow to be, and how they might take from the national Government some of the loyalty the citizens owed to it, he made three historic tours during his Presidency. One was through New England in 1789, another through the Northern States in 1790, and still another through the Southern States in 1791. He did this, as he said—and the words sound good nearly a century and a half later—"In order to become better acquainted with their principal characters and internal circumstances, as well as to be more accessible to numbers of well-informed persons who might give him useful advices on political subjects."

6. But Washington did more to stimulate patriotism than merely to travel and mingle with the people. He knew that Nations grow as their commerce and manufactures and agriculture grow, and that all of these grow as the means of transportation are extended. He sought to knit the sections together by their common interest in these great enterprises; and he projected highways and canals as aids not to sectional, but to national, development.

7. But the Nation expanded geographically after the death of Washington far more rapidly than the Nation's means of inter-communication. The small national area of 1789 grew to the great expanse of the Nation in 1860. Even in terms of the crude transportation of that day, the first thirteen States were still within "driving distance" of each other.

8. With the settling of and the peopling of the Continent to the shores of the Pacific, there developed the problem of self-contained territories because the Nation's expansion exceeded its development of means of transportation, as we learn from our history books. The early building of railroads did not proceed on national lines.

9. Contrary to the belief of some of us Northerners, the South and the West were not laggard in developing this new form of transportation; but, as in the East, most of the railroads were local and sectional. It was a chartless procedure; people were not thinking in terms of national transportation or national communication. In the days before the Brothers' War not a single line of railroad was projected from the South to the North; not even one from the South reached to the national capital itself.

10. In those days, it was an inspired prophet of the South who said: "My brethren, if we know one another, we will love one another." The tragedy of the Nation was that the people did not know one another because they had not the necessary means of visiting one another.

11. Since those days, two subsequent wars, both with foreign Nations, have measurably allayed and softened the ancient passions. It has been left to us of this generation to see the healing made permanent.

12. We are all brothers now, brothers in a new understanding. The grain farmers of the West and in the fertile fields of Pennsylvania do not set themselves up for preference if we seek at the same time to help the cotton farmers of the South; nor do the tobacco growers complain of discrimination if, at the same time, we help the cattle men of the plains and mountains.

13. In our planning to lift industry to normal prosperity, the farmer upholds our efforts. And as we seek to give the farmers of the United States a long-sought equality, the city worker understands and helps. All of us, among all the States, share in whatever of good comes to the average man. We know that we all have a stake—a partnership in this Government of this, our country.

14. Today, we have many means of knowing each other—means that at last have sounded the doom of sectionalism. It is, I think, as I survey the picture from every angle, a simple fact that the chief hindrance to progress comes from three elements which, thank God, grow less in importance with the growth of a clearer understanding of our purposes on the part of the overwhelming majority. These groups are those who seek to stir up political animosity or build political advantage by the distortion of facts; those who, by declining to follow the rules of the game, seek to gain an unfair advantage over those who are willing to live up to the rules of the game; and those few who, because they have never been willing to take an interest in their fellow Americans, dwell inside of their own narrow spheres and still represent the selfishness of sectionalism which has no place in our national life.

15. Washington and Jefferson and Jackson and Lincoln and Theodore Roosevelt and Woodrow Wilson sought and worked for a consolidated Nation. You and I have it in our power to attain that great ideal within our lifetime. We can do this by following the peaceful methods prescribed under the broad and resilient provisions of the Constitution of the United States.

16. Here, here at Gettysburg, here in the presence of the spirits of those who fell on this ground, we give renewed assurance that the passions of war are moldering in the tombs of Time and the purposes of peace are flowing today in the hearts of a united people.

Most striking for a contemporary reader of the Roosevelt speech, bringing to the text what we might take to be stable and universal memories of Lincoln, Roosevelt, and Gettysburg, is the near absence of Lincoln and Gettysburg from the speech itself. Lincoln himself is mentioned by name only once in the speech, in paragraph 15, along with five other presidents. Gettysburg, although it is mentioned in the first sentence of paragraph 2, is by no means the central subject or image of the speech. Far from being stable or universal, both Lincoln and Gettysburg were and are contested, contingent rhetorical constructions; moreover, in this speech even the contingency and contestation are largely effaced.

In trying to account for the near-absence of Lincoln and Gettysburg from Roosevelt's 1934 speech, we might turn to the circumstances of its composition for a clue to his plans for appropriating and shaping public memory at the Gettysburg site. The Franklin Delano Roosevelt Library retains five separate draft typescripts of the address. The first is a draft of the speech by an unknown author, clipped to a cover memo to Steve Early from "D.J." asking Early to check a fact in the draft with "Mr. Barbee." This draft contains source annotations as endnotes. Attached to that draft and the memo to Early is another typed draft, based on the first draft and itself marked up for further revision. The third is a single-spaced press release version of the speech as prepared for delivery, on which H. M. Kannee has recorded in shorthand Roosevelt's deviations from the prepared text. Next there is a large-type reading copy of the speech. The fifth is a typewritten transcript of the speech identified in a covering memo as having been prepared by the White House stenographer from notes taken during delivery. "Underlining indicates words extemporaneously added to the previously prepared reading copy text. Words in parenthesis are words that were omitted when the speech was delivered, though they appear in the previously prepared reading copy text."[3] The final copy is that which appears in Roosevelt's published papers and which is transcribed in full here. All five typescripts differ in significant ways from the printed version edited by Roosevelt speechwriter Judge Samuel Rosenman. Although the details of authorship and composition are somewhat murky, the surviving copies of the speech do reveal significant shaping by Roosevelt.

Based on the surviving documents and Roosevelt's long-standing habits of speech composition, it appears that a speechwriter prepared the initial draft. Using it as a starting point, Roosevelt himself probably dictated the second draft to a stenographer, after which he made some further revisions in longhand on the resulting typescript, in turn using that amended typescript as the basis for the dictation of a version for release to the press, which he further revised just before or during delivery. In preparing Roosevelt's papers for publication, Rosenman relied on the corrected reading copy, but omitted an opening paragraph in which Roosevelt praised Gov. Gifford Pinchot of Pennsylvania.[4]

Who actually wrote the first draft of the speech? Almost certainly, the author was David Rankin Barbee (1874–1958), a southern journalist who migrated to a job as a feature writer for the *Washington Post* in 1928 and who took a job as a public relations writer for the Federal Alcohol Control Administration in 1933. Barbee was well known to Steve Early, Roosevelt's press secretary, who had placed public relations writers in several federal agencies; it was Early who was asked to send the initial draft to Barbee for fact checking and who may have suggested that Barbee write it.[5] If Roosevelt's de-emphasis of Lincoln seems odd, Barbee's draft for the speech, in comparison, seems astonishing.

But rather than assume that Barbee wrote the first draft, let us examine the evidence. Mechanical evidence is consistent with Barbee as author. The typewriter on which Barbee wrote eleven footnotes to the first draft, headed "Annotations" and sent back to the White House in response to Early's request, appears to be identical to that used to write the first draft. It is consistent with Barbee's authorship for the draft to have been sent back to him for fact checking—why else would Barbee, out of all possible historians, have been chosen for fact checking if he were not the author of the draft itself?

Contextual evidence further supports the possibility of Barbee as author or collaborator on the first draft of the speech. Roosevelt sometimes worked from first drafts that had been submitted by various writers in or out of the administration, and so the practice would not have been unusual. Years later, for example, Roosevelt's undelivered "last speech" was based on a first draft submitted by Josef Berger, a writer at the Democratic National Committee.[6] Harry Hopkins recalls an informal, after-dinner meeting with Roosevelt and some others on September 23, 1934, to discuss a radio speech scheduled for September 25. "It was perfectly clear that the President did not know what he was going to talk about. . . . He asked Moley if he had anything, and Moley promptly pulled a manuscript from his pocket—and the conversation indicated that he had either asked Moley to prepare something or knew that he was doing so. . . . It then developed that Felix Frankfurter and some of his bright boys had prepared Moley's manuscript."[7] Such practices were common for Roosevelt.

Barbee was positioned to help out with the speech. Throughout the New Deal, he kept up a correspondence with Early, the press secretary, and with Marvin McIntyre, the appointments secretary and himself a former campaign press secretary to Roosevelt. He volunteered to write for the White House, and apparently did write for Early on occasion. In December, 1933, in a note thanking McIntyre for helping him secure a post as director of public relations in the Federal Alcohol Control Administration, Barbee wrote: "Some day you may need a humble pen to write something for the Administration which you would not care to ask the able pens now at your command to write. If you think mine worthy of that office, command it."[8]

Barbee continued throughout the Roosevelt era to correspond with his apparent protector, Steve Early. As early as December, 1933, several months before the first Gettysburg speech, Barbee stepped into a controversy that had apparently begun when Herbert Hoover's press secretary, Theodore Joslin, charged that the New Deal was trying to control the news by hiring former newspapermen to engage in public relations work in various government agencies. On January 9, 1934, Barbee drafted for Early's use a long memorandum responding to Joslin's charges and including a short history of relations between the government and the press.[9] Barbee followed the controversy closely, collecting several file folders of clippings and a mimeographed copy of a press release on which someone, apparently Barbee, has written in red pencil, "This started the d-n controversy." The press release, headed "From CONGRESSIONAL INTELLIGENCE, 601 Albee Building, Washington, D.C., Release October 10," claims that "at least 150 ex-newspapermen are holding important posts in the Roosevelt Administration." One of those listed is Barbee.[10] The controversy over the New Deal and the press continued at least through 1935. In January of that year, Rep. Martin Dies (D-Texas), later the chair of the infamous Dies Committee, an early version of the House Committee on Un-American Activities, proposed that a congressional committee investigate White House censorship of the news. In June, Barbee delivered the baccalaureate address at Emory and Henry College on the theme, "The New Deal and the Freedom of the Press." Barbee defended the New Deal's employment of public relations workers and former journalists, and gave a short history of government-press relations. In one passage, Barbee's characteristic hostility to Lincoln and the Republicans emerges directly, when he describes Lincoln's suppression of the Democratic press: "The Democratic press was ruined beyond the power of redemption. To this day it has not recovered what it lost in the first year of Lincoln's Administration."[11]

Barbee cultivated his relation to FDR's speaking on several occasions, at the same time revealing his familiarity with Roosevelt's habits of speech composition. From time to time throughout the Roosevelt presidency, Barbee sent to Early materials that he suggested might be helpful additions to Roosevelt's speech material file.[12] When, in the summer of 1940, it appeared that Barbee might lose his job because of an agency reorganization, he appealed to Early to help him find another post. In one of a series of letters, he wrote to Early: "When the political campaign begins to warm up, it may be that you will be asked to suggest some writers or researchers to help in the press section. If so, I might fit in there in some capacity. I have written many political speeches and speeches for members of Congress and for Government officials on all sorts of topics, and research is a field in which I have long worked with some degree of success."[13]

Barbee's sense of the relationship between public memory and partisan maneuver was highly developed. In March, 1940, Barbee suggested to Early that Works Progress Administration employees be hired to index back years of Democratic newspapers, thereby making them accessible to historians and influencing the writing of history. "Our American history and biography has been written chiefly by Republican authors, using Republican source material."[14]

Although there is no direct documentary evidence proving that Barbee was the author of the first draft, there is considerable contextual evidence of Barbee's relation to Early, of Barbee's composition of various confidential documents, and of Barbee's commitment to the ideas that appear in the first draft of the 1934 speech.

Stylistic evidence strongly suggests that Roosevelt himself was not the author of the first draft. Compare the first full paragraph of that draft with the reading copy:

Initial Draft of Proposed Address at Gettysburg, May 30, 1934 (first paragraph)	Reading Copy of Gettysburg Address, May 30, 1934 (first paragraph)
On these beautiful hills two great armies of brave, gallant and chivalrous Americans once met in bloody combat. Not far from here, in another vale, consecrated to American valor ["valor" is inserted in pen; "history" is crossed out], a ragged Continental army starved through a terrible winter while keeping alive the expiring hopes of our ancestors in their ultimate freedom. And contiguous to this battlefield and that vale is the invincible city of Philadelphia, where the Declaration of Independence was born and the Constitution of our country was drafted. Surely all this is holy ground.	On these hills of Gettysburg two brave armies of Americans once met in combat. Not far from here, in a valley likewise consecrated to American valor, a ragged Continental Army survived a bitter winter to keep alive the expiring hope of a new Nation; and near to this battlefield and that valley stands that invincible city where the Declaration of Independence was born and the Constitution of the United States was written by the fathers. Surely, all this is holy ground.

Roosevelt kept the structure of Barbee's paragraph but considerably simplified it in his characteristic way. He pruned away adjectives. "Great armies of brave, gallant, and chivalrous Americans" becomes "brave Armies of Americans," omitting in the process those adjectives most closely associated with southern myths of the Lost Cause. "Starved" changes to "survived," gaining a more optimistic flavor, but diminishing the force of the original, with its parallel to "expiring," which is retained in the revision. The stuffy "contiguous" is changed to "near." Roosevelt worked similar stylistic simplifications throughout his revision of Barbee's draft.

Roosevelt's changes, although they retained most of the structure and logic of Barbee's draft, went far beyond stylistic revision, however, to produce a speech considerably different in its argument. Roosevelt's draft is much shorter than Barbee's. The omissions give Roosevelt's version a compactness and clarity of argument that focuses on the New Deal and its appeal for national unity. Barbee's draft, on the other hand, clearly wants to rewrite the nation's memory of the Civil War according to his own view—a view that at least partly survives into Roosevelt's final version.

David Rankin Barbee's authorship of the first draft is supported not only by circumstantial implications and stylistic resonance, but also by the doctrines he embedded in the draft. Barbee spent his career actively contributing to the myth of the Lost Cause, which depicted the South as fighting not for slavery but for liberty and which offered, as the grounds for a national reunion, a vision of "the Brothers' War" between equally heroic and gallant white soldiers of North and South. Although Barbee professed himself to be in some ways an admirer of Lincoln, he complained in *An Excursion in Southern History* of "the attempt being made by Northern infidels and iconoclasts to destroy Washington in the affections of the American people and to elevate Lincoln to a place next to God."[15]

The deliberate emphasis in Barbee's draft on Washington rather than Lincoln—an emphasis largely retained by Roosevelt—is clearly part of Barbee's attempt to diminish Lincoln's reputation. Barbee writes that "The more I study the causes of the Civil War, the more I am led to believe that Mr. Lincoln was as much of a hot head as Yancey, as much of a fanatic as many of our Southern people said Jefferson Davis was."[16]

Barbee held the view shared by some other southern writers that abolitionist sentiment had been gaining ground as a native movement in the South itself until the beginnings of the northern abolition movement in 1830, at which point the South, partly as a reaction to northern hostility and interference, turned away from abolition and to the greater task of preserving its sectional freedoms, accusing the North of neglecting "the tenderer and gentler side of the relation between master and slave," in which the slave was Christianized and civilized.[17] Lincoln, according to Barbee, "was no demi-god, but a human being of very coarse fibre, with a great brain and with many ugly spots in his character. His ambition and his vanity were no less causes of the war than the militant hatred of the Northern parsons against the South."[18] Barbee called for a new generation of historians to write "a correct history of the South. . . . Such a history will teach you that the South was always for Union, and that the War of Secession was no Civil War but a War of Freedom, the South emptying her veins in a futile effort to protect liberty on this continent."[19]

It might seem that sectional passions would have cooled in the long years from the Civil War to the administration of Franklin Delano Roosevelt. But the passion of David Rankin Barbee to continue rewriting public memory had lost none of its force. Barbee was energetically committed to recasting the public memory of the Civil War era. He devoted one long article, for example, to defaming Lincoln's secretary of war, Edwin M. Stanton, en route to redeeming the reputation of Confederate president Jefferson Davis from the charge that Davis had ultimately been captured by a Union army detachment that found him fleeing in his wife's dress. As Barbee tells the story in *The Capture of Jefferson Davis,* the infamous Stanton, whose bust greeted any visitor to the War Office through seventy-five years of unhappy memory, had hidden in a safe next to the secretary's office—a secret of great historic importance, long concealed from the American people." When, according to Barbee's account, the safe was finally opened in 1945 under pressure from Barbee, it was found to contain evidence of Stanton's plot to defame Davis: "a waterproof coat and a shawl supposedly worn by Jefferson Davis at the time of his capture in Georgia in May, 1865." Barbee complained that Stanton's supposed plot—supported by generations of his successors—was meant to conceal the true nobility of Davis, who was, according to Barbee, a "very great man . . . the chiefest in a galaxy of great Americans." Barbee is particularly outraged that Davis's reputation suffers when "our Southern newspapers are joining in the foolish idolatry of Lincoln."[20] On the opening of the safe, Barbee comments: "It was not until we had a President who is the son of a Confederate soldier [Harry Truman] that the truth—the awful truth—of Mr. Davis' 'disguise' is revealed to the public. Even now the public is not permitted to see those garments."[21]

Barbee's draft of Roosevelt's 1934 Gettysburg Address contained no "foolish idolatry of Lincoln." Lincoln's name appears nowhere in it. Instead, the first draft celebrates Washington, emphasizing his Virginia origins and loyalties and quoting his letter to James Madison (another Virginian) claiming that "we are all children of the same country." The absence of Lincoln from the first draft is underscored by the presence, astonishing in the circumstances, of Lincoln's rival, Stephen A. Douglas.

> Historians seem to agree that the issues which caused our Brothers' War had their beginnings in 1850. In the decade which followed there was an intense development of our country along many lines, conspicuously in railroads. But it was a haphazard and local development. Only one statesman in that period had caught Washington's vision of the future of America—Stephen A. Douglas. For years he devoted his genius to constructive planning along the lines mapped out by our first President. A New England man, he had, in early manhood, settled in Illinois, among a population drawn from all the sections. By marriage with a daughter of North Carolina, he became the owner of plantations and slaves in that State and in Mississippi. This gave him a surer grasp of the problems of his day than any of his competitors had. In order to develop the Mississippi Valley, and tie in the Northwest with the deep South, he projected a railroad from Chicago to New Orleans and another from Cairo to Mobile. Had these been built; had other North and South lines been built in the older States, connecting New York with Savannah, Philadelphia with Memphis, and Washington with New Orleans, could there have been a war between the North and the South?

Hence, by implication, it was Douglas, not Lincoln, who could have kept the country on the course of peaceful national development set out by Washington. Lincoln, too contemptible to merit even a mention in this draft for a presidential speech at Gettysburg, and on the very site of the first Gettysburg Address, becomes a sectional fanatic, in contrast to Washington, the Virginian; Douglas, the popular sovereignty Democrat; and Lucius Q. C. Lamar, who is quoted in the speech as "an inspired Prophet of the South who said, 'my brethren, if we know one another, we will love one another.'" Lincoln's incapacity to avoid an unnecessary war is attributed in part to Lincoln's failure to own slaves, hence conceding to Douglas "a surer grasp of the problems of his day."

Barbee's rhetoric may be understood as a tributary of the larger torrent of reunionist sentiment that had begun with the end of Reconstruction and that in the 1930s—and to some extent today—was and is still the reigning public memory of the Civil War. David W. Blight describes how, as early as the 1880s, North and South found grounds for an end to Reconstruction and a rebirth of national sentiment in the myth of the South's Lost Cause. "The war became essentially a conflict between white men; both sides fought well, Americans against Americans, and there was glory enough to go around." Blight describes an "inner" Lost Cause myth promoted by belligerent diehards (including Stephen Early's grandfather, Lt. Gen. Jubal Early) and a "national" Lost Cause movement that appealed to the North with sentimental tales such as those of John Esten Cooke, who "found a vast and vulnerable audience for his stories of the genteel and romantic heritage of old Virginia." Blight describes the "inner" Lost Cause as having an "influence" that "persisted until World War I," but it seems clear that Barbee and Early were peddling this more belligerent strain of the Lost Cause myth in the draft they sent to Roosevelt for delivery at Gettysburg.[22]

The Civil War as a war of gallant white brothers is a part of public memory so widespread as to seem universal, but it is important to notice the rhetorical contingency of such reunionist sentiment as the product of political coalitions and the product, as well, of energetic mythmaking over many decades. To be sure, there was some resistance to the reunion, especially from those who pointed out how reunionism swept aside the memory of the Civil War as an ideological conflict precipitated by slavery and who pointed to reunionism itself as an act of forgetting that stood in the way of racial justice. Frederick Douglass was one of the first and most eloquent resisters of reunionism. W. E. B. DuBois, in his turn, wrote that "of all historic facts there can be none clearer than that for four long and fearful years the South fought to perpetuate human slavery," even as he laments the imperfect politics of the North. Both Douglass and DuBois warned that forgetting slavery as a cause of the Civil War was a way of forgetting civil rights as well.[23]

Visitors to Gettysburg in the 1930s and in the 1990s saw a commemorative landscape on which is inscribed in myth and monument the history of a gallant battle between brothers. Although there is a statue of Lincoln near the site of the original Gettysburg Address, the battlefield, maintained as a historic site by the National Park Service, seems to have no memory of the causes of the Civil War. This amnesia is a rhetorical construction of considerable complexity that draws in and inspires thousands of tourists every year. In her study of Gettysburg in public memory, Amy Kinsel writes that in remembering the battle and the war, "the nation avoided dealing with the race issue, preferring to concentrate on the battlefield heroism and the growing myth of the South's Lost Cause. . . . Celebrations of American heroism that accepted southern valor as indistinguishable from northern sacrifice served to exclude from the war's historical legacy the idea that black freedom and equality might be as worthy of commemoration as was the valor of the white soldiers." Kinsel continues, "Battlefield memorialization at Gettysburg confirmed Americans' collective cultural amnesia regarding slavery. . . . The war to preserve the Union seemed in battlefield commemorations to have little if any connection with the fight to limit or abolish slavery."[24]

The evidence suggesting that Barbee wrote or collaborated with Early in writing the first draft of FDR's 1934 Gettysburg Address is strong. But what does this suggest for rhetorical interpretation? There is a sense in which it may be fair to read FDR's speech backward to its sources in Barbee's sectionalism, his Lost Cause reunionism, and his Democratic partisanship. Traces of these elements survive in FDR's speech, and, equally important, a detailed reconstruction of the authorship of the speech helps us to understand the complex ways in which the presidential creation of public memory is itself constructed and negotiated. Hence, it is important for rhetorical scholars to retrace the authorship and the ideological ancestry of speech texts. If presidential speech shapes our public memory, it is surely useful to understand the practices that in their own turn shape presidential speeches.

Roosevelt's 1934 speech was importantly "motivated," in the sense in which that term is employed by Kenneth Burke, by David Rankin Barbee's first draft, which in its own turn had a complex of "motivations."[25] But the speech, even in its first draft, is motivated, too, by the writer's appeal to what he took to be the larger motives of FDR and the New Deal. When FDR undertook his own revision of the speech, his strategic motives, historical and local, ideological and political, conscious or unconscious, shaped the resulting drafts.

How, then, are we to account for the absence of Lincoln and of the race question from Roosevelt's speech? Partly, such an omission was an example of Roosevelt's complacency about issues of civil rights—a complacency that is likely to strike our own generation as evidence of insensitivity or outright racism on FDR's part. Kenneth O'Reilly describes Roosevelt as personally "lacking . . . an appreciation of or sympathy for problems of race and racism in America."[26] Whatever his personal habits of mind, in the first years of the New Deal, Roosevelt seems clearly to have subordinated civil liberties and civil rights to larger issues of national and economic recovery, which he took to have more immediate urgency and which he saw as the basis for lasting change. In his account of civil rights in the New Deal era, John Egerton writes:

> The great contribution of the New Deal to the cultural and political life of the South was that it turned a mock debate into a real one and offered a genuine alternative to the Old South/New South philosophy. The liberal agenda of Franklin Roosevelt and his administration called for a massive economic reformation to bring higher living standards to all: far-reaching new programs in support of labor, education, health, housing, and the general welfare; major reforms in agriculture and industry; and an opening of the democratic political process to virtually all adults. . . . Eventually, inevitably, such transforming changes would challenge the continued existence of white supremacy and extreme socioeconomic class stratification.[27]

Within the Roosevelt administration, according to Patricia Sullivan, black leaders such as Robert C. Weaver and John Preston Davis "determined to obtain a hearing for black workers. . . . The New Deal provided a new opportunity to get federal action that could counter the . . . system that had brutally proscribed the opportunities of black Americans."[28] Black American voters, who had many legitimate reasons to be disappointed with administration rhetoric and with such legislative failures as the refusal of FDR to support antilynching legislation, nevertheless left the Republican party and turned decisively to the Democrats. In *Farewell to the Party of Lincoln: Black Politics in the Age of FDR*, Nancy Weiss argues: "Despite the fact that Roosevelt had done very little for blacks as a racial minority, he had managed to convey to them that they counted and belonged. . . . The simple fact that blacks were not excluded from the New Deal was a sufficient departure from past practice to make Roosevelt look like a benefactor of the race."[29] Celeste Condit and John Lucaites contend: "Franklin Delano Roosevelt and Harry S. Truman . . . created the conditions that would invite substantial egalitarian rhetoric. Dramatically reversing the presumption of federal inaction across the board, Roosevelt opened up the possibilities for presidential and congressional action to stamp out state-enforced inequality, even though his own achievements in racial equality were modest."[30] On the other hand, John B. Kirby has argued that even the white "race liberals" of the New Deal supported economic development rather than appeals for changed attitudes, resulting in a "certain dependence" on the part of blacks and, for whites, "an intense loyalty to reform liberalism that encouraged them to work for improvements in black life but not to attack the racial as well as the political patterns of American society which frequently compromised their interracial hopes and their reform goals.[31]

David Rankin Barbee's old-style, unreconstructed, Lost Cause sectionalism, and his conditional reunionism partly account for the words spoken by Franklin Delano Roosevelt at Gettysburg on May 30, 1934. But FDR's speech is not reducible to Barbee's first draft. Roosevelt's listeners did not hear or read Barbee's draft. To understand what FDR's speech might have meant for his audience, and what it might mean for us to recover the speech as part of our own memory of Roosevelt and of Gettysburg, we must take a fresh look at the delivery text and the later published text as they diverged from Barbee's text and as they might have appeared to hearers and readers. But our own reading of FDR's text, even when it attempts to reread the speech from the perspective of author and hearers, cannot exhaust the meaning of the speech heard on May 30, 1934, nor is it in turn reducible to that speech.

Serious attention to the origins and dissemination of Roosevelt's 1934 speech throws into question the very notion that we can, with confidence, identify a single text as *the* text of the speech. Roosevelt's speech *is* partly the Barbee first draft, but it is not reducible to that draft. The speech exists in contrasting but equally authoritative versions as heard and seen by its immediate audience, as heard by a national radio audience, as reprinted in newspapers, as edited for inclusion in Roosevelt's official public papers, as having been forgotten by history, and, perhaps, as having been resurrected here as a many-layered text.

The text also, necessarily, exists for us with its intertextual resonance and whatever contextual knowledge we bring to it as audience or as reconstructive historians. Hence, for example, even if, having examined the history of the Barbee draft, we then turn to the delivery text, the Barbee text becomes part of our own memory of the speech, just as Lincoln before it and the civil rights movement after it are part of our own memory of Roosevelt's heretofore forgotten speech. Nevertheless, in an act of imagination aided with some historical detective work, we can come to understand something more about American rhetoric in the 1930s by imagining ourselves back in the time of the speech and seeing the world through that speech.

From Barbee's partisan sectionalism, Roosevelt wove an aesthetic and ideological vision of unity. Roosevelt's rhetorical mastery, while it slips at times, is still impressive. He begins the speech by putting aside any echoes of northern triumphalism or of mourning, calling the day "glorious" and twice using the word *rejoice* in his opening paragraph.

The emotional lift established by these two words becomes a metaphorically spatial lift in the second paragraph, when the view rises from the "hills of Gettysburg" to a perspective that takes in Valley Forge and Philadelphia. From the spatial height thus metaphorically gained, Roosevelt asserts a spiritual height, closing the second paragraph with the assertion that "all this is holy ground."

The spatial height that permits our taking in of Gettysburg, Valley Forge, and Philadelphia is also a temporal, historical height, since as the view broadens in space it also lengthens in time, going from 1934 briefly back to the 1860s and quickly beyond to take in the decades of the Revolution, the Declaration of Independence, and the Constitution. Hence, from its very first words, what is later to be announced as the thesis of the speech is already enacted in style, metaphor, and perspective, in the act of rising to a "glorious" height from which we can take in American time and American space, space and time that embrace the civil religion of a "consecrated" valley, an "invincible" city—holy ground."

In a series of phrases, Roosevelt again links his own audience not only to the Civil War but also to the founding fathers. Washington's "solemn, tender, wise words of farewell" were addressed "not alone to his generation, but to the generation of those who laid down their lives here and to our generation and to the America of tomorrow." Those who came before are "our fathers and grandfathers"—two generations.

Roosevelt depicts multiple generations and, in effect, multiple historical epochs as united in time. The unity of time is reinforced by a potential unity of space—both in Roosevelt's sweeping encompassment of the geography of the country and in his appeal to an end to sectionalism. Washington, Roosevelt says in paragraph 4, described himself as both a Virginian and an American. In paragraph 4, Washington is shown speaking as a national and not a sectional patriot. In paragraph 5, Washington is shown moving, making "three historic tours" as president, knitting together the pieces into a Nation. In paragraph 6, Washington is depicted as an agent of national economic development, a precursor of the New Deal.

Roosevelt often spoke of his own wish to achieve Jeffersonian ends by Hamiltonian means. Roosevelt's Washington here becomes a spokesman and an example of the ways in which patriotism, stimulated by material development, leads to improvement of the lot of the individual. Roosevelt's method is, so far, almost entirely narrative and descriptive. Whatever there is of argument seems to flow naturally as interpretation of the narrative rather than as assertion and proof. Rhetorically, the narrative leads the interpretation, rather than subordinating the narrative as proof to a structure of assertions.

In paragraph 7, the fall from grace begins, with a narrative of the causes of sectional conflict that led to the Civil War. As in a sermon, the fall from grace is shown to have been stimulated in a way by success—the nation's rapid geographic expansion. But the success is undermined by a failure not, at least at first, of spirit, but by a failure of materialism. Roosevelt's history lesson is that the failure to plan for a national system of railroads—and attendant lines of communication—led to the growth of a sectionalism that was the cause of the Civil War.

The tale of the fall from grace is deceptively simple; in fact, Roosevelt is negotiating tricky rhetorical territory. In the speech's most direct reference to sectional prejudice so far, Roosevelt ascribes the prejudice to "some of us Northerners" who believe that "the South and the West were . . . laggard in developing" railroads. In a speech that has already implicitly associated patriotism with civil religion, Roosevelt's confession/accusation in ascribing sectional prejudice to his own section is both a gesture of humility and a politically calculated message to senators and representatives from the solid South upon whose votes the New Deal absolutely depended.

In alleging that the causes of the Civil War were sectional misunderstanding brought about by inadequate regional material development, Roosevelt leaves himself open to the warnings of Frederick Douglass and W. E. B. DuBois about the dangers of forgetting slavery as a cause of the war. At the same time, the appeal to national patriotism, an end to sectional prejudice, and massive federal involvement in economic development may be seen as setting in motion the conditions that made the civil rights movement—the next phase of emancipation—possible. Hence, Roosevelt is offering to the South a new bargain in which the North agrees to forget slavery as a cause of the Civil War if the South will agree that the misunderstanding was caused by the absence of precisely what the New Deal proposed to provide: a vastly increased role for the federal government in national life. Roosevelt's bargain is very different from the policy of sectional autonomy that ended Reconstruction in 1877.

Roosevelt ends this section of the speech in paragraph 10 by quoting, without attribution, Lucius Q. C. Lamar, identified only as "an inspired prophet of the South who said: 'My brethren, if we know one another, we will love one another." Southerners might have identified Lamar's words as quoted from his eulogy of Charles Sumner.[32]

This passage of the speech repeats a figure of effacement that has occurred at least twice before in it. Roosevelt builds an extended narrative of the material causes of the Civil War, but just as he gets to the point of narrating—or even naming—the conflict, he jumps entirely past it, skipping the war itself and more than fifty years of intervening events. After summing up his narrative of the railroads with an indirect allusion to the war ("The tragedy of the Nation was that the people did not know one another because they had not the necessary means of visiting one another"), Roosevelt skips to the twentieth century: "Since those days, two subsequent wars, both with foreign Nations, have measurably allayed and softened the ancient passions. It has been left to us of this generation to see the healing made permanent" (paragraph 11).

The passions of those days may have been allayed and softened, but they are still, evidently, so powerful that they can be mentioned only indirectly, as Gettysburg itself is mentioned only very gingerly in the speech. We have seen how, in paragraph 2, Roosevelt retreats from Gettysburg, returning to it again only briefly at the end of paragraph 3. There runs throughout the speech a peculiar sense that Gettysburg is everywhere in it—but as a presence so horrible, so potentially divisive, that it must be treated with caution. This quality of the almost unmentionable danger of Gettysburg serves as an implicit rationale for what might otherwise seem to be the crude opportunism of Roosevelt's turning of the Civil War into a text for the defense of the New Deal. The near absence of the Civil War serves, under the circumstances, to intensify it as a rhetorical presence in the speech. To acknowledge this effect is not necessarily to endorse, from our own greater distance of years from the Civil War, and from the Roosevelt era, the absence of the Civil War, Lincoln, and slavery from the speech. In fact, I believe it is our job at least partly to recover Lincoln and slavery in our own reading of the speech, but to do so in a way that accepts the cultural memories of the Roosevelt era as their reality. Merely to reject the Roosevelt era's memories and appeals as incorrect by our own standards could too easily become a way for us to avoid interrogating our own responsibility to remake our own collectively shared memories—which are sure in their turn to seem at least partly blind to our own sons and daughters.

Roosevelt depicts the period after the Civil War with contrasting sections on responses to the New Deal. On one hand, the common people accept one another as brothers. On the other hand, "three elements" resist the New Deal with precisely the sort of thinking that, by implication, led to the Civil War: "These groups are those who seek to stir up political animosity or build political advantage by the distortion of facts; those who, by declining to follow the rules of the game, seek to gain an unfair advantage over those who are willing to live up to the rules of the game; and those few who, because they have never been willing to take an interest in their fellow Americans, dwell inside of their own narrow spheres and still represent the selfishness of sectionalism which has no place in our national life" (paragraph 14).

Roosevelt's passage on the enemies of the New Deal is remarkably combative in tone, especially for a commemorative speech. Sadly, it may be the extreme statement in the speech of a quality that is latent throughout—the sense that patriotism and national unity require a unanimity of opinion that discredits public deliberation. Whatever the merits of Roosevelt's characterization of his opponents, they are associated with "the passions of war," whereas his own and the only feasible alternative is presented as working with great former presidents for "a consolidated Nation" and "a united people."

Roosevelt's association of his opponents with the "passions of war" is a variation on a strain in early New Deal rhetoric that appealed for unity on the grounds of a national economic emergency that was compared in severity and structure to a state of war.[33]

Franklin Delano Roosevelt's 1934 Gettysburg Address is a minor ceremonial address that, when read in context, vividly recalls the conflicted spirit of its day. At the same time, the speech bristles with paradoxes characteristic of the texts of public memory. Roosevelt's text is itself a document under revision both before and after its delivery—even as a literal text, it survives as a multiple text. As a rhetorical text, Roosevelt's speech is even more complex, paradoxical, and many-layered. Roosevelt evoked the awesome power of Gettysburg by rendering it nearly absent from his speech. He advanced the cause of civil rights by mentioning Lincoln only once and slavery not at all in the course of the speech. He adopted a draft text that was full of southern sectionalism and in his revisions as well as in his embodiment of the speech, turned it into a strong appeal for an end to sectionalism. He advocated a spiritual renewal brought about by material means. Though evoking presidents of many parties and policies, Roosevelt called for a public unity and brotherhood that would strengthen his partisan advantage and disparage those who resisted. Instead of praising Lincoln, Roosevelt in effect took his place beside Lincoln, remembered the past by appealing to his fellow citizens to forget old quarrels, and celebrated Memorial Day by looking to the future.

The paradoxes of Roosevelt's speech may be useful for us to recover and reflect upon, but it is useful to remember, too, that the speech did not appear paradoxical to those who heard and read it in 1934.

All but one of the several letters sent by citizens to the White House in the days immediately following the speech were positive. They came from all regions of the country; those from the South often sounded a note of deep appreciation for Roosevelt's conciliatory language. Positive or negative, the letters seemed to agree that the United States was in a time of special peril and that Roosevelt was acting decisively, for good or ill.

Samuel Sinaink of Philadelphia wrote to the president that he had "sounded a new hope and era of emancipation" that was threatened by "the forces of reaction" which "are bitter over the loss of power; they are desperately fighting your regime with a false hope to return to the old days of reaction and special privilege."[34]

Donald J. Eaton, depicting himself as a champion of free enterprise, and who attributed to himself the power to bring about the downfall of the administration by a campaign in the press and radio, sent the only negative letter, expressing his "contempt at hearing the most nauseating repulsive speech it has ever been my misfortune to hear. . . . You are a disgrace to the name of Roosevelt."[35]

Dan Stephens sent a radiogram from Nebraska that underscored the hope and turmoil widely felt and characteristically evoked in the rhetoric of the New Deal era:

> your gettysburg address stirred the country profoundly millions of our people hear [*sic*] under brazen skies and withering heat are suffering from dust storms and droung that is unparalleled they feel that they have a sympathetict government at washington and are deeply grateful for your inspiring leadership and support they are also stirred by inspiring defense of the recovery act by your lieutenant hugh johnson who so ably castigated the enemies of these reform measures in his speech yesterday.[36]

B. J. Campbell of Memphis telegraphed that Roosevelt's speech had "touched the heart of the whole American people. It was brim full of patriotism, kindness, affection, good will to the nation regardless of section."[37]

Several writers compared Roosevelt's speech favorably with Lincoln's. V. Y. Dallman of the *Illinois (Springfield) State Register* called the speech "Lincoln-like." Walter L. Kirschenbaum of New York "considered your Gettysburg Address next to the one given by Abraham Lincoln."[38]

Roosevelt's speech was widely reprinted in newspapers throughout the country, together with descriptions of his fifty thousand to one hundred thousand listeners at the Gettysburg cemetery and the cheering throngs along the route leading to it.[39] Virtually every newspaper report emphasized first Roosevelt's call for national unity, closely followed by an account of his condemnation of—in the condensation offered in a *New York Times* headline—"Breeders of Political Animosity, Chiselers and Exponents of Sectionalism."[40] The *Atlanta Constitution,* one of many papers that reprinted the speech in full, reported it in sympathetic detail with a lead paragraph sounding the myth of Gettysburg as the high tide of the Confederacy: "Close by the ridge where Lee flung the flower of the south into one desperate charge against northern steel, President Roosevelt today called upon the nation to heal the scars of sectional strife."[41]

The African-American press showed no interest in the speech at Gettysburg, but it was clearly paying close attention to the administration's attitude toward the race question. In its June 2, 1934, edition, the *Pittsburgh Courier* reported that on May 30, Senators Wagner and Costigan, sponsors of an antilynching bill then stalled in the Senate, met with Roosevelt at the White House, "but no word on the anti-lynching measure was given out although it is known they discussed it thoroughly with the chief executive. They were accompanied to the White House by Walter White, N.A.A.C.P. secretary, but Mr. White did not share in their conference with the President."[42]

Franklin Delano Roosevelt's Gettysburg Address of May 30, 1934, delivered during the rising tide of the first New Deal, appears to have been a highly successful stroke in the formulation of Roosevelt's Progressive coalition. Four years later, Roosevelt delivered a second Gettysburg Address, after his landslide 1936 reelection, but at a time when the New Deal coalition had begun to unravel and when the high tide of the New Deal itself had come and gone, although the outcome was not yet clear to political partisans on either side. In July, 1938, on the seventy-fifth anniversary of the battle at Gettysburg, Roosevelt returned to dedicate the Peace Memorial on the battlefield at the last great reunion of Civil War veterans.

The original commemorative site at Gettysburg was in the form of the Soldiers' National Cemetery, created to bury the Union dead, state by state, and to remember "not only sacrifice, but victory."[43] Throughout the rest of the nineteenth century, Gettysburg was preserved as essentially a Union memorial. In addition to the cemetery itself, the battlefield as a whole was preserved in work that began soon after the battle and which was conducted by the Gettysburg Battlefield Memorial Association from 1863 to 1895. Monuments to Union veterans and units were placed about the field of battle. The Soldier's National Cemetery had been sponsored by the Northern states; the Gettysburg Battlefield Memorial Association was a private group, dedicated to preservation and memorialization of the battlefield.[44]

In 1895, the War Department assumed control over the Gettysburg site, managing it until 1933 as the Gettysburg National Military Park. Under War Department management, the park began to include Confederate monuments. "By the time of the grand fiftieth anniversary reunion of the Blue and the Gray in 1913, Gettysburg National Military Park exemplified the theme of reunionism in the United States."[45]

The Virginia monument, with its equestrian statue of Robert E. Lee, appeared in 1917, and other southern monuments were gradually added. After Roosevelt took office in 1933, the Gettysburg site came under the administration of the National Park Service.[46]

The Peace Memorial that Roosevelt dedicated in 1938 at the seventy-fifth reunion had been planned since before the fiftieth reunion in 1913.[47]

"AVOIDING WAR, WE SEEK OUR ENDS THROUGH THE PEACEFUL PROCESSES OF POPULAR GOVERNMENT UNDER THE CONSTITUTION," ADDRESS AT GETTYSBURG, JULY 3, 1938

Governor Earle, Veterans of the Blue and the Gray:

1. On behalf of the people of the United States I accept this monument in the spirit of brotherhood and peace.

2. Immortal deeds and immortal words have created here at Gettysburg a shrine of American patriotism. We are encompassed by "The last full measure of devotion" of many men and by the words in which Abraham Lincoln expressed the simple faith for which they died.

3. It seldom helps to wonder how a statesman of one generation would surmount the crisis of another. A statesman deals with concrete difficulties—with things which must be done from day to day. Not often can he frame conscious patterns for the far off future.

4. But the fullness of the stature of Lincoln's nature and the fundamental conflict which events forced upon his Presidency invite us ever to turn to him for help.

5. For the issue which he restated here at Gettysburg seventy-five years ago will be the continuing issue before this Nation so far as we cling to the purposes for which the Nation was founded—to preserve under the changing conditions of each generation a people's government for the people's good.

6. The task assumes different shapes at different times. Sometimes the threat to popular government comes from political interests, sometimes from economic interests, sometimes we have to beat off all of them together.

7. But the challenge is always the same—whether each generation facing its own circumstances can summon the practical devotion to attain and retain that greatest good for the greatest number which this government of the people was created to ensure.

8. Lincoln spoke in solace for all who fought upon this field; and the years have laid their balm upon their wounds. Men who wore the blue and men who wore the gray are here together, a fragment spared by time. They are brought here by the memories of old divided loyalties, but they meet here in united loyalty to a united cause which the unfolding years have made it easier to see.

9. All of them we honor, not asking under which flag they fought then— thankful that they stand together under one flag now.

10. Lincoln was commander-in-chief in this old battle; he wanted above all things to be commander-in-chief of the new peace. He understood that battle there must be; that when a challenge to constituted government is thrown down, the people must in self-defense take it up; that the fight must be fought through to a decision so clear that it is accepted as being beyond recall.

11. But Lincoln also understood that after such a decision, a democracy should seek peace through a new unity. For a democracy can keep alive only if the settlement of old difficulties clears the ground and transfers energies to face new responsibilities. Never can it have as much ability and purpose as it needs in that striving; the end of battle does not end the infinity of those needs.

12. That is why Lincoln—commander of a people as well as of an army— asked that his battle end "with malice toward none, with charity for all."

13. To the hurt of those who came after him, Lincoln's plea was long denied. A generation passed before the new unity became an accepted fact.

14. In later years new needs arose, and with them new tasks, worldwide in their perplexities, their bitterness and their modes of strife. Here in our land we give thanks that, avoiding war, we seek our ends through the peaceful processes of popular government under the Constitution.

15. It is another conflict, a conflict as fundamental as Lincoln's, fought not with glint of steel, but with appeals to reason and justice on a thousand fronts—seeking to save for our common country opportunity and security for citizens in a free society.

16. We are near to winning this battle. In its winning and through the years may we live by the wisdom and the humanity of the heart of Abraham Lincoln.[48]

How are we to read this speech, to imagine it in its own time and place, and to catch its echo through the years? The 1938 speech shares much with the 1934 address. In doctrine and theme, the two are similar, and yet the 1938 speech appears to have a sadder and more serene music.

Though the speech is clearly meant to be heard by all Americans, it is addressed specifically to the aged Civil War veterans encamped in the summer heat for the seventy-fifth anniversary of the great battle fought at Gettysburg. Roosevelt employs this mode of address to formalize and solemnize his opening words, adopting a tone that runs throughout the speech.

The tone of Roosevelt's address is both simple and formal. In a few places, the style may strike our own ears as falsely elevated, even trite: "immortal deeds and immortal words" (paragraph 2); "glint of steel" (paragraph 15). Yet even these phrases stick close to Roosevelt's theme, and by every account that we have of Roosevelt's skills in delivery, FDR could sing even a commonplace script into grandeur. The "glint of steel" phrase first appears in the third draft of the speech, in a handwritten paragraph written as an insert by Roosevelt. In delivery, Roosevelt actually dropped "glint of," although Samuel Rosenman overlooked the stenographer's correction and carried the phrase into the Roosevelt papers.[49]

The themes of the 1934 Gettysburg Address are in many ways repeated in 1938. Roosevelt appeals to patriotism and national unity, urges that particular desires be subordinated to the general good, and describes the current situation as the equivalent to war.

In contrast to the 1934 speech, the 1938 speech is centered on Abraham Lincoln. Lincoln becomes the unifying presence that unites the energetic texture of the address. And yet, though the speech everywhere uses Lincoln as a touchstone and mythic hero, Roosevelt does not merely fall into hero worship. After his reverent invocation of Lincoln in paragraph 2, FDR reflects in paragraph 3 that "it seldom helps to wonder how a statesman of one generation would surmount the crisis of another." Here Roosevelt introduces a theme common to his rhetoric throughout the New Deal era: We are to be guided by a fundamental faith, and yet we must respond experimentally and flexibly, dealing "with concrete difficulties—with things which must be done from day to day. Not often can [the President] frame conscious patterns for the far off future" (paragraph 3). And yet it is about the future, more than about the past, that Roosevelt speaks. The frequent references to the past of Lincoln are all employed to draw from Lincoln the inspiration to face the challenges of the 1930s.

In the opening paragraphs of the speech, Roosevelt alternates between sharing Lincoln's faith and reminding his audience of the need for change and adaptation. This alternating pattern not only states but also repeatedly rehearses his hearers in the act of comparison, in effect stimulating and enacting in form the theme he is urging as doctrine.

Alfred Haworth Jones has described the ways in which Roosevelt benefited, especially in his second-term appeals for his foreign policy in the period immediately preceding World War II, from an explicit identification of himself with Lincoln. Much of the stimulus for the Lincoln-Roosevelt connection came from three popular writers of the period whose works mythologized Lincoln and who were also liberals and supporters of Roosevelt: Carl Sandburg, Stephen Vincent Benét, and Robert E. Sherwood.[50] Sherwood, author of *Abe Lincoln in Illinois*—first a stage play and then a popular Hollywood film—later became a Roosevelt speechwriter.[51]

In looking to the future, Roosevelt casts himself in the role of Lincoln. In comparing Lincoln's Gettysburg Address with the Gettysburg speech of Edward Everett and with Pericles's funeral oration, Garry Wills argues: "Lincoln was an artist, not just a scholar. Classicism of Everett's sort looks backward; but the classic *artifact* sets standards for the future. . . . It was the challenge of the *moment* that both Pericles and Lincoln addressed."[52] Roosevelt's rhetorical art, his mode of looking forward, of recreating the past for the use of the future, might well be compared with that of Lincoln and Pericles.

By the standards Roosevelt teaches us to apply to this speech, and by the standards of the modernist rhetoric of effect and efficiency characteristic of the period, every element in the speech is designed to constrain the audience's judgment. Such an effect is, in a sort of circularity that is not necessarily illogical, itself a sort of proof, in the sense that Roosevelt's claim to leadership and authority is based partly on his being able to give rhetorical evidence of his ability to command the situation and to control the forces of change. In the same way, though the speech alternates between reverence for the past and evocation of needs of the moment, the two are united by their appeal for a mode of unified assent—on one hand to the authority of a Lincolnesque civil religion, and on the other to the exigencies of an economic crisis—the moral equivalent of war—requiring us as listeners to unite in obedience to the tactical experiments of the president.[53] As a rhetorical accomplishment, Roosevelt's uniting of appeals to permanence and change, sentiment and economic efficiency, ancestor worship and tactical experiment, is masterful, and masterfully adapted to the thought of his time. This was a period in which academic rhetoricians were rereading classical rhetoric and eighteenth-century British parliamentary debate through the lens of a modernism that was summed up in Herbert Wichelns's enduring claim, published in 1925, that rhetoric "is not concerned with permanence, nor yet with beauty. It is concerned with effect."[54]

Roosevelt explicitly compares himself with Lincoln: "It seldom helps to wonder how a statesman of one generation would surmount the crisis of another. A statesman deals with concrete difficulties" (paragraph 3). He also presents himself both as an interpreter of Lincoln and as a successor to Lincoln. Such a comparison surely presents for Roosevelt, as president, problems of decorum that would not apply to other speakers on the occasion. Roosevelt handles the problem of decorum by the appeal to practical necessity and by an utter avoidance of either false humility or self-promotion. He is in addition supported by the funerary tradition that requires both reverence for the dead and a ritualized burying of the past, a turning to the future. The living must leave the burial place, our rituals seem to tell us, and get on with their lives.[55]

As an interpreter, Roosevelt depicts Lincoln—and himself—in terms of an ideology that is strikingly explicit in its utilitarianism: "But the challenge is always the same—whether each generation facing its own circumstances can summon the practical devotion to attain and retain that greatest good for the greatest number which this government of the people was created to ensure" (paragraph 7).

The utilitarian philosophy of the greatest good for the greatest number was surely consistent with the rhetoric of the New Deal, which asked various constituencies to postpone their own claims in favor of the greater good. Was it—and was it understood to be— Lincoln's philosophy?

Roosevelt's Lincoln seems partly at odds with the Lincoln of Garry Wills, a Lincoln who is depicted, at Gettysburg, as the champion of equality, rereading the Constitution, in his own speech at Gettysburg, in terms of the Declaration's claim that "all men are created equal." According to Wills, Lincoln won at Gettysburg the battle over the ideological significance of the Civil War, purifying the air and rewriting the Constitution "by appeal from its letter to the spirit. . . . By implicitly doing this, he performed one of the most daring acts of open-air sleight-of-hand ever witnessed by the unsuspecting. Everyone in that vast throng of thousands was having his or her intellectual pocket picked. The crowd departed with a new thing in its ideological luggage, that new constitution Lincoln had substituted for the one they brought there with them. They walked off, from those curving graves on the hillside, under a changed sky, into a different America."[56]

Must we understand Roosevelt as falling short of Lincoln's ideal of equality, or even as interpreting the Constitution in a less progressive way? Possibly. Once again Roosevelt had come to Gettysburg, and once again he was silent about the fate of African Americans seventy-five years after their emancipation. But Wills reminds us that Lincoln, too, was silent about slavery in the Gettysburg Address. "Slavery is not mentioned, any more than Gettysburg is."[57] Instead of mentioning slavery, or Gettysburg, or emancipation, or the Union, says Wills, "the 'great task' mentioned in the Address is not emancipation but the preservation of self-government."[58] If Wills is right in this assessment, then we may reasonably argue that Roosevelt forcibly echoes Lincoln both in doctrine and in strategy. Perhaps Roosevelt discerned in Lincoln what Edwin Black observed when writing on the Gettysburg Address: "As an actor in history and a force in the world, Lincoln does not hesitate to comprehend history and the world. But he never presumes to cast his mind beyond human dimensions. He does not recite divine intentions; he does not issue cosmic judgments. He knows, to the bottom, what he knows. Of the rest, he is silent."[59]

Roosevelt calls for a democratic procedure—"the peaceful processes of popular government under the Constitution" (paragraph 14)—to achieve a fundamental social goal—"seeking to save for our common country opportunity and security for citizens in a free society" (paragraph 15). The appeal to democracy is the fundamental for both Lincoln and Roosevelt. Roosevelt's appeal to economic security becomes an implicit extension of Lincoln's appropriation of Jefferson's "all men are created equal." Lincoln was silent about a system of slavery that his words and actions were designed to abolish. Roosevelt was silent about a continued denial of basic rights that his economic reforms were in part designed to abolish.

Roosevelt's two Gettysburg addresses show a remarkable similarity to the Lincoln depicted by J. David Greenstone in his *The Lincoln*

Persuasions. Lincoln, argued Greenstone, achieved his historical success as a coalition builder who united two diverging strains of American liberalism—the reform liberals who respond to the consummatory and perfectionist strain and the humanist liberals who appeal to instrumental rationality. Greenstone sees Lincoln as a master rhetorician, whose "practical humanitarianism achieved coherence and intelligibility—and attracted great popular support—because it drew broadly on beliefs and practices deeply rooted in American culture. That is, whereas the personal humanitarianism of the abolitionists was an expression primarily of the tradition of Protestant separatism and piety, Lincoln's ethic asserted a union of piety with prudential rationality and of sainthood with citizenship."[60]

Roosevelt's silence about civil rights at Gettysburg was deliberate—a self-conscious appeal to instrumental rationality in the name of a progressive spirit. No clearer evidence can be given of Roosevelt's self-consciousness about the limits of coalition than by examining an anonymous draft submitted for the 1938 Gettysburg speech. Among the various drafts of that speech is an eight-page version filed as an "unused draft."[61] Some phrases and something of the general structure of the unused draft survive in the speech Roosevelt delivered, although FDR radically abbreviated and altered the speech to make of it an entirely new creation and worked through several drafts to refine and polish what became the final speech. But it is clear that he read and used the unused draft, even where he rejected it. Furthermore, the draft was itself so artful and eloquent that Roosevelt clearly rejected it not only because he favored brevity but also because he thought the time had not yet come for plain speaking about civil rights. The anonymous speechwriter proposed a much more discursive and explicit treatment of America's past and present than Roosevelt adopted. The draft acknowledged the South's complaint about Reconstruction:

> But the weight of military victory, uniting the states, was overbalanced by the weight of human shortcomings, driving them once more apart.
>
> So we had the tragedy of Reconstruction. With Lincoln dead at the hand of a half-mad assassin, President Andrew Johnson was overwhelmed by those sinister forces of fanatical reaction that seem to gain power at the end of every war, and the South went through the terrors of economic ruin, social chaos and political exploitation.

Against its extended concession to Southern feelings, the draft balanced a remarkable appeal for racial reconciliation.

> Speaking to the people of the South, I say but this: You need not have, nor should you tolerate, a lower level of living than the rest of the country. But to escape from such a level, more is needed than to build up the income of the factory workers in your new industrial empire. It is impossible, in any commonwealth of men, to have one large group prosperous while pitted against a lower group. The welfare of the white race in the South, the well being of the millions who work in factories and upon southern farms, depends in the last analysis upon the welfare of the Negro race. You may not have, perhaps you will not have for centuries, economic parity between the races, but they will rise together or go down together in any industrial economy based on political democracy and individual freedom.
>
> And just as there can be no sectional prosperity where men and women are stratified in varying levels of poverty, so there can be no national prosperity where one great section is below the national level. By common efforts, the section below that level can be lifted up, but in the unrelieved interplay of competitive forces it will drag the other down.

These astonishing paragraphs, which so many yearned to hear and which to so many seemed the logical next step for the administration, disappeared into silence. We may, in retrospect, admit that in composing his speech as he did, Roosevelt followed Lincoln's example, saying and doing what he could to move in the right direction. Nevertheless, it is proper that these unsaid words should be part of our own memory of Roosevelt's speech at Gettysburg. Roosevelt stirs, even when he disappoints, our hopes and expectations.

The hopes and expectations of the African-American press often turned to the administration, but as in 1934 Roosevelt's speech was not the story. On July 9, 1938, when it might have taken notice of the president's speech, the *Pittsburgh Courier* instead described Roosevelt's brief "message of greeting" to the twenty-ninth congress of the National Association for the Advancement of Colored People (NAACP), meeting in Columbus, Ohio. The *Courier* story reprints the president's brief letter, in which he wrote to the NAACP what he would not say to a national audience: "I have watched with interest the constructive efforts of your organization, not only on behalf of the Negro people in our nation, but also in behalf of the democratic ideals and principles so dear to the entire nation. For it is evident that no democracy can long survive which does not accept as fundamental to its very existence the recognition of the rights of its minorities."[62]

In its only story on the Gettysburg reunion, the *Courier* reported that the oldest Civil War veteran at the Gettysburg encampment was 112-year-old William A. Barnes, "a Negro Union soldier."[63] The *Philadelphia Afro-American* ran a front-page photograph of Roosevelt speaking with the oldest veteran, but Roosevelt's speech went unreported, despite otherwise full coverage, with several photographs of African-American veterans at the Gettysburg reunion. Peyton Gray reported that "All traces of discrimination, both as to racial identity and geographical location, were absent as approximately 58 colored and 1,950 white Civil War veterans gathered here last week to mark the seventy-fifth anniversary of the Battle of Gettysburg and the final reunion of the Blue and Gray."[64]

Roosevelt's 1938 speech was broadcast by radio and widely reprinted in Fourth of July editions of the mainstream press, which estimated the immediate audience at 150,000 to two hundred thousand people. The press stories focused on the tale of the last reunion and on Roosevelt's invocations of Lincoln.[65]

Franklin Delano Roosevelt's speeches at Gettysburg in 1934 and 1938, especially when read in the context of their times and with close attention to their processes of composition, reveal a president entirely in command of his own views, able to avoid David Rankin Barbee's insinuations of Lost Cause sectionalism and an anonymous author's temptation to speak out forcefully on civil rights. Roosevelt kept his own attention—and that of his audience—focused on the exigencies as he understood them, appealing for national unity and economic recovery in the name of a renewed memory of the American past.

In retrospect, Roosevelt's silence about civil rights makes us rightly impatient. An abiding theme of American civil rights rhetoric was captured in a short poem by Langston Hughes, who asked, "What happens to a dream deferred?" Years later, writing from Birmingham jail, Martin Luther King Jr., reminded his readers: "justice too long delayed is justice denied."[66] Roosevelt's silence on this subject at Gettysburg asks us to believe that the dream there deferred is not necessarily a dream denied. Roosevelt implicitly claimed that his silence was imposed by political circumstances and that the dream would be fulfilled by the material improvement of all regions, by the construction of a national economy, and by a patriotism shifted from state and region to the nation.

For us, as for Roosevelt, public memory must always make its own compromise with history—trying to be realistic about historical constraints, but without becoming accomplices in accommodating reaction. We are rightfully uneasy in the presence of these silences and these words from our past. In cultivating our own guilty conscience through a revision of public memory, we, too, may be tempted to use the past as an alibi for postponing the duties to which we are called.

NOTES

1. Robert Lowell would rank only Jefferson with Lincoln in eloquence. On the centennial of the Gettysburg Address, Lowell wrote, "Abraham Lincoln was the last President of the United States who could genuinely use words. He and Thomas Jefferson are perhaps the only presidents with this gift" ("On the Gettysburg Address," in *Lincoln and the Gettysburg Address,* ed. Allan Nevins [Urbana: University of Illinois Press, 1964], 88). On Jefferson's rhetoric, see also Stephen E. Lucas, "Justifying America: The Declaration of Independence as a Rhetorical Document," in *American Rhetoric: Context and Criticism,* ed. Thomas W. Benson (Carbondale: Southern Illinois University Press, 1989), 67–130; and Jay Fliegelman, *Declaring Independence: Jefferson, Natural Language, and the Culture of Performance* (Stanford, Calif.: Stanford University Press, 1993).

2. "The Selfishness of Sectionalism Has No Place in Our National Life" in *The Public Papers and Addresses of Franklin D. Roosevelt,* ed. Samuel I. Rosenman, 13 vols. (New York: Random House, 1938), 3:272–75.

3. Master speech file, box 19, speech no. 706, Franklin Delano Roosevelt Library, Hyde Park, New York (hereafter FDR Library).

4. The opening paragraph, added by Roosevelt in delivery but dropped by Rosenman in the printed work, reads: "What a glorious day this is. I rejoice in it and I rejoice in this splendid celebration of it. I am especially happy to stand here on the field of Gettysburg at the side of a man, who, through all his life, has so splendidly served the cause of progressive government and the cause of humanity, Gifford Pinchot, Governor of Pennsylvania. (Applause)" (master speech file, box 19, speech no. 706, [draft 5], FDR Library).

5. Roosevelt biographer Kenneth S. Davis describes Early as a "fiery-tempered southerner who would become White House press secretary and whose white southerner racist attitudes would sometimes clash with Eleanor's championship of black rights, but whose overall performance would prove of immense value to Roosevelt personally and to the New Deal" (Davis, *FDR: The New Deal Years, 1933–*

1937 [New York: Random House, 1986], 20). Early was a grandson of Confederate general Jubal Early. Based on internal evidence, including the many references to Virginia and Democratic partisanship, it is possible that Steve Early wrote the first draft, or that he wrote it in collaboration with Barbee.

6. Thomas W. Benson, "Inaugurating Peace: Franklin D. Roosevelt's Last Speech," *Speech Monographs* 36 (June, 1969): 138–47.

7. "Harry L. Hopkins memo (handwritten) on FDR speechwriting," pt. 3, box 6, folder 19, Harry L. Hopkins Papers, Special Collections, Georgetown University Library, Washington, D.C.

8. Barbee to McIntyre, Dec. 9, 1933, box 11, folder 613, David Rankin Barbee Papers, Special Collections, Georgetown University Library, Washington, D.C. (hereafter Barbee Papers).

9. Memo, Barbee to Early, Jan. 9, 1934, box 14, folder 746, Barbee Papers. Another memo or draft written by Barbee for Early, now apparently lost, is referred to in a letter from Barbee to Early on Aug. 10, 1937: "Does this hit the spot? If not, send it back to me and I will do it over. I had to type it myself, as I did not want anyone here to know that this memo is being prepared. No carbon was kept, so the original with such corrections as you desire will have to come back to me for typing" (box 11, folder 613, Barbee Papers).

10. Press Release, "From CONGRESSIONAL INTELLIGENCE," box 14, folder 747, Barbee Papers. See also folders 743, 744, 745. The Congressional Intelligence press release was probably released in October, 1933, or October, 1934, based on contextual evidence in the Barbee files, but I have not yet been able to locate the original.

11. The Dies clipping is from the *Washington Post*, Jan. 19, 1935, box 14, folder 744, Barbee Papers. Barbee's speech titled "The New Deal and the Freedom of the Press" is in folder 743, ibid. The quotation is taken from page 13.

12. See, for example, Early to Barbee, Mar. 30, 1939, and Barbee to Early, Aug. 10, 1942, box 11, folder 613, Barbee Papers.

13. Barbee to Early, July 22, 1940, ibid.

14. Barbee to Early, Mar. 14, 1940, ibid.

15. David Rankin Barbee, *An Excursion in Southern History* (Richmond, Va.: Langbourne M. Williams, 1928), 6. This work is a reprint of a series of articles that originally appeared in May, 1927, in the *Asheville (North Carolina) Citizen*, of which Barbee was managing editor. The copy I have consulted is in the collection of the libraries of the Pennsylvania State University, catalogued as item 000020060251, marked as the gift of Mrs. A. K. Anderson, to whom it was given by Barbee himself, according to an inscription in Barbee's hand on the title page. The Penn State copy is annotated at various places by Barbee. One of the eleven endnotes that Barbee provided in response to Early's request is to *An Excursion*, which provides fairly strong evidence that Barbee was the author of the draft.

16. Barbee, *An Excursion*, 7. In another essay, Barbee again attempted to diminish Lincoln's reputation; see David Rankin Barbee, *A Lost Incident in Lincoln's Life*, a reprint from *Tyler's Quarterly Historical and Genealogical Magazine*, July, 1945, as a pamphlet that is bound with others and held at the Columbia University libraries as *Abraham Lincoln: Pamphlets*, vol. 10 (973.701 Z). In this article, Barbee tells the story

of Lincoln's pardon of a convicted New Bedford, Massachusetts, man on a charge of engaging in the slave trade. The pardon had not been certified at the time of Lincoln's death and was later granted by Pres. Andrew Johnson. Barbee uses the story to condemn both Johnson and Lincoln of hypocrisy and political expediency. As is often the case with Barbee, the story of hypocrisy is sharpened by a sense of conspiracies: "There were many strange happenings in the life of that strange man [Lincoln], but none was stranger than that he, the emancipator of the slaves and the Northern hero of a war which slavery had so much to do with bringing on, should have, in the final weeks of his life, pardoned a New England slave-runner; and that a clerk in the Department of Justice should have held up the execution of that order" (ibid., 1). At the Library of Congress itself, says Barbee, "the Lincoln Collection is kept under lock and key in a special stack of its own," as if someone had something to hide (ibid.).

17. Barbee, *An Excursion*, 27.

18. Ibid., 53.

19. Ibid., 64.

20. David Rankin Barbee, *The Capture of Jefferson Davis* [a bound offprint, "Reprinted from *Tyler's Quarterly Historical and Genealogical Magazine*, July 1947" and presented by Barbee to the library of the University of North Carolina, Chapel Hill], 1, 2, 36–37. The copy in the University of North Carolina library is inscribed by Barbee: "University of North Carolina with Compliments of David Rankin Barbee" (ibid., 1).

21. Barbee, ibid., 4. In 1949, after Truman had appointed Early undersecretary of defense, Barbee send a copy of *Capture of Jefferson Davis* to Early along with a letter asking Early to get the Department of Defense to release from its archives the coat Davis wore when captured, so that it could be sent to the Confederate Museum in Richmond, Virginia. He pleaded that Davis's family "wish this to be done," and reminded Early that both Early and the president were descendants of Confederate soldiers (Barbee to Early, Aug. 15, 1949, box 11, folder 613, Barbee Papers).

22. David W. Blight, "'For Something beyond the Battlefield': Frederick Douglass and the Struggle for the Memory of the Civil War," *Journal of American History* 75 (Mar., 1989): 1166–67. The classic work on the end of Reconstruction and the birth of reunionist sentiment in American public memory is Paul H. Buck, *The Road to Reunion, 1865–1900* (1937; reprint, New York: Vintage Books, 1959).

23. W. E. B. DuBois, "The Propaganda of History," in *W. E. B. DuBois: A Reader*, ed. David Levering Lewis (New York: Henry Holt, 1995), 205 (the passage is from DuBois, *Black Reconstruction in America* [1935]); Blight, "'For Something beyond the Battlefield,'" 1156–78. See also Michael C. Leff, "Lincoln Among the Nineteenth-Century Orators," in *Rhetoric and Political Culture in Nineteenth-Century America*, ed. Thomas W. Benson (East Lansing: Michigan State University Press, 1997), 131–55.

24. Amy Kinsel, "'From These Honored Dead': Gettysburg in American Culture, 1863–1938" (Ph.D. diss., Cornell University, 1992), 550–51. Jim Cullen reports that Civil War reenactors from the North and South agree that slavery was not really the cause of the Civil War; see Jim Cullen, *The Civil War in Popular Culture: A Reusable Past* (Washington, D.C.: Smithsonian Institution Press, 1995), 197. See also Kirk Savage,

"The Politics of Memory: Black Emancipation and the Civil War Monument," in *Commemorations: The Politics of National Identity,* ed. John R. Gillis (Princeton, N.J.: Princeton University Press, 1994), 127–49; Ivan Karp and Steven D. Lavine, ed., *The Poetics and Politics of Museum Display* (Washington, D.C.: Smithsonian Institution Press, 1991); Gabor S. Boritt, "Lincoln and Gettysburg: The Hero and the Heroic Place," and Eric Foner, "Ken Burns and the Romance of Reunion," in *Ken Burns's The Civil War: Historians Respond,* ed. Robert Brent Toplin (New York: Oxford University Press, 1996), 81–100, 101–18; John S. Patterson, "From Battle Ground to Pleasure Ground: Gettysburg as a Historic Site," in *History Museums in the United States,* ed. Warren Leon and Roy Rosenzweig (Urbana: University of Illinois Press, 1989), 128–57; G. Kurt Piehler, *Remembering War the American Way* (Washington, D.C.: The Smithsonian Institution Press, 1995), 47–91; Michael Kammen, *Mystic Chords of Memory* (1991; reprint, New York: Vintage Books, 1993), 294.

25. Kenneth Burke, *A Grammar of Motives* (1945; reprint, Berkeley: University of California Press, 1969), and *A Rhetoric of Motives* (1950; reprint, Berkeley: University of California Press, 1969).

26. Kenneth O'Reilly, *Nixon's Piano: Presidents and Racial Politics from Washington to Clinton* (New York: Free Press, 1995), 110.

27. John Egerton, *Speak Now Against the Day: The Generation Before the Civil Rights Movement in the South* (New York: Alfred A. Knopf, 1994), 81.

28. Patricia Sullivan, *Days of Hope: Race and Democracy in the New Deal Era* (Chapel Hill: University of North Carolina Press, 1996), 46, 48.

29. Nancy J. Weiss, *Farewell to the Party of Lincoln: Black Politics in the Age of FDR* (Princeton, N.J.: Princeton University Press, 1983), 210–11.

30. Celeste Michelle Condit and John Louis Lucaites, *Crafting Equality: America's Anglo-African Word* (Chicago: University of Chicago Press, 1993), 177.

31. John B. Kirby, *Black Americans in the Roosevelt Era: Liberalism and Race* (Knoxville: University of Tennessee Press, 1980), 234.

32. Lucius Quintus Cincinnatus Lamar (1825–93) was elected to Congress from Mississippi in 1857 and 1859 but resigned to join the Confederacy, drafted the Mississippi secession ordinance, and served in the Confederate army and other posts. After the war, Lamar served in the House of Representatives (1873–77) and the Senate (1877–85), as secretary of the interior (1885–88), and as associate justice of the Supreme Court (1888–93).

33. The classic statement of this theme is William E. Leuchtenburg, "The New Deal and the Analogue of War," in *The FDR Years: On Roosevelt and His Legacy* (New York: Columbia University Press, 1995), 35–75. On the war metaphor as applied to domestic policy, see also David Zarefsky, *President Johnson's War on Poverty* (Tuscaloosa: University of Alabama Press, 1986). On presidential rhetoric as antideliberative, see Jeffrey Tulis, The Rhetorical Presidency (Princeton, N.J.: Princeton University Press, 1987).

34. Sinaink to Roosevelt, May 30, 1934, PPF 200B, box 16, "Public Reaction, May 30, 1934" folder, FDR Library.

35. Eaton to Roosevelt, May 31, 1934, ibid.

36. Radiogram, Stephens to Roosevelt, June 1, 1934, ibid.

37. Telegram, Campbell to Roosevelt, May 31, 1934, ibid.

38. Dallman to Roosevelt, with attached clipping, May 31, 1934, and Kirschenbaum to Roosevelt, May 30, 1934, ibid.

39. The estimate of one hundred thousand is from Dorothy D. Bartlett, "Roosevelt Weary and Unsmiling in Gettysburg Talk," *Philadelphia Inquirer,* May 31, 1934, 1. See also Leon Dure Jr., "United Nation Urged by Roosevelt," *Washington Post,* May 31, 1934, 1; "Unity Gains Acclaimed," *Los Angeles Times,* May 31, 1934, 1; "President Hails Spirit of Unity in Gettysburg Talk," *Harrisburg Patriot,* May 31, 1934, 1; "Unity Urged by Roosevelt as U.S. Ideal," *Philadelphia Inquirer,* May 31, 1934.

40. "Roosevelt Hails New Unity in Nation in Gettysburg Battlefield Speech," *New York Times,* 31 May 1934, 1.

41. "Heal War Scars, President Urges," *Atlanta Constitution,* 31 May 1934, 1.

42. "Faint Hope for Anti-Lynch Bill Passage Remains," *Pittsburgh Courier,* June 2, 1934, sec. 2, p. 5.

43. Kinsel, "'From These Honored Dead'," 94

44. Kinsel argues that the goals of memorialization and preservation were essentially in conflict, since the memorials placed about the battlefield altered its appearance (ibid., 160–61).

45. Ibid., 225.

46. John Bodnar describes how the National Park Service assumed management of all national parks during the New Deal with a self-conscious aim of imposing "a nationalistic framework upon the public's perception of the past in a more systematic way" (*Remaking America: Public Memory, Commemoration, and Patriotism in the Twentieth Century* [Princeton, N.J.: Princeton University Press, 1992], 170).

47. *Pennsylvania at Gettysburg: The Seventy-Fifth Anniversary of the Battle of Gettysburg; Report of the Pennsylvania Commission,* vol. 4, ed. P. L. Roy (Harrisburg, Pa.: W. S. Ray, State Printer, 1914). See Kinsel, "'From These Honored Dead,'" 302–304; Frederick W. Hawthorne, *Gettysburg: Stories of Men and Monuments* (Hanover, Pa.: Sheridan Press, 1988), 27; D. Scott Hartwig and Ann Marie Hartwig, *Gettysburg: The Complete Pictorial of Battlefield Monuments* (Gettysburg: Thomas Publications, 1995), 17.

48. Samuel I. Rosenman, ed., *The Public Papers and Addresses of Franklin D. Roosevelt,* vol. 7 (New York: Macmillan, 1941), 419–21.

49. "Gettysburg 75th Anniversary, Speech of the President at Gettysburg," draft no. 2, July 3, 1938, FDR speech file, folder no. 1142, FDR Library.

50. Alfred Haworth Jones, *Roosevelt's Image Brokers: Poets, Playwrights, and the Use of the Lincoln Symbol* (Port Washington, N.Y.: Kennikat Press, 1974). For changing popular and scholarly interpretations of Lincoln in collective memory, see Merrill D. Peterson, *Lincoln in American Memory* (New York: Oxford University Press, 1994). On Roosevelt's appropriation of Lincoln, see Cullen, *Civil War in Popular Culture,* 46–48.

51. Sherwood's *Abe Lincoln in Illinois* opened on Broadway on Oct. 15, 1938. Sherwood joined the Roosevelt speechwriting team in 1940.

52. Garry Wills, *Lincoln at Gettysburg: The Words That Remade America* (New York: Simon and Schuster, 1992), 52.

53. There is a considerable literature in rhetorical studies on presidential crisis management. Such works typically argue that the president uses or even manufactures crises as a method of controlling assent. See, for example, Denise Bostdorff, *The Presidency and the Rhetoric of Foreign Crisis* (Columbia: University of South Carolina Press, 1994); and Amos Kiewe, ed., *The Modern Presidency and Crisis Rhetoric* (Westport, Conn.: Praeger, 1994). Most of the rhetorical studies have treated presidents after FDR. It might well be argued that Roosevelt's entire presidency employed crisis rhetoric from start to finish—first the depression, then World War II.

54. Herbert A. Wichelns, "The Literary Criticism of Oratory," *Studies in Rhetoric and Public Speaking in Honor of James Albert Winans,* ed. A. M. Drummond (New York: Century, 1925), reprinted in *Landmark Essays on Rhetorical Criticism,* ed. Thomas W. Benson (Davis, Calif.: Hermagoras Press, 1993), 26.

55. Donovan Ochs demonstrates how deeply embedded and how double-edged our funeral rituals are in *Consolatory Rhetoric* (Columbia: University of South Carolina Press, 1993).

56. Wills, *Lincoln at Gettysburg,* 38.

57. Ibid., 37. For an analysis of the discussion of slavery in the Lincoln-Douglas debates and the displacement of the moral issue by "surrogate" arguments based on conspiracy theories, history, and legal themes, see David Zarefsky, *Lincoln, Douglas, and Slavery: In the Crucible of Public Debate* (Chicago: University of Chicago Press, 1990).

58. Wills, *Lincoln at Gettysburg,* 90.

59. Edwin Black, "Gettysburg and Silence," *Quarterly Journal of Speech* 80 (Feb., 1994): 35.

60. J. David Greenstone, *The Lincoln Persuasion: Remaking American Liberalism* (Princeton, N.J.: Princeton University Press, 1993), 244.

61. The "unused draft" is accompanied by a note stating that until 1957 it had been mistakenly filed among the drafts for an August 11, 1938, speech at the University of Georgia ("Gettysburg 75th Anniversary," unused draft, FDR speech file, folder 1142, FDR Library).

62. "'Minority Rights Must Be Recognized,' Says President Roosevelt," *Pittsburgh Courier,* July 9, 1938, 4.

63. "Negro Vet Is Oldest at Gettysburg Re-Union," *Pittsburgh Courier,* July 9, 1938, 4.

64. Peyton Gray, "58 Vets at Gettysburg," *Philadelphia Afro-American,* July 9, 1938, 1.

65. For example, Alexander Kendrick, "Roosevelt is Winning His 'Battle,' He Tells 200,000 at Gettysburg; Sun Lights Beacon for Eternity," *Philadelphia Inquirer,* July 4, 1938, 1; Richard L. Harkness, "Roosevelt Likens Fight to Lincoln's," *Philadelphia Inquirer,* July 4, 1938, 1; "Roosevelt Calls on People to Fight for Security in Touching off Eternal Light at Gettysburg," *Atlanta Constitution,* July 4, 1938, 1; "150,000 on Battlefield as President Calls for Nation United in Peace," *Harrisburg Patriot,* July 4, 1938, 1; W. A. MacDonald, "President at Gettysburg Sees Victory Near in Battle 'Fundamental as Lincoln's,'" *New York Times,* July 4, 1938, 1; "President Dedicates Eternal Peace Light at Gettysburg," *Los Angeles Times,* July 4, 1938, 1; Marshall

Andrews, "Roosevelt at Gettysburg Sees Victory in 'Another Conflict as Fundamental as Lincoln's,'" *Washington Post*, July 4, 1938, 1.

66. Langston Hughes, "Harlem," in *The Norton Anthology of African American Literature*, ed. Henry Louis Gates Jr. and Nellie Y. McKay (New York: W. W. Norton, 1997), 1267; Martin Luther King Jr., "Letter from Birmingham Jail," ibid., 1856. Hughes's poem provides the title for Lorraine Hansberry's play, *A Raisin in the Sun*.

CHAPTER 8

The Hidden
Hand vs. the
Bully Pulpit

The Layered Political Rhetoric

of President Eisenhower

Meena Bose and Fred I. Greenstein

I N THE TWENTIETH CENTURY, rhetoric has become an increasingly important factor in presidential leadership. In examining presidential rhetoric, scholars typically focus on public communications, particularly speeches and remarks made at press conferences. But much of the communication of chief executives goes on in private interactions with their aides and others in their political environments. A president's private communications represent an important source of influence within an administration.[1]

A president's private communications may be oral or written, oblique or direct, and verbal or nonverbal. They also may be consistent or inconsistent with his public communications. Whatever the case, they warrant attention for a variety of reasons. They are an antecedent of the president's public communications and other actions. They provide a window into the president's motivations. They afford insights into such difficult to analyze aspects of public political communication as trial balloons and leaks. And, when they become available in the archives, they help shape historical judgments of the legacies of particular presidents.

Our aim in this chapter is to explore the relationship between private and public presidential rhetoric by examining selected communications on national security of Pres. Dwight D. Eisenhower. While scholars have studied extensively Eisenhower's political style and policy-making process, an aspect of his presidency that has received less attention is his skill as policy communicator. Eisenhower is an excellent subject for our purposes because his complex and layered political style was marked by differing approaches to public and private communication. His communications on national security are particularly instructive because his views on that topic were highly developed and explicitly formulated and because national security was the central concern of his presidency.[2]

We begin our analysis with a schematic account of Eisenhower's political style. We then review Eisenhower's national security policies and the larger strategic perspective from which they arose. Having situated our analysis, we explicate Eisenhower's rhetorical style by examining his verbal products at three levels. First, we lower our lens on a specimen of his famously ambiguous discourse in press conferences. Then we analyze an example of his closely reasoned private communications.

Our third account is not of a single rhetorical example but an extended pattern of public political communication: the unsuccessful efforts of the Eisenhower administration in the late 1950s to refute the charge that the United States had fallen dangerously behind the Soviet Union in the development of intercontinental ballistic missiles. Assertions that the United States trailed the Soviet Union in missile development were first made in the mid-1950s, after an earlier alleged "bomber gap" proved to be nonexistent. The "missile gap" controversy was of modest proportions, however, until the Soviet launching of the artificial earth satellite *Sputnik* in October, 1957. At that point the controversy intensified sharply, continuing through the 1960 presidential campaign and contributing to the massive buildup of American strategic weapons in the Kennedy administration. That, in turn, led to a spiraling arms race that continued throughout the Cold War and left the post–Cold War world with the deadly legacy of tens of thousands of nuclear warheads.[3]

EISENHOWER'S POLITICAL STYLE

Dwight Eisenhower was uniquely popular among post–World War II American presidents. He served two full four-year terms, with an average public approval rating of 64 percent. In this he was exceeded only by John F. Kennedy, who was president for less than three years and did not live to reap the consequences of the increased U.S. military involvement in Vietnam over which he presided. Apart from Kennedy, Eisenhower is the only chief executive who received more positive than negative ratings from the public throughout his entire presidency.[4]

In spite of the American people's affection for him, Eisenhower found little favor with students of the presidency until well after he left office. Echoing the views of many of Eisenhower's contemporary critics, scholars held him to have been good-natured and well intentioned, but politically naive and passive. He seemed to have been little more than a presidential figurehead whose policies were made by such nominal subordinates as White House chief of staff Sherman Adams and Secretary of State John Foster Dulles.

However, by the 1980s, scholars had transformed their assessments of Eisenhower. They were prompted not by changing assessments of his policies but by new evidence about his performance. As the inner records of the Eisenhower presidency became available in the Dwight D. Eisenhower Library in Abilene, Kansas, and other archives, it became evident that Eisenhower in fact was a presidential activist, but that his activism took an unconventional form.

The impression that Eisenhower reigned rather than ruled was engendered by the way he resolved the contradiction between what Americans expect from their president in his dual capacity as head of state and principal national political leader. As head of state, the American president is a symbol of unity. Like a constitutional monarch, he is expected to be a noncontroversial representative of the entire nation. As the nation's chief political leader, however, he must engage in the intrinsically divisive prime ministerial tasks of political problem solving. The tendency of presidents to sully their public images by conspicuous displays of politicking may be one reason why their public support often erodes in the course of their presidencies.

Eisenhower's solution to the contradictory role demands of the presidency was to maintain the public stance of a head of state who transcended politics. He did so by playing down those aspects of the job that lead a president to be perceived as "just another politician." He employed a number of tactics in this effort, which, considered together, have come to be called "hidden-hand leadership."

One such tactic was concealing his role in political machinations by making extensive use of intermediaries. Another was what he called not "engaging in personalities." He made it a strict policy never to criticize another public figure by name, adopting this detached stance so as not to bring the presidency down to the level of everyday politics and to avoid personal animosities that might impede political consensus building. Still another was to employ "lightening rods"—that is, to leave it to others in his administration to institute its more controversial policies.

Most relevant to this discussion is Eisenhower's instrumental use of language. Eisenhower was studiously variable in his rhetorical practices. In working with his speechwriters on public addresses, he chose language that was at once elevated and simple. As he put it in a prepresidential cabinet review of his 1953 inaugural address, "I deliberately tried to stay at the level of talk that would make as good reading as possible at the Quai d'Orsay or at No. 10 Downing," but that also "would sound good to the fellow digging the ditch in Kansas."[5]

Eisenhower struck a quite different note in his weekly press conferences. Bolstering the impression that he was removed from political specifics, he was often ambiguous in reply to reporters' questions, sometimes professing ignorance of matters because he believed they were best not discussed. He expressed himself in a homely, idiomatic way that went over well with the public but that led many political observers to doubt his political sophistication. As New York Times columnist Arthur Krock wrote in 1957, in Eisenhower's press conference prose "numbers and genders collide, participles hang helplessly and syntax is lost forever."[6]

There is another category of Eisenhower's rhetoric that could scarcely be more different from the tortured language of his press conferences. As noted above, Eisenhower also was the writer of rigorously argued private communications. Perhaps because of his long years as a military staff officer and strategist, it became Eisenhower's practice to set his thoughts down on paper, doing so to clarify as well as communicate his ideas. During both his military and his political careers, Eisenhower composed numerous lucid and often artfully written memoranda and personal letters to friends, family members, and associates, as well as a variety of diary entries. Eisenhower's private communications are an invaluable guide to the rationale behind his policies, revealing a keenly analytical mind and an impressive capacity to analyze policy alternatives and to anticipate their consequences.[7]

EISENHOWER'S CONCEPTION OF NATIONAL SECURITY

Eisenhower ran for president in 1952 with great reluctance, having rejected bids from representatives of both parties to become a candidate in 1948. He was motivated by a desire to place the United States on a firm footing for waging the Cold War. It was his conviction that the Truman administration's enormous expenditures on the military establishment were counterproductive. In Eisenhower's opinion, the long-run security of the nation resided in the strength of its economy and society. Unnecessary military spending sapped the nation's economic system and moral fiber and diminished its national security.

A further stimulus to Eisenhower's candidacy was his firm commitment to cooperation with the Western democracies. As the first military commander of the North Atlantic Treaty Organization, Eisenhower had been deeply involved in welding the NATO alliance. To his great distress, the almost certain 1952 Republican candidate was Ohio Senator Robert A. Taft, whose isolationist leanings meant he could not be counted upon to support NATO.[8]

In his capacity as military strategist, Eisenhower adhered to what diplomatic historian John Lewis Gaddis calls an asymmetrical view of how to meet the nation's national security needs. His conviction, which became the basis of his administration's "New Look" national security stance, was that the United States should defend itself against the communist world by developing its military resources *selectively* rather than by seeking to equal the Soviet Union in all aspects of military endeavor. In particular, it should rely more on its nuclear forces to deter Soviet expansionism and not attempt to match that nation's huge standing army.[9]

As Gaddis points out, Eisenhower rejected the notion that the greater a nation's military force level the stronger it is, even in the realm of nuclear weapons. Instead, he advanced what has come to be known as the doctrine of nuclear "sufficiency," holding that once a nation has the strategic capacity to deter aggression it has no need to add to its nuclear arsenal. Eisenhower made this point on a number of occasions, once caustically reminding his party's legislative leaders that it is possible to kill a person only once.[10]

THE RHETORIC OF AMBIGUITY

Although Eisenhower was the architect of his administration's national security policies and the dominant figure in its internal deliberations, his press conferences left outside political observers with the false impression of a president who was in firm control of neither his administration's policies nor of the English language. That was far from the case, but it sometimes served Eisenhower's purposes to be less than precise in answering reporters' questions.

A striking instance of obfuscation on Eisenhower's part is his reaction to a question about the use of nuclear weapons at his March 16 and March 23, 1955, news conferences. At issue was Communist China's bombardment of Quemoy and Matsu, two tiny islands within sight of mainland China but under the control of the Nationalist government in Taiwan. On March 16, reporters asked whether Eisenhower would consider using tactical nuclear weapons to defend the islands. The president refused to comment on that particular case, but he made the general observation that "in any combat where" tactical nuclear weapons "can be used on strictly military targets and for strictly military purposes, I see no reason why they shouldn't be used just exactly as you would use a bullet or anything else."[11]

Before his press conference the following week, the State Department relayed through Press Secretary James C. Hagerty the suggestion that Eisenhower refuse to answer if the question came up again. Eisenhower's reply was, "Don't worry, Jim, if that question comes up, I'll just confuse them." It did, and Eisenhower replied with a comment that was convoluted and grammatically flawed but politically deft:

I must confess I cannot answer that question in advance. The only thing I know about war are [*sic*] two things: the most changeable factor in war is human nature in its day-by-day manifestation; but the only unchanging factor in war is human nature. And the next thing is that every war is going to astonish you in the way it occurred, and in the way it is carried out. So that for a man to predict, particularly if he has the responsibility for making the decision, to predict what he is going to use, how he is going to do it, would I think exhibit his ignorance of war; that is what I believe. So I think you just have to wait, and that is the kind of prayerful decision that may some day face a President.[12]

For insight into what the United States would do in the event of an actual attack on the offshore islands, the answer was uninformative. But as a political statement, it accomplished a number of purposes. It warned the Communist Chinese government that Eisenhower had not ruled out an attack on Quemoy and Matsu, while not committing the United States to defend those vulnerable outposts. It avoided antagonizing the influential members of Eisenhower's party who were ardent supporters of the Nationalist Chinese. And, to the public, it conveyed a reminder that any action would result from a "prayerful decision" on the part of the trusted General Ike.

THE RHETORIC OF LUCIDITY

Unlike his press conferences, Eisenhower's private communications are a model of logical analysis. The common theme underlying his private communications on national security is the need for the United States to keep its ends and means in balance. Early in 1952, when he had not yet agreed to seek the presidency, Eisenhower learned that President Truman had submitted a budget to Congress with a proposed deficit of $14 billion, much of it a function of proposed military expenditures. Eisenhower made this entry in his diary: "I am greatly afraid that certain basic truths are being forgotten or ignored in our public life today. The first is that a democracy undertakes military preparedness only on a defensive, which means a long-term, basis. . . . Everything done to develop a defense against *external* threat, except under conditions readily recognized as an emergency, must be weighed and gauged in the light of probable *internal* effect."[13]

Eisenhower went on to note that after World War II the government had cut the military budget too sharply, but during the Korean War arms spending had soared. Now his concern was the "danger of internal deterioration through the annual expenditure of unconscionable sums on a program of indefinite duration extending far into the future."[14]

The Eisenhower administration's New Look strategy was intended to provide the nation with adequate security as far into the future as the Cold War continued, without spending "unconscionable sums" on defense. To accomplish this goal, Eisenhower conducted a comprehensive national security policy review in his first year in office, using its results to bring about substantial reductions in military expenditures in the budget proposal of the outgoing Truman administration. That was the beginning, however, of eight years of political controversy in which military representatives and hawkish members of the political community argued that Eisenhower was allowing the nation's military capacity to fall behind that of the Soviet Union.[15]

Even before there was a "missile gap" controversy, the word *gap* had entered the vocabulary of American political controversy in the mid-1950s, when critics of the New Look claimed that the Eisenhower administration had allowed a "bomber gap" to develop between the United States and the Soviet Union. While this fear proved to be unfounded, the same critics soon took up the cry that the United States was falling behind the Soviet Union in missile development.[16]

Those controversies became the stimulus for one of the most eloquent and instructive of Eisenhower's private communications on national security—a seven-paragraph personal and confidential letter to publisher Richard Leo Simon. Simon wrote to Eisenhower in 1956 in reference to arguments by columnists Joseph and Stewart Alsop that the Soviet Union was making great progress in missile development and that the United States should drastically increase its defense spending.[17]

Eisenhower's reply was so succinct and penetrating that nearly three decades later *Washington Post* columnist David Broder reprinted it in its entirety in the context of the Reagan-era debate over whether the United States should undertake a massive defense buildup, including the visionary and costly Strategic Defense Initiative.[18] "The true security problem of the day," Eisenhower wrote, "is not merely man against man or nation against nation. It is man against war."

I have spent my life in the study of military strength as a deterrent to war, and in the character of military armaments necessary to win a war. The study of the first of these questions is still profitable, but we are rapidly getting to the point that no war can be *won*. War implies a contest: when you get to the point that contest is no longer involved and the outlook comes close to destruction of the enemy and suicide for ourselves—an outlook that neither side can ignore—then arguments as to the exact amount of available strength as compared to somebody else's are no longer the vital issues.

When we get to the point, as one day we will, that both sides know that in any outbreak of general hostilities, regardless of the element of surprise, destruction will be both reciprocal and complete, possibly we will have enough sense to meet at the conference table with the understanding that the era of armaments has ended and the human race must conform in its actions to this truth or die.[19]

"[A]rguments as to the exact amount of available strength as compared to somebody else's are no longer the vital issues." Herein lay the nub of Eisenhower's rejection of the demand that the United States exceed the Soviet Union in its military power—including its missile capacity. This brings us to the response of Eisenhower and his administration to *Sputnik*-driven demands for a massive U.S. missile buildup.

THE NOT-SO-BULLY PULPIT

Eisenhower's hidden-hand leadership style served his purposes in many respects. It enabled him to maintain the strong public support that derived from his wartime popularity and continued through his presidential years. That, in turn, provided him cover for holding down defense and other spending during his time in office and for crisis management in the international arena. But it would be a mistake to suggest that his unconventional presidential style was without weaknesses.

Eisenhower's flat-footed actions in the missile-gap controversy point to a basic limitation in a leadership style that underplays the role of the chief executive as public enunciator of policies. The shock to Americans of the 1957 launching by the Soviet Union of an artificial space satellite can be compared only to that of Pearl Harbor. It was less worrisome that the ostensibly backward Russians had won a victory in the "space race" than that it had developed rockets that appeared powerful enough to project nuclear warheads to the American heartland.

Eisenhower's reaction to *Sputnik* was, in effect, to stand pat. Worse yet, his administration initially responded with an arrogance and complacency that seemed all the more extreme because of the level of alarm in the nation. Word of the Soviet launching reached Washington on the evening of October 4, 1957, by which time Eisenhower had left town for a golfing weekend in Gettysburg. He made no immediate personal response, leaving it to Press Secretary Hagerty and Secretary of State Dulles to comment.

The public statements of Hagerty and Dulles made light of the Soviet achievement. The launch of a satellite by the Soviet Union was "no surprise," they declared, adding that the U.S. space program was not meant to be "a race with the Soviets." Other members of the Eisenhower administration were even more dismissive. Secretary of Defense Charles E. Wilson called the orbiting Soviet satellite a "nice scientific trick"; trade adviser Clarence Randall called it a "silly bauble"; and White House chief of staff Sherman Adams dismissed it as an "outer space basketball game."[20]

Eisenhower's first public response to *Sputnik* was in his October 9 press conference. It seemed a lackluster performance. His answers to questions were long and digressive. His attempt to convey a sense of calmness came across as self-satisfaction. At one point he seemed to disparage the Soviet feat, calling *Sputnik* "one small ball in the air." Only when pressed did he grant that the Soviet Union had gained "a great psychological advantage throughout the world," adding the qualification, "I think in the political sense that is possibly true; but in the scientific sense it is not true."[21]

Eisenhower also made several rather mild speeches designed to reassure the nation. After the Soviets launched a second, more technically advanced satellite in November, this one carrying a dog, Eisenhower gave a radio and television address in which he insisted that "we are ahead of the Soviets in the nuclear field, both in quantity and in quality." He noted that "although the Soviets are quite likely ahead in some missile and special areas, and are obviously ahead of us in satellite development, as of today the over-all military strength of the free world is distinctly greater than that of the communist countries."[22]

Throughout his remaining time in office, Eisenhower consistently denied there was a missile gap favoring the Soviet Union. He resisted demands for rapid acceleration of the U.S. space and missile programs, contending that the nation was already proceeding in those areas at a pace sufficient for national security. As he put it in 1960, in response to a press conference question about whether he felt "any sense of urgency in catching up with the Russians": "I am always a little bit amazed about this business of catching up. What you want is enough, a thing that is adequate. A deterrent has no added power, once it has become completely adequate, for compelling the respect of any potential opponent for your deterrent, and therefore, to make him act prudently."[23]

Eisenhower's response to the missile-gap controversy was based partly on evidence he could not make public. He knew from the findings of highly secret spy plane flights over Russia that the Soviet missile program was well behind that of the United States. But he had a more fundamental reason for holding the line on defense spending that derived from his own authoritative conception of the nation's strategic needs. It was the view implicit in his letter to Simon that the United States did not need to exceed, or even equal, the Soviet Union in missile power. It needed only enough to be able to *deter* a Soviet attack. This position *was* well-suited for public communication and merited a higher profile than Eisenhower gave it.[24]

One of Eisenhower's missed opportunities for addressing the missile-gap charges was his farewell address to the nation on January 17, 1961. In addressing the nation, Eisenhower outlined the accomplishments of his administration and the challenges the United States would continue to face. In particular, he discussed the growth of the "military establishment," noting that the nation's annual military expenditures exceeded "the net income of all United States corporations." Eisenhower then went on to issue a now-famous warning: "In the councils of government, we must guard against the acquisition of unwarranted influence, whether sought or unsought, by the military-industrial complex. The potential for the disastrous rise of misplaced power exists and will persist. We must never let the weight of this combination endanger our liberties or democratic processes."[25]

Neither in his farewell address nor earlier did Eisenhower develop the doctrine of nuclear sufficiency with the force and clarity of his 1956 letter to Simon. Just three days after Eisenhower bid the nation farewell, it was regaled with the inaugural address rhetoric that presaged the vast increase in nuclear forces of the Kennedy administration: "we shall pay any price, bear any burden, meet any hardship, support any friend, oppose any foe to assure the survival and the success of liberty."[26]

CONCLUSION

Putting the missile-gap controversy to rest called for the bully pulpit, not the hidden hand. Therein Eisenhower was deficient. His rational mind-set made him insensitive to the importance of emotion in the thinking of others, his habits of indirection made him ill suited for presidential pedagogy, and he felt no need for historical vindication. As he wrote in his diary during the Taiwan Straits crisis in 1955, "I have so often been through these periods of strain that I have become accustomed to the fact that most of the calamities that we anticipate never really occur."[27] The result of Eisenhower's complacent approach was that John F. Kennedy entered the White House in 1961 pledged to close a nonexistent missile gap. For that and other reasons, Kennedy spawned a dangerous and costly arms race with the Soviet Union.

An Eisenhower who did more to be publicly articulate might have prevented that outcome. It is impossible to know whether it was in Eisenhower's capacity to make better use of the presidential pulpit, but in retrospect two possibilities come to mind. One would have been to make public such eloquent private communications as his letter to Simon in order to stimulate a more searching strategic debate than was possible by means of formal addresses and news conferences.

The second would have been to capitalize in public on the great private persuasiveness that was abundantly evident in Eisenhower's interventions in the internal counsels of his administration. One way this might have been accomplished is suggested by a bravura media performance on his part three and one-half years after he left the White House. On the eve of the twentieth anniversary of D-Day, Eisenhower broadcast a ninety-minute televised interview with Walter Cronkite on the Columbia Broadcasting System. The interview, which was filmed on the Normandy beaches, conveyed a powerful sense of Eisenhower's force of personality and command of specifics. Above all, it dramatized his authoritativeness on matters of war and peace.

The effectiveness of this display of Eisenhower's rhetorical capacity in face-to-face settings is captured in the respectful language of a front-page account in the next day's *New York Times:* "The terror-filled hours of D-Day were recalled with simple eloquence last night by Gen. Dwight D. Eisenhower. . . . In an almost matter-of-fact voice, General Eisenhower, recalled the fearful decision to go ahead with the landings on June 6, 1944, despite predictions of barely tolerable weather."[28]

The entire tone of the article made the power and persuasiveness of Eisenhower's presentation evident. It is highly plausible that some such dramatization of Eisenhower's authoritative views on the nation's security would have scotched claims that the nation's security depended on winning an arms race with the Soviet Union.[29]

If Eisenhower had prevailed, the Kennedy arms buildup might have been averted, and the post–Cold War world might have been preserved from its huge and perilous nuclear inheritance. In short, Eisenhower's failure to be persuasive about the missile gap had genuine political consequences. It would be difficult to imagine a more compelling demonstration of the importance of political rhetoric.

NOTES

1. On the emergence of public rhetoric as a political tool for presidents in the twentieth century see Jeffrey K. Tulis, *The Rhetorical Presidency* (Princeton, N.J.: Princeton University Press, 1987). Also see Samuel Kernell, *Going Public: New Strategies of Presidential Leadership,* 3d ed. (Washington, D.C.: Congressional Quarterly Press, 1997). Theodore Windt discusses the focus in studies of presidential rhetoric on public communication in "Presidential Rhetoric: Definition of a Discipline of Study," in *Essays in Presidential Rhetoric,* 2d ed., ed. Windt and Beth Ingold, (Dubuque, Iowa.: Kendall/Hunt, 1987), xxiii–xxvii. A recent article that does analyze private communication, namely, a recently declassified transcript of a telephone conversation between then–Vice President Lyndon B. Johnson and presidential adviser Theodore C. Sorensen on June 3, 1963, about civil rights, is Roderick P. Hart and Kathleen E. Kendall, "Lyndon Johnson and the Problem of Politics: A Study in Conversation," in *Beyond the Rhetorical Presidency,* ed. Martin J. Medhurst (College Station: Texas A&M University Press, 1996), 77–103.

2. A study that examines both policy making and policy communication in the Eisenhower administration is Meena Bose, *Shaping and Signaling Presidential Policy: The National Security Decision Making of Eisenhower and Kennedy* (College Station: Texas A&M University Press, 1998). See also Martin J. Medhurst, *Dwight D. Eisenhower: Strategic Communicator* (Westport, Conn.: Greenwood Press, 1993).

3. For an analysis of how the missile-gap debate fostered the major strategic buildup of the 1960s, see Desmond Ball, *Politics and Force Levels: The Strategic Missile Program of the Kennedy Administration* (Berkeley: University of California Press, 1980).

4. For a fuller explication of Eisenhower's leadership style and its implications, see Fred I. Greenstein, *The Hidden-Hand Presidency: Eisenhower as Leader* (New York: Basic Books, 1982), which was published with a new preface in 1994 by Johns Hopkins University Press. See especially chap. 3 passim.

5. "Cabinet meeting of Jan. 12–13, 1953," Ann Whitman file, Dwight D. Eisenhower Library, quoted in Greenstein, *Hidden-Hand Presidency*, 109.

6. Arthur Krock, "Impressions of the President—and the Man," *New York Times Magazine*, June 23, 1957, cited in Greenstein, *Hidden-Hand Presidency*, 8.

7. For an extensive collection of Eisenhower's private communications from Pearl Harbor through the end of his first term in the White House see Alfred D. Chandler, Louis Galambos, and Daun Van Ee, eds., *The Papers of Dwight D. Eisenhower* (hereafter *PDDE*), 17 vols. (Baltimore: Johns Hopkins University Press, 1970–96). This series will continue to include the remainder of Eisenhower's private presidential papers. See also Daniel D. Holt and James W. Leyerzapf, eds., *Eisenhower: The Prewar Diaries and Selected Papers, 1905–1941* (Baltimore: Johns Hopkins University Press, 1998).

8. For a more complete discussion of the factors that shaped Eisenhower's decision to run for president in 1952, see Robert R. Bowie and Richard H. Immerman, *Waging Peace: How Eisenhower Shaped an Enduring Cold War Strategy* (New York: Oxford University Press, 1998), 70–71.

9. John Lewis Gaddis, *Strategies of Containment: A Critical Appraisal of Postwar American National Security Policy* (New York: Oxford University Press, 1984), chap. 5 passim.

10. Ibid., 187.

11. "The President's News Conference of March 16, 1955," in *Public Papers of the Presidents: Dwight D. Eisenhower, 1955* (Washington, D.C.: GPO, 1959), 329–43 (hereafter *PPOP* followed by the year). For background on the 1955 offshore islands crisis, see Chester J. Pach Jr. and Elmo Richardson, *The Presidency of Dwight D. Eisenhower*, rev. ed. (Lawrence: University Press of Kansas, 1991), 98–104.

12. "The President's News Conference of March 23, 1955," *PPOP, 1955*, 350–65. Eisenhower recalls his comment to Hagerty in his memoirs, *The White House Years: Mandate for Change, 1953–1956* (Garden City, N.Y.: Doubleday, 1963), 478. For a film clip of the press conference exchange, see Public Broadcasting Corporation videotape *The American Experience: Eisenhower* (Boston: WGBH Educational Foundation, 1993).

13. Eisenhower diary entry, Jan. 22, 1952, in *NATO and the Campaign of 1952*, vol. 13, *PDDE*, 896–902.

14. Ibid.

15. For an analysis of Eisenhower's national security policy review in 1953, see Bowie and Immerman, *Waging Peace*, chap. 8 passim, and Bose, *Shaping and Signaling*, chap. 2 passim.

16. Edgar M. Bottome, *The Missile Gap: A Study of the Formulation of Military and Political Policy* (Rutherford, N.J.: Farleigh Dickinson University Press, 1971), 34–38, 73–75. A more recent study of the missile-gap debate based on the declassified record is Peter J. Roman, *Eisenhower and the Missile Gap* (Ithaca, N.Y.: Cornell University Press, 1995).

17. For representative columns by the Alsop brothers, see Joseph and Stewart Alsop, *The Reporter's Trade* (New York: Reynal, 1958), esp. 273–85.

18. Eisenhower to Richard L. Simon, Apr. 4, 1956, reprinted in David Broder, "Negotiate or Die—Eisenhower," *Washington Post*, Sept. 7, 1983, and in *Eisenhower: The Middle Way*, vol. 16, *PDDE*, 2113–15.

19. Ibid.

20. For the Eisenhower administration's initial response to *Sputnik*, see Robert A. Divine, *The Sputnik Challenge: Eisenhower's Response to the Soviet Satellite* (New York: Oxford University Press, 1993), xiv–xvi. See also David Henry, "Eisenhower and Sputnik: The Irony of Failed Leadership," in *Eisenhower's War of Words: Rhetoric and Leadership*, ed. Martin J. Medhurst (East Lansing: Michigan State University Press, 1994), 223–49.

21. "The President's News Conference of Oct. 9, 1957," in *PPOP, 1957* (Washington, D.C.: GPO, 1958), 719–32. See also Divine, *Sputnik Challenge*, 7–8.

22. Eisenhower, "Radio and Television Address to the American People on Science in National Security," Nov. 7, 1957, in *PPOP, 1957*, 789–99. Eisenhower follows up on this speech one week later in "Radio and Television Address to the American People on 'Our Future Security'," Nov. 13, 1957, ibid., 807–17. For a more detailed analysis of both addresses, see Divine, *Sputnik Challenge*, 45–47, 52–58.

23. "The President's News Conference of Feb. 3, 1960," in *PPOP, 1960–61* (Washington, D.C.: GPO, 1961), 144–54. Eisenhower's insistence on not drastically expanding the U.S. space budget is analyzed in David Callahan and Fred I. Greenstein, "The Reluctant Racer: Eisenhower and U.S. Space Policy," in *Spaceflight and the Myth of Presidential Leadership*, ed. Roger D. Launius and Howard E. McCurdy (Urbana: University of Illinois Press, 1997), 15–50.

24. Many scholars have analyzed the "missile gap" myth, notably: Ball, *Politics and Force Levels*, 89–93; McGeorge Bundy, *Danger and Survival: Choices about the Bomb in the First Fifty Years* (New York: Random House, 1988), 334–57; and Roman, *Eisenhower and the Missile Gap*, passim. For a study of the Eisenhower administration's decision to use U-2 reconnaissance flights over the Soviet Union, see Michael R. Beschloss, *Mayday: Eisenhower, Khrushchev, and the U-2 Affair* (New York: Harper and Row, 1986). See also Beschloss, *The Crisis Years: Kennedy and Khrushchev, 1960–1963* (New York: HarperCollins, 1991), 25–26.

25. Eisenhower, "Farewell Radio and Television Address to the American People," Jan. 17, 1961, in *PPOP, 1960–61*, 1035–40. For an analysis of the origins of "military-industrial complex," perhaps the most oft-quoted phrase from Eisenhower's farewell address, see Charles J. G. Griffin, "New Light on Eisenhower's Farewell Address," in Medhurst, ed., *Eisenhower's War of Words*, 273–84.

26. Kennedy, "Inaugural Address," Jan. 20, 1961, in *PPOP, 1961* (Washington, D.C.: GPO, 1962), 1–3.

27. Eisenhower, Mar. 26, 1955 diary entry, in *The Eisenhower Diaries*, ed. Robert H. Ferrell (New York: W. W. Norton, 1981), 294.

28. "Eisenhower Recalls the Ordeal of D-Day Assault 20 Years Ago," *New York Times*, June 6, 1964.

29. A new biography of Eisenhower notes that while Eisenhower never became completely comfortable with television appearances, he did better on television when he spoke directly and naturally to the people instead of following a script. See Geoffrey Perret, *Eisenhower* (New York: Random House, 2000), 489–93.

CHAPTER 9

Ronald Reagan and the American Dream

A Study in Rhetoric Out of Time

G. Thomas Goodnight

I N THE MID-TWENTIETH CENTURY, the American presidency rose to great prestige. The popular, quiet leadership of Dwight Eisenhower navigated the turbulent postwar world, and the dynastic rhetoric of John Kennedy rang with Tennyson-like cadences. According to political theorists of the time, the ascent was not untroubled. The growth of bureaucracy, use of secrecy, and invocation of emergency powers seemed to take the executive branch to the fringes, if not wholly beyond, the limits of constitutional authority. Arthur Schlesinger called this condition of leadership the "imperial presidency," a state in which the demands of the Cold War generally, and nuclear weapons in particular, had rendered the restrictions of shared power, the constitutional checks and balances of the federal system, outmoded. Was the imperial presidency an artifact of the Cold War or is it a permanent condition of executive leadership? This is the perdurable question this chapter addresses.

Whether conducted in a plain or an imperial style, at base all presidential leadership is a civic art constituted by public enactments of the presidency. Civic performances distinguish each administration as the executive deploys inherent and implied powers within the federal arenas of shared and separated authority. Individual presidential actions constitute interpretations of Constitutional text, original intent, and historical practice in light of contemporary governmental and political constraints and opportunities. Collectively, administration performances achieve shape and significance by virtue of the public arguments among all those whose prerogatives and responsibilities are affected by the policies and fortunes of a presidency. Public and elite gestures of support, compliance, or opposition comprise the ongoing legitimation drama of American government. In cycles of election and rule, normal business and crisis, policy adoption and defeat, majority and minority standing, the national stage sets and resets for a new (and sometimes renewed) administration. That the basic civic drama of the presidency itself is invariably "imperial" appears to be a difficult claim to sustain. Indeed, if the mid–Cold War years were characterized by a gathering high style for presidential rhetoric, post-Nixon presidents were all but denuded of the pomp and circumstance the prestige of office brings.

Imperial rhetoric was never more out of fashion than in Gerald Ford's and Jimmy Carter's Washington. Rarely, did a less majestic view of America reign than during the post-Nixon 1970s. From lame WIN buttons to the "Poland is free" gaffe, Ford was blown about by every political squall; and by the minute, the land of plenty became the land of limits for the unlucky Carter administration.

Without vision, the people do not necessarily perish, but they do not feel that well either. The malaise-ridden Georgia farmer, nuclear engineer, and New South Democrat transposed presidential style from the inside out—replacing martial courage with technocratic caution, patrician glamour with dour rectitude, and high tone with plain speaking. During the Carter years, American know-how and aims seemed ever at odds. It was found that big technology was more problem than solution; that supporting human rights was not the same as fighting communism; that economic growth and environmental preservation were not compatible; that civil rights could be put at odds with unfettered opportunity; and that power projection offered little protection from terrorists. From double-digit inflation, to Soviet intransigence, to the Iran hostages, Carter's America was an America that would not work.

Nowhere were the public performances of the presidency more sharply distinct than between Carter and Reagan. As George Edwards wrote: "The symbols of the 'post-imperial presidency' such as modesty, openness, and integrity, which Jimmy Carter worked hard to portray, were 'weak,'" or at least insufficient for the "mastery" of the times. It was not that Carter did not try to project an image of toughness, it was just that his rhetoric, as Aristotle might have observed, was more on the milder side. "You show me a good loser and I will show you a loser," he said.[1] "Carter tried to be sports minded and athletic by playing tennis, softball, and jogging, but his image as a sports participant was probably best captured when he faltered and collapsed in total exhaustion in the 10 kilometer race over the Catoctin Mountain trail in Maryland in 1979."[2] Even when fishing, a sturdy image of Eisenhower stolidity, he had the misfortune to be attacked by a killer rabbit.

Peanuts are a sturdy, rough, useful staple; jellybeans are colorful, smooth, and sweet. To conjure the blue-jean-wearing, heavy-sweatered, sometimes-flanneled Carter squirming through a fireside chat in contrast with the flashily tuxed, sometimes-open, Western-shirted, striding Reagan is to at once see the difference a tone fit for the times makes. A brash, new style dashed into Washington at the end of the dowdy 1970s. "Following the 1980 San Francisco debate with Jimmy Carter, for example, Reagan was asked, 'Governor, weren't you intimidated by being up there on stage with the President of the United States?' 'No,' responded Reagan, 'I've been on the same stage with John Wayne.'"[3]

From John Wayne to George Gipp, Ronald Reagan was familiar with the mileage that could be gained from a stew of part Irish wit, part Hollywood acting, and part Western grit—a recipe for the all-American image. "Even his personal attributes—his horseback-riding, sagebrush-clearing, wood-chopping persona, with the 'right stuff' to take a bullet in the chest and still oppose gun control—all projected the image of a President and a country unwilling to be pushed around." Reagan made us realize, as Garry Wills put it, that "people who keep talking about the age of limits are really talking about their own limitations, not America's.'"[4] Clearly, Reagan returned a high-toned style to the presidency, but an assessment of the administration's "imperial" qualities requires that the couplings of power and persuasion be brought into clear focus—a not undifficult task—due to the administration's still controversial legacy.

Public memories are especially tricky. As administrations depart from the scene and the buzz of politics moves on to confect other images of leadership, it is difficult to recollect what made the rhetoric of an era go exactly, much less to bring a presidential legacy into perspective for evaluation. This is especially true for Ronald Reagan. On one hand, he is given high marks as a "superb political strategist" by Aaron Wildalvsky and heralded as a president who "after eight years in office . . . had succeeded in redefining the parameters and the vocabulary of political discourse in America."[5] Indeed, his public popularity was at 70 percent when he left office and continues to grow. On the other hand, 62 percent of a large group of American historians rank Reagan in the "'below average' category, between Zachary Taylor and John Tyler." Schlesinger writes: "The administration was incoherent, incompetent, duplicitous, and dedicated to rash, mindless policy."[6] Such a tempered conclusion notwithstanding, Michael Foley gets to the heart of the issue. How Reagan achieved success and personal popularity is "something of a mystery." Referring to mushrooming deficits and limited success on the conservative agenda, Foley observes: "The president's promises were not delivered. His proposals were shown not to work. His objectives were not achieved. His policies remained unpopular."[7] Richard Neustadt puts the question in perhaps its most blunt form: "How could a man so inattentive seem to do so relatively well?"[8] I will explain how by analyzing Reagan's mobilization of the American Dream in setting a controversial course for presidential leadership.

PRESIDENTIAL LEADERSHIP AS PUBLIC ARGUMENT

The perspective I take on presidential leadership goes back to Neustadt himself who authored a germinal definition in 1960: "Presidential power is the power to persuade." The idea here is that the exercise of power involves more than commands flowing from legal authority. Rather, the president must convince elites, especially in crises, that it is right for them to take action in fulfilling their independent duties. "The essence of a President's persuasive task . . . is to induce them to believe that what he wants of them is what their own appraisal of their own responsibilities requires them to do in their interest, not his."[9] To this definition, I would add a brief corollary: Presidential power *is* the power to persuade, and presidential power *is the power to appear to need to be persuaded.* The added clause is not negligible.

The corollary affirms Neustadt's placement of presidential power within the ambit of civic discourse generally, and a strategic bargaining, a give-and-take among potentially independent actors specifically (I would explicitly say bargaining with *and* before public and private constituencies, too). The chief difference rests with Neustadt's one-way obligation of a president to harmonize his own aims with the duties of elites. This is a misleading interpretative and evaluative norm because it plops the president in a frozen center, as the Tatalovich and Daynes model of concentric rings of constituencies shows.[10] If one acknowledges that any president has a choice in affirming or denying conventional expectations of role enactment, however, it is easy to see that presidential action is a two-way street. Indeed, historically the president's approval has been an elite and public object of desire avidly sought, anticipated, and debated. Thus, it is fair to say that the signature of a specific rhetorical presidency is constituted in the ongoing emphasis, interpretation, and enactment of a democratically elected candidate *within and against* the expected roles of chief executive, legislative leader, opinion/party leader, commander in chief, chief diplomat, and member of the first family of the United States—as these performances unfold to meet and cross the elite and public expectations of an era.

The corollary answers Craig and Kathy Smith's objection that Neustadt miscasts presidential persuasion as bargaining because, unlike negotiations, the president does not have "to relinquish anything for the sake of compliance" in going public.[11] The enactment of one presidential role rather than another, the ordering of issues and strength of support for policies, rhetorical grants of or attacks on institutional legitimacy—all the public gestures of cooperation and division a presidency can muster—are stakes in defining or conceding preferred civic practices (and concomitant political aims). The controversies waged by allies and enemies within and without a presidency always play out conceptually, stylistically, and ideologically in elections, crises, and normal business for the length of an administration. Debates over what the president did, could, should, or will do constitute legitimation disputes over the uses of power and thus inevitably shape and reshape the domestic and foreign policy landscapes of democratic politics. These rhetorical efforts constitute the public argument of an American presidency. Such argumentation begins long before election time. In fact, the 1980s began on October 27, 1964.

CITIZEN ORATOR AS CONTROVERSIALIST

Citizen Ronald Reagan understood the power of controversy. He told us so himself. "I am going to talk of controversial things. I make no apology for this," reads the first two lines of "The Speech" in Reagan's autobiography. Too controversial for General Electric, he carried this high voltage message to the national stage in the fall of 1964. "A Time for Choosing," delivered to a national television audience on behalf of a flagging Goldwater campaign, vaulted Reagan into the national spotlight. David Broder described the speech as the "most successful political debut since William Jennings Bryan electrified the 1896 Democratic Convention with his 'Cross of Gold speech'."[12] Apart from historical interest, "A Time for Choosing" bears analysis because of the constancy that is the signature of Reagan's public speaking. As Kurt Ritter and David Henry note: "Reagan's orations over a span of four decades were astonishingly repetitive. Reagan [himself] was untroubled by this."[13] The following passage is drawn from the conclusion of the speech and yields a summing of a field of persuasion:

> You and I know and do not believe that life is so dear and peace so sweet as to be purchased at the price of chains and slavery. If nothing is worth dying for, when did this begin—just in the face of this enemy?—or should Moses have told the children of Israel to live in slavery under the pharaohs? Should Christ have refused the cross? Should the patriots at Concord Bridge have thrown down their guns and refused to fire the shot heard round the world? The martyrs of history were not fools, and our honored dead who gave their lives to stop the advance of the Nazis didn't die in vain! Where, then, is the road to peace? Well, it's a simple answer after all.
>
> You and I have the courage to say to our enemies, "There is a price we will not pay." There is a point beyond which they must not advance! This is

the meaning in the phrase of Barry Goldwater's "peace through strength!" Winston Churchill said that "the destiny of man is not measured by material computation. When great forces are on the move in the world, we learn we are spirits—not animals." And he said, "There is something going on in time and space, and beyond time and space, which, whether we like it or not, spells duty." You and I have a rendezvous with destiny. We can preserve for our children this, the last best hope of man on earth, or we can sentence them to take the first step into a thousand years of darkness. If we fail, at least let our children and our children's children, say of us we justified our brief moment here. We did all that could be done.[14]

So, "the voice of the Cubs became the Great Communicator and approached his own rendezvous with destiny," speech critic Paul Erickson concludes.[15]

James MacGregor Burns says not without some restraint that the speech "reads disappointingly today." "It was a talk that had been given a thousand times not only by Reagan but by Herbert Hoover, Alf Landon, Wendell Wilkie, Robert A. Taft, and Barry Goldwater—a long denunciation of big government, creeping socialism, the threat to private property, government planning, federal spending, the 'schemes of the do-gooders,' planned inflation, and the kind of moral, economic, and military weakness that would provoke communist aggression, war, and defeat."[16] The contradiction between Reagan's anti-Vietnam stance and the Cold War apocalyptic vision notwithstanding, most critics credit the speech as the moment American conservatism turned into a choice and not an echo. Goldwater lost, but Reagan's America loomed just over the horizon for the 27 million Americans who voted for Goldwater and refused to jump on board the Great Society.

There is a broad, academic consensus that Ronald Reagan's public speaking gave conservatism a friendly face. Robert Dallek put it this way: "unlike Goldwater, the ex-Governor of California was a 'soft sell' spokesman for the conservative ideology" who "exploited resentments and emotions not be being a loud and threatening figure but by making wisecracks or poking fun at his enemies.'" Or, as Mary Stuckey observed: "Rather than ranting and raving in Goldwater fashion, and instead of offering to lob a grenade into the men's room of the Kremlin, he offered audiences a calm and poised presentation." Stylistically, according to Burns, this unexpected turn gave Reagan a great advantage. "The media had a hard time understanding Reagan because they had never quite encountered his type before—an ideologue with charm. [He] . . . could say the most terrible things with a disarming quip or smile."[17]

"Soft sell," "calm and poised," "charm"—truly amazing words for a speech (given a thousand times in more sophisticated variations) that itself reads as much an anticommunist incendiary as any Cold War tract given by Joe McCarthy. This gap between commentary and text is puzzling. (1) Was Goldwater really *that* crazed? (2) Does acting ability alone create such presence as to submerge content—permanently? Are the American people really *that* unsophisticated? (3) Or is there some other feature of leadership— some heretofore unnoticed code—at work in the peculiar positioning of a friendly performance and a fighting rhetoric?

To answer this question and assay the qualities of a line of public address, one need observe *ingenium* in play—the stamp of wit for a rhetoric.[18] What I see as the signature of Reagan's rhetoric is the displacement of time in the interests of persuading and being persuaded. This distinctive fusion of imagination and memory retarding time is there in the Goldwater speech and remains throughout key to Reagan rhetoric. True, the concluding passage reads more as rhetorical folk art than polished prose. That would come later. But, the eddies of time in the speech constellate an inventional field from which the future president would draw arguments to persuade and to be persuaded.

The field of Reagan's persuasion is clear. In the span of two paragraphs, the orator assembles an all-star cast (Patrick Henry, Moses, Jesus, Concord patriots, Coral Bell, Winston Churchill, Abraham Lincoln, FDR, a host of martyrs who would rather kill than appease Nazis, and Barry Goldwater) to play the communists in a game for the ages. As Burns discovered, but insufficiently appreciated when placing Reagan's speaking within the domain of Republican tracts, sometimes rhetoric is noteworthy not for its novelty, conceptual distinction, or even word brilliance. Rather, the measure of a rhetoric can be taken in how it assembles symbolic resources from momentous public discussions that are sufficiently durable, flexible, and distinctive enough to form an anointment-in-waiting for a rhetor who claims to be the bearer of a historic message. Reagan would claim to keep the faith and journey the road to presidential power with these heroic figures *and* contemporary "true" American heroes, all alike challenging present government planners and other do-gooders passing from the scene. This was his posture of persuasion.

The posture from which Reagan would appear to be persuaded—either to concretize national purpose in public policy or to grant exception for pragmatic politics—appears in the last few sentences. These contain a remarkable fusion of FDR's "rendezvous with destiny" signaling Reagan's commitment to domestic political ambitions, Lincoln's "best hope on earth" presaging American exceptionalism, and Churchill's "thousand years of darkness" foreshadowing a fight to the death with Soviet communism. Reagan mobilized these voices again and again to caption the present in terms of allies who lived the drama of freedom and enemies who would deny (or insufficiently appreciate) America its destiny. Would the United States await its destiny, act shrewdly with hope, or leap into an apocalyptic abyss? To work prudently within these horizons Reagan would "need" to be persuaded, case-by-case, by advisers and opponents alike. But what was the historic message, displayed in a thousand speeches across a hundred topics, of which Reagan found himself destined to be the bearer? It was nothing less, I believe, than that of his own life bound to . . .

THE AMERICAN DREAM

There was little distinctive about Reagan's conservative philosophy. Although it took a while for social conservatism to emerge as a mainstream discourse after the Johnson-Goldwater election, Reagan propounded general conservative views through his elections as governor of California and bids for the presidency. The simplicity, repetition, and populist qualities of these themes have lead some interpreters to a rather basic explication of the rhetoric. Larry Berman, says, for example: "He was truly the 'Great Communicator' because what he had to communicate were bumper sticker slogans with resonance to the general public: taxes are bad, communists are bad, bureaucrats are bad, liberals are bad, abortion is bad, individualism is good, prayer is good, the flag is good, God is good, morality is good, the family is good, balanced budgets are good."[19] Rhetoric past its era does taste flat, especially when reduced and captioned as a "public philosophy." What such abstractions leach out is the play of discourse—the dreams of times past and future ingeniously connected to the present through visions of leadership that can be supported, refuted, and even scorned but never safely ignored.

The American Dream was Reagan's vision. John White writes: "Before Reagan became president, pollster Richard Wirthlin told him, '[By] symbolizing the past and future greatness of America and radiating inspirational confidence, a President can pull a nation together while directing its people toward fulfillment of the American dream.'"[20] Jane Blankenship and her colleagues find the dream set to use in the presidential debates. Reagan's enveloping vision put him in the position of a "liberator" who removes government in the larger sweep and allows us to "dream our dreams." The position allowed Reagan to identify with a larger historical scene of purpose and diminish the recent present as a deviation. According to Mary Stuckey, the American Dream constitutes the core of Reagan's "vision" which permits "Americans to forget the struggles of the present and focus on 'the lost summertime of the nation's past when neighborhoods were safe, when families held together, when U.S. power bestrode the world.'" Significantly, Reagan himself "revalidated the American dream by living it out publicly."[21]

That the American Dream of individual success was at odds with social concerns seems confirmed by the children the Reagan era gave birth to: the self-indulgent Yuppies and the destitute homeless, stark reminders of the success and failure of place in America. Yet it is not as simple as these images suggest. The American Dream is not one of ease or self-interest. As articulated by James Truslow Adams in the midst of the depression, the American Dream is above all the world through the restless eyes of an immigrant; as such, it is a dream of family. As a collective vision, the Dream invites publics, not to forget struggle, but to clothe work and effort in the hopes for betterment in the next generation. As part of a first family, Reagan's own mixed family history allowed him purchase in the Dream—even with alcoholism, divorce, estrangement, and distance, the Reagans had risen.

Reagan's rhetoric succeeds not by virtue of its request to simplify or "forget" the particulars of American history. Americans can do that well enough on their own. Rather, it succeeds because the Dream releases family members from pain of loss caused by the economic displacements, change, and scattering over which there could be scant control. Reagan's rueful, self-critical humor shared the suffering and softened the sharper emotions of rage or despair. Using his edged wit to blame bureaucrats and politicians, he inscribed almost-human faces on the economic forces driving people from the family farm, small-town America, and whole regions of the industrial Midwest during the early 1980s.

Gradually, Reagan rhetoric transformed the Republican Party into the party of "family values" through extolling the ordinary heroism it takes to thrive in eras of change. "We have every right to dream heroic dreams," the president said in first inaugural. "Those who say that we're in a time when there are not heroes, they just don't know where to look." This dynastic vision of place celebrates and values the strength of the America family; it was the dynamic that made social conservatism go.[22]

The Dream was both more and less than a vision. While enticing Americans to share a rhetoric out of time, the Dream was also deployed strategically to wage controversy. In the domestic policy realm, the American Dream became translated into a preprogressive performance of the Gospel of Wealth that emphasized Reagan's public speaking as opinion and party leader, diminished the role of chief executive, and played off both adventitiously against the expectations of the president as a legislative leader. In foreign policy, the American Dream became translated into a performance of American exceptionalism that played the president's commander in chief obligations against his initiatives as chief diplomat. Reagan's speeches were rhetoric and reality enveloped in controversy.

THE PERSUADABLE PRESIDENT

Controversies surrounding Reagan played continuously for the length of the administration. Four examples are drawn from these debates and presented here to illustrate how grants of presidential legitimacy were sought by bargaining in the interests of pragmatic decision making. The disputes concerned how far Reagan would go in dismantling the New Deal, in satisfying the Moral Majority, in ignoring reigning standards of policy competence, and in confronting the Soviet Union. In the first two cases, I will show how Reagan was persuaded and used persuasion to adopt or frame a prudent stance in relation to political exigencies concerning welfare and the Moral Majority. In the second two examples, I will show how resources of *ingenium* were deployed inventively to redefine the landscapes on which prudential intelligence itself could be assessed in domestic and foreign policy.

Could Reagan be persuaded to maintain a social safety net should his philosophy of self-reliance not work for everyone?

Pursuit of the American Dream became the pretext in which government aid for the poor became recaptioned as "welfare dependency." "Cuts in discretionary domestic spending from 5.7 percent of the gross national product in 1981 to 3.7 percent in 1987 focused heavily on the poor. Education and training, community development, welfare, nutrition, housing assistance, and antipoverty programs were cut the most." There was more than enough blame for economic pain to go around, especially in the recession of the early 1980s. But if government was a cause rather than a solution to the problem, then the engine of capitalism alone could pull America out. As Richard Reeves writes: "The idea of Reaganism from the beginning was to change the political reflexes of a working majority of the nation, to get Americans to stop instinctively turning to government with their problems."[23]

The locus of controversy turned from concerns of the 1960s, such as whether or not poverty could be eliminated to what constituted a "safety net" for those who could not or would not produce labor.[24] Is ketchup a vegetable? How do we count homeless if they are not at home? What in-kind services do the poor really have? How do we get welfare cheats and bureaucrats off the tax roles? These questions constituted much of the social debate of the 1980s. The administration thus began to dismantle the Great Society's extension of social welfare, even while letting itself be persuaded that maintaining FDR-style entitlement programs was a necessary exception. The burden of recovery fell on those least able to afford it.[25] Although the inflexibility on social issues created an opportunity for the press to portray Reagan as cold and indifferent, the American Dream provided a center of warmth and a position from which the debate would center on give-and-take. As Matthew Kerbel concludes: Reagan "won a popular reputation as a likeable salesman, whose reluctance to bend on budget and tax issues could be written off to the admirable tendency to stand by long held beliefs" and his efforts were captioned that way.[26] In the end, compromise over tax increases in 1982 was explained not as the president moving from his principles, but instead that his advisers had persuaded him to satisfy critics in the interests of ending a political logjam. This is how presidential rhetoric could function both as ideological lever and political pragmatism at the same time within a consistent administration script.

Even while tax policy found compromise, the vocabulary of social welfare was turned upside down. The "needy" became the "greedy" when Reagan returned to nineteenth-century social theory that associated economic failure with sin, beginning the long argument that welfare was responsible for poverty because it encouraged dependency. On the other hand, "the greedy" became the "needy" when Reagan expanded the vision of the "common man" to encompass all people trying to provide for family in the face of taxes and government regulations—again, reversing field to a nineteenth-century view of the chief executive whose duties were limited to a nonprogressive understanding of the Constitution. In both cases, prudent federal action was defined from an inventional field secured by a discourse thought past. In both cases, a rhetoric out of time allowed Reagan to wage controversy in opposing and compromising with liberals.

Would Reagan be captured by the moral majority? Or could he be convinced to stray from his rhetoric in the interests of pragmatic politics?

Were rhetoric reality, the answer to the first question would have been an unequivocal yes. It is certain that Reagan put his verbal support behind neoconservatives and campaigned constantly against "the counterculture and moral laxity" of the '60s generation "claiming that hedonism, the pursuit of instant gratification, leads to selfishness, the abdication of responsibility and social instability." As Ritter and Henry report, in fact, Reagan's oratorical success itself "owes as much to his capacity to imbue secular political events and issues with the trappings of religious ritual." Indeed, so great was the success, that Foley concluded: "[T]he office may be in the process of becoming a necessarily ideological agency whose power and authority are becoming increasingly dependent upon the mobilizing force of national ideals, faiths and symbols."[27] It is also certain that Reagan mobilized Moral Majority rhetoric to polarize debate, attacking those who disagreed with his policies as "politically motivated, seeking to drag the dirt of politics into an issue that should be clear of any such taint." The rhetoric provided ample room for moral and economic conservatives to capitalize on "middle class resentments" left in the wake of Vietnam and the Great Society.[28]

Reagan's moral appeals were never more prominent than at election time, but his rhetoric shifted to economic priorities soon afterward. Although he continued to associate himself with "the New Christian Right crusade against abortion and for school prayer, Reagan did not throw the weight of the presidency behind the cause." To put it in a positive light, Burns notes that the Reagan coalition was able to unite the moral and the economic right by alternatively prioritizing the president's efforts at election and governing times. In this regard, Congress made a wonderful foil because the administration was never in a dominant position on Capitol Hill, so responsibility for barring the Moral Majority's agenda could always be fobbed off on the Democrats.[29]

Perhaps it was for this reason that many persuaded themselves that Reagan was "both an ideologue and a pragmatist."[30] After all, he was just an actor playing a role, and he could be expected to do what politicians do: compromise. The 1982 support of tax increases lent some support for this interpretation. More significantly, the gap between denunciations of federal spending and the growth of the federal deficits seemed to prove the point. Yet to discount Reagan as a compromiser is to miss the way even compromise was leveraged through controversy to continue to shift the terms of political debate. Indeed, one of the most remarkable features in Reagan's politics "is the extent to which he rationalized contradictory actions or denied responsibility for them."[31]

Reagan's rhetoric was hardest at work not in branding New Dealers, Fair Dealers and Great Society children with the "L" word. Rather, the challenge was to explain to conservatives his own compromises in the interest of government. Tactical explanation began early in his California career. In signing an abortion bill, he acceded to the liberals but insisted on a conservative provision; in signing an income tax increase, he insisted on a property tax cut.[32] In both cases, he could blame the liberals for undesirable policy, claim a minor victory that shows success, and express hope for the future. He asked his right-wing critics: "It is one thing to stand for something—and I do, and I know they do, also—but it's another thing to have to make a choice if you can't get all you want at once, when you are faced with hostility in at least one house of the legislature. Do you jump off the cliff with the flag flying and never get any of it, or do you say, 'O.K., I'll work as hard and get as much of a chunk as I can, and come back later and go for the rest of it'?" Overall, the tactical position was successful in both avoiding responsibility for logjams in Congress (at least in the first administration and the beginning of the second) and in sustaining belief in the Reagan Revolution. Harris found that "66 percent of the respondents in a survey . . . agreed. '[Reagan] is no ordinary politician because he really wants to cut federal spending and cut back the federal bureaucracy.'" Clearly, Reagan had a hierarchy of conservative issues that favored the economy first, as Martin Medhurst has observed, and clearly the reasons for delaying the social agenda could be laid at the door of Democratic obstructionism.[33]

In the second two examples, we turn from acute, contested political speech to illustrations of a different kind. It is well known that political leaders are feared for their power, but loved for their imperfections. The studied imperfections constitute a special manifestation of *ingenium*— fusing the wit of the speaker with the audience's playfulness. Such inventive play permits people to escape businesslike prudential reasoning, if only momentarily. At play is a wish for an uncommon common sense that triumphs over, or at least relieves, the workaday tedium of conventions, criticisms, and corrections. This *ingenium* may be captioned as a quality of a president's speaking, but it also inheres in the collective (sometimes strategically critical) support given by people who play along with moves of their own. First, the president, then the play.

Would Reagan be convinced to master the technical duties of the chief executive?

The answer was definitely no. "According to former Budget Director David Stockman, 'Ronald Reagan seemed as far above the detail work of supply side as a ceremonial monarch is above politics."[34] "He takes long vacations from the White House, leaves difficult matters requiring expertise to his aides, and goes home from the Oval Office after short days to his television set. He even, we learned during the campaign, occasionally falls asleep during Cabinet meetings." Reagan could delegate, and it was up to his staff to persuade him to take action. "No one could doubt either that his personal values dominated his administration or that his subordinates, far from manipulating him, labored to make administrative and policy sense out of his bundle of prejudices." To put this in the language of leadership studies, Reagan played up a transformational inspiration by playing down transactional definitions of competence as he "burned the mid-day oil."[35]

Gaffes that would have felled a dozen politicians bounced off the Gipper. The "Teflon president," a moniker given Reagan by Pat Schroeder, was a name spoken as much in awe as criticism. The press of the 1980s loved to find "erroneous statements" that were "palmed off as facts" by the president. Reagan used Rubik's Cube as an example of American free enterprise when its inventor was Hungarian; he confused a report of a Medal of Honor recipient with the movie *A Wing and a Prayer;* he introduced Sugar Ray Robinson's wife as Mrs. Ray; he referred to Liberia's president Samuel Doe as "Chairman Moe."[36] The White House tried to limit these minor storms by restricting press conferences. Stuart Spencer stopped Reagan from giving off the cuff answers and tried to "goof proof" his election. "This stabilized the campaign, although Reagan fell off the wagon at least one more time when he declared that trees, not industry or cars, caused most air pollution. The next day, during a Reagan speech at Claremont College, students hung signs on trees which read 'chop me down before I kill again.'"[37] Still goofs came. Much of the fascination came from "trying to decide whether Reagan's gaffes were deliberate distortions, conscious acts of deception, or simply evidence of ignorance of the subject."[38] That was the point.

Reagan's targets of delegitimation were bureaucrats of all stripes; technocratic competence, or even knowledge of detail, was not a value for a president. As Kathryn Olson has shown, his knowledge resided not in scientific or bureaucratic competence, but in a larger sense of purpose—articulating an American vision and playing a dramatic role. If a few facts were wrong or even if others were made up, it was the point, not the details, that mattered; and, the press's pointless, dogged nattering provided the show. The actor-president put caviling commentators in the position of either (1) not getting a joke, (2) not appreciating a performance, or (3) nastily insisting a small thing mattered when it did not. Eventually, "the White House staff came to realize that such lapses really didn't matter. . . . For example, Speaks breezily responded to a gaff: 'It made its point, didn't it?'" Even Arthur Schlesinger was forced to conclude: "the fact that he [Reagan] does not command or even comprehend the details of policy need not be of major political consequence."[39]

H. W. Brands has argued that Theodore Roosevelt was so revered by many Americans because his reckless courage and colorful exploits disrupted the spreading, gray conformity of the machine age.[40]

Reagan's shameless trumping of accusations—that he missed details transformed to signs of the small purpose on the part of his adversaries—plays a similar role. The president's befuddled cunning constitutes a charming release from the tedious prudential grids of the information age. With Reagan, the public outwits, for now, the demanding perfections of expert epistemics and restores an uncommon common sense. Nuclear weapons, however, offered quite a different story.

Could Reagan be convinced to continue detente with the Soviets? Could he be convinced by Gorbachev to accept the arms deal Reagan himself had proposed in the first administration?

The answers to these questions, although performed on a larger stage, nevertheless follow the pattern of "bargaining" characteristic of domestic policy debate. Ronald Reagan never entered the nuclear age. His foreign policy thinking seemed to be fixed on VE-Day, a moment of ascendant American power and nascent Soviet antagonism. The nuclear age itself had been created by world acknowledgment of the ineradicable existence of nuclear weapons, the inescapability of massive retaliation, and the eventual inevitably of war by madness, miscalculation, or accident. A balance of terror, mutually assured destruction, détente, a long twilight struggle bound by ideological antagonism, and shared interests in survival—these were the permanent and best conditions of the age. Reagan was not interested in peaceful coexistence, détente, or any other forms of "appeasement" or unilateral disarmament. He came to the presidency committed to just one thing: Roll back.

The world was a larger stage upon which the Reagan rhetoric played. On it, the American Dream was reconfigured as American exceptionalism—a language of special purpose, divine providence, and epochal destiny. At a dozen summits, the president practiced his rhetoric in places where visions soar and dangers lurk, from fickle domestic supporters to crafty allies and implacable foes. Ronald Reagan's anticommunism never wavered and at times rose to levels higher than his Cold War pro-Goldwater speech. Fortunately, such "Red or Dead" rhetoric never became social reality.

Interestingly, critics conclude that apocalyptic fears were outweighed by what became known as Reagan's "feel good" American optimism. Ritter and Henry explain: "From 1947 to 1965 Reagan developed the ability to speak to divergent audiences simultaneously. Even within a single speech, he could subtly shift the fundamental assumptions implied by his rhetoric, moving from the desperate prospect of a secular Armageddon to the reform motive of restoration rhetoric."[41] Anticommunism had long played a role in domestic politics, but the 1980s Cold War was not bound utterly to grim Cold War ideological struggle.[42] While the domestic side provided the affirmative moment, and balance, the appeal to ultimates could be discounted as "bargaining" within the context of international arms control talks. Peace-through-strength put the Soviets in the position of having to persuade the president to play in the rational dialectic of history. It also provided a rational interpretation for an otherwise mad script. In nuclear strategic doctrine there is even a desired place for a slightly crazy president. Who else could act out of sheer vengeance and push the button?

The early Reagan administration was controversial because it talked of winnable nuclear wars, warning shots, and postnuclear survival. In the argot of the day, new first-strike weapons technologies made war more winnable, hence more thinkable.[43] When the $1.5 trillion defense build-up was hooked up to a history of strident anti-Soviet denunciations, Reagan's friendly smile and charming lack of command of details—which had served him well in the domestic arena—became scary. The result was a divided discourse and a global-domestic political contest to capture and define weapons' deployments, procurements, and international summits as leading toward peace not war. The controversial style spawned a whole new peace movement at home to "freeze" nuclear weapons, just as in the domestic area the question became: Who, and under what conditions, could persuade the president to avoid the ultimate?

A single telling example illustrates how the rhetoric was mobilized. The speech followed on the heals of the nuclear-freeze movement, the "Evil Empire" speech, the "Star Wars" announcement, and three years of tempestuous negotiations with the Soviets. The incident occurred amid widespread newspaper reports that the gap between rich and poor was growing rapidly in Reagan's America and that the septuagenarian president himself was beginning to doze at cabinet meetings.

"My fellow Americans," Reagan said jokingly while doing a voice check prior to a radio address, "I'm pleased to tell you today that I've signed legislation that will outlaw Russia forever. We begin bombing in five minutes."

What had been charming errors in domestic matters became something else entirely when displayed on the world stage.

The foreign press went wild. West Germany's Social Democratic
Party stated: "'The lord over life or combustion of all Western Europe
. . . is obviously an irresponsible old man, who gets grinning pleasure
from the action element of mass destruction and who probably can no
longer distinguish whether he is making a horror movie or commanding a superpower.'"[44] The Soviet news agency TASS, recalling that his
aides had talked about warning shots and winnable wars, reported that
"there was no doubt that Reagan's joking remarks would be seen as
the 'proof of the fact that his hypocritical speculation' about improv-
ing relations with the Soviet Union and seeking arms-control agreement was simply intended to 'camouflage' his intentions."[45] On page
one, *Le Monde* "suggested that it would take a battery of psychologists
to shed any light on the subconscious significance—if any—of President Ronald Reagan's grotesquely playful remark," calling the bombing wish either an "expression of repressed desire or the exorcism of a
dreaded phantom."[46]

The domestic press had a term for such a moment in presidential
rhetoric, too. It was called a "gaffe." Democratic sources underplayed
the mistake with mild criticism. "I don't think it is very funny," weighed
in presidential contender Walter Mondale. Many newspapers called
the pre-speech warm-up a mistake in judgment and then went on to
explain how television reporters are not bound by the same rules as
print reporters. Most blamed the press for taking the joke out of proportion. Others saw recompense in the remark. "[I]t is refreshing, in a
way, to know that the president is not so dour that he can't laugh. He
was probably doing a satire on himself, or on some public perception
of what he's like," *The Forum* editorialized. Only Gary Hart tried to make
hay: "Maybe it's the early stress of the national election. It could be
that he's not getting enough vacation time. Who knows? Or, on the
other hand, more frightening perhaps, it's in moments of that sort that
his real feelings come out." Other Republicans reported they were glad
they had a tough bargainer in command and it was time the Soviets
watched their own bellicose rhetoric.[47]

Just as Reagan's domestic gaffes were reconfigured by controversy
to serve the interests of the presidency, so this foreign policy error reinforced a productive frame for the president. The bombing "joke" (not
revelation, wish, phantom, or fantasy) became at worst a mistake and

at best a further reason for the Soviets to be highly motivated to reduce confrontation with the United States. There seemed to be a tacit agreement among U.S. commentators not to allow themselves to be played into a hypercritical affiliation with the foreign press, and so commentary found a milder range of collective invention, leaving the president and American presidency little the worse for wear on this occasion.

"Peace through strength" rhetoric—a rich, mix of ambiguously tough and tender speech acts—fabricated ways to convince Americans that Reagan embraced the shared goals of avoiding nuclear war and that a nuclear weapons buildup was needed to reach a point where stockpiles could be frozen at mutual and verifiable levels. Unfortunately for the administration, the public controversy necessary to build defense budgets and sustain rollback on the nonnuclear–foreign policy side set a scene for covert operations that ended up in Iran-Contra, an episode that pushed controversy over into the contemporary politics of fragmentation.[48]

In sum, Reagan's domestic and foreign policy rhetorics were characterized by strategic controversy. Reagan reversed the terms of the social welfare debate by taking the New Deal opposition between the common man and the wealthy and turning the "plutocrats" into bureaucrats who were blind to the American Dream. When inconsistencies between radical rhetoric and political compromise arose, he dumped blame for government deficits onto the "tax and spend" liberals who would not cut government programs enough, called for the line-item veto, and collected compromises without concession—at least on his own part. Leadership is relative to opposition. Hugh Heclo surmises that the strategy was successful in large part because "the articulate portions of the Democratic party seemed dumbstruck in the face of events, unwilling to retreat on the New Deal–Fair Deal–Great Society commitments or to go forward toward some more social democratic vision of an egalitarian, solidaristic order."[49] Democratic Congresses never seemed to quite catch on. Reagan rhetoric both sustained ideology and pragmatism because each compromise was never a concession, an effort to appease, or a cooperative reality construction. Rather, compromise was always captioned as an aggressive strategy to sustain by public argument a challenge to the definition of legitimate governmental action.

On the foreign policy side, the American Dream became translated into American exceptionalism, a place where scientific competence at arms control was not as important as announcements of national purpose drawn from another historic field of invention, prenuclear international politics. Before 1945, world wars were winnable and the "arsenal of democracy" defensible. The Democrats did mount a more successful opposition in this area, but the nuclear-freeze campaign would ultimately be turned to serve the interests of the administration, which claimed to increase the chances of peace by building up the weapons of war. A $1.5 trillion defense buildup was inspiration enough for the language of *glasnost* and *peristroika* to be spoken by Russians who wooed Reagan avidly throughout his second administration.[50]

Conclusion

Studies in the American presidency nowadays share a common premise: "The effectiveness of a president's leadership in the late twentieth century depends heavily on his persuasive abilities." However, within this consensus is a deeply fractured view of the meaning and significance of "going public." On one side, rhetoric is held to be a matter of skill and organized image manipulation. Presidential speech is a policy supplement to constitutional government necessitated by the exigencies of the media age. Perhaps Fred Greenstein put this view most bluntly: "[O]ratory without results is as dead as faith without works." In contrast, other scholars hold that rhetoric is reality—a matter of linguistic definition and symbolic inducement in the social construction of elite and public beliefs. Each side would leave us with very different conclusions about the Reagan administration.[51]

For supplementarians, presidents need persuasive skill because the Constitution is an imperfect document with ambiguous or imperfect legal authority.[52] Public opinion leadership requires adaptation of policy to the public through "simplification."[53] A president who goes over the heads of Congress may do so for good reasons or bad, but the extraconstitutional action is always dangerous. If modern conditions have made popular appeal a lamentable necessity, however, the more skilled a president the better.

There are dangers to these habit-forming acts of public persuasion, however. Rhetoric leads presidents (a) to avoid difficult decisions and pander to the public, (b) to overpromise and cause disillusion, (c) to create differential expectations and polarize parties, (d) to reduce concern for issues and overemphasize staging and spin, or (e) to fail at crucial times, thus weakening the presidency itself.[54] As Edwards and Wayne put it: "The problem is with the system, particularly its constitutional, institutional, and political structures. The Constitution divides authority; institutions share power; and parties lack cohesion and often a sustained ideological thrust."[55]

The view of presidential persuasion as a necessary evil would give Reagan high marks as an actor and point out his skills in delivery, voice modulation, posture and gesture—even should the speeches be found light on content or performances overestimated and successful only by virtue of staff preparation and spin. This conclusion, however, leaves the puzzle of why there have not been a string of professional actor-presidents; or why successful presidents have not always been great speakers. Nor does it explain the self-referential quality of "acting" itself as part of a persona deployed to build support and discount opposition.

For social constructivists, a president communicates a vision, and Reagan *was* the Great Communicator. "Today, as never before, presidents want not only to please the public and avoid irritating them" Denton and Hahn report. Presidential power "is derived from the public's identification with presidential representations of reality," Kiewe concludes. The Smiths identify the dimensions of this reality in pointing out that: "To study presidential communication is, therefore, to study the ways in which presidents use the resources of laws, language, logic, and ideology to lead." Constructivism includes more than mere ingratiation for the Smiths. They observe that the many interpretative communities engage in a "struggle" to impose definitions of social reality.[56] Yet these definitions once again contain anomalies in explaining the Reagan administration, which rather than pleasing everyone seemed instead to deliberately provoke controversy. For the many, many controversies of the Reagan years, success appeared not so much to depend upon "reality" construction, but upon taking advantages of controversies *within* as much as *between* interpretative communities. The constructivist position does not take into consideration that discounting, not belief, sometimes plays the larger role in the public's reception of politics.

To be sure, presidential leadership depends upon persuasion that requires speaking skills; and presidential words and deeds *do* have consequences for the symbolic milieu within which different groups and activities become defined. However, at base presidential leadership is neither sheer instrumental persuasion nor symbolic inducement. Rather, presidential persuasion is an irreducible civic discourse, a public argument invested in an ongoing disagreement over distributions of duties and authority among the presidency, Congress and the judiciary, among opposing political parties, between national and local interests, between mainstream constituencies which embrace incremental political adjustments and ideological visionaries and movements, and between the United States and its foreign adversaries and allies. William Lammers observes that: "The proper role for the Presidency in American politics has long been in dispute." Contestation is an inherent, not accidental, feature coded by discursive practices into presidential leadership precisely because the checks and balances, separation and sharing of power, are riven throughout Constitutional government. Moreover "divided party control of government at the federal level has been the norm in modern U.S. politics."[57] Therefore, all evaluations of a presidency are not politically neutral and cannot help but be part of the very discourse over the proper role of democratic influence that constitutes the historic constitutional experiment. Within this context, I draw three orders of conclusion.

First, the Reagan presidency challenges scholars to reconnect studies of presidential influence with traditions that lend insight into civic discourses, including classical rhetorical traditions. The reason contextual study is important is that without understanding the codes—the ways public argument has been enacted within historic institutional contexts—scholars are likely to be drawn into replicating, without explicating, civic discourse. For example, Roderick Hart observes that rhetoric in classical times was taught to facilitate deliberation and statecraft. Since Gerald Ford onward, he says, "[p]residential speech has become so plentiful and so strategic that it has become almost pure performance. The self-checking process of public argument envisioned by the ancients is now a parody of dialectical give-and-take." Hart's strong assertion of republican virtue offers a vigorous declinist critique of how politicians persuade, but in being persuaded we need turn to a different moment of the classical tradition.[58]

A new, nondeliberatively oriented rhetoric became the rage after the republic in the nascent Roman imperium. Everyone was doing it, even the emperor. This rhetoric involved declamation aimed at speaking to an issue of choice (resembling the old rhetoric), but the crises that once evoked deliberation turned more on display, self-expression, and release than labored prudence. The disputed cases mixed history, fiction and myth to provide a strange attractor for argument. The positions involved well-known repetitive *divisions* of issues spectacularly presented. The performances featured *colores* or interpretations spun to favor one's own side and characterize opponents as misinformed, foolish, or worse. Speech emphasized the *sententiae*, the witty phrase or "sound bites" in sandals. The New Rhetoric of the imperium was the *controversia*.[59]

Analogically, then, the controversial Reagan administration was an imperial presidency, Republican style. Reagan enacted rhetorical resources available to U.S. presidents since the inception of the Constitution when the office was occupied by George Washington, the American Cincinnatus and first American leader who was not-quite-king. Not merely a "drama of courtiers circulating around the king"— although it was at times every bit of that—Reagan policy coursed powerfully on the most ancient lines of challenge to republican government itself and so cannot be dismissed easily as a matter of peculiar "manners," or the manners were of deeper significance to democratic practice than can be assumed at first glance.[60]

To appraise a rhetoric of personage, hierarchy, circulating commentary, and ancestral duty—a rhetoric out of time—leadership studies need to reanalyze how "controversy" operates within the history of constitutional government where the president is both a democratic leader and a not-quite-king. The pragmatic leader persuades through deliberation and its variations to get elite and public constituencies to do the right and prudent thing. The not-quite-king leads as an anointed figure whose motives, intentions, and beliefs center interpretative political controversy. For the former, political address stands as an open invitation to criticism within prudential norms; for the latter, public criticism must be defended as proper and redeemed against affiliation with greater purpose secured in a generative mix of personal and public memory and imagination. In the acts of an administration the relationship between prudence and *ingenium*, between what a president "does" and "is" laminates onto the contemporary political scene a (re)newed decorum which itself leaves an enduring model for reading and reinventing political practice. The model continues to unfold, even after the "end" of an administration. Thus, observation number two.

Second, the Reagan administration invites examination of the consequences of the presidency in the contexts of a national discourse—an ongoing debate over the terms of politics and society. Isocrates would have us examine the relationships between the general and particular as a field of political invention. In this regard, the legacy of the 1980s is mixed for party and politics.

Undeniably, Reagan's strategic vision grounded a comeback for the Republican Party that was sustained by the Bush administration, then surged forward in an angry populism, reached its peak in the "Contract with America," and receded after the bombing in Oklahoma City. It seems that while most members of the public could discount populist fire as a bargaining strategy, a few were out in the boonies living the dream. More broadly, Reagan's efforts to exploit, rather than cement, an alliance between the economic and moral right left Republicans in a strategically vulnerable position. New Democrats moved in on the economic side and left Republican "extremists" beholding to the Moral Majority—which, it seems, was not a majority not after all.

For Democrats, the deficit issue provided a route back to the center. But to do this, New Democrats abandoned or disguised the party's twentieth-century heritage of social activism. The failure to sell a national health-care policy suggests that disguise holds little surprise for the ever-vigilant, who see the welfare state haunting any and all federal policy. Further to the Left, 1990s-style liberal movements embraced the politics of victimization—perhaps a legacy of the Carter years. The results are not beneficial for everyone. As Michael Schaller summarizes: "The [Reagan] administration's approach to a variety of social problems, such as teenage pregnancy, drug abuse, and AIDS remained essentially negative. Teenagers were urged to remain chaste, ghetto youth to 'just say no to drugs,' and everyone cautioned to be monogamous and heterosexual to avoid disease. The result, not surprisingly, was a surge in the teenage pregnancy rate, a drug scourge among poor and minority youth, and the rapid spread of AIDS. Meanwhile, the prison inmate population doubled and the homeless emerged as a national scandal."[61] Americans eventually will have to recover, if not reinvent, visions of a Greater Society—or else face the consequences of diminished social justice.

Third, the Reagan administration itself is a metaphor, a way to conceptualize and imagine cultural practice as a window into the contested formation of "American" self-understanding and identity.[62] In this respect, Reagan both expanded and contracted the public sphere. Since the 1980s, talk-show populists and book-deal "revolutionaries" have tried to out-Reagan Reagan by upping the heat and souring the humor. The campaign industry has transformed Reagan's delegitimating barbs into expensive, biannual avalanches of cutely cynical negative advertising. Continuing delegitimation battles have taken a heavy toll on the public sphere—fueling the general attitude of skepticism toward public institutions characterizing the 1990s.

The modern Right has no monopoly on incivility, of course. Reaganism could be viewed as a complement to the strong ideological fare of the 1960s. Of course, such antideliberative rhetorics, albeit in different forms, continued to be the rage even toward the century's end. For example, the Clinton administration's efforts to ignite "volunteerism" and the Republican governors' post-1998 election efforts to address policy alike were ignored largely in lieu of wringing the last ratings spike from the Clinton-Lewinski scandal. The media's and Washington's obsession with elected officials' sex lives suggests that ideological struggle may be invested in a virulent politics of the personal among elites—even as *public rejection* of this aristocratic plot of televisual senatorial assassinations appears for the moment to have restored some sense. Still, by making a court of Congress and the "person" of the politician the prevailing locus of mystery and dispute, the nation's politics-for-now moved from the "permanent campaign" to the "permanent controversy."

Interestingly, all parties decry this fix, but all agree that such titanic controversy is inevitable. For those who remember their classical rhetoric, it may be recalled that leadership scandals like these signaled the devolution of the rhetoric of imperium. Rhetorical outcomes are not inevitable, though, and criticism may yet reshape the political. Toward that goal, the controversies of the 1980s deserve understanding and appraisal on their own grounds.

In the end, the Reagan administration was a rhetoric out of time. The past anchored Reagan's inventional field of leadership. The immigrant ever-moving West and GIs triumphant in Europe constituted defining experiences, from whose lessons domestic and foreign policy advocates would stray at their own hazard. In this regard, the Great Society and detente were but mutable political presents which the citizen-actor and the citizen-governor never entered. The secret of Reagan's rhetoric is that he waited for the times to come to him, rather than adapting to the moment, and then mobilized his talents, experience, and staff to animate a national discourse by performing the presidency.

As citizen-president, Reagan forwarded the aspirations of the immigrant family, in its connections with generations past, to diminish consensus over the present field of policy options, thereby refashioning a future for the American people. The rhetoric is both a reality construction and a bargaining position simultaneously. The leadership stance was a powerful, even unique achievement. David Mervin concludes that, although the administration did not rise to the level of consequence equal to its rhetoric, Reagan did bring "about a change in the terms of debate with regard to both foreign and domestic policy, revitalized the office of chief executive and made possible his replacement by a candidate of his party. No one but Roosevelt among modern presidents could claim a comparable record." No one but Reagan could so fuse, for a time, Hollywood, Washington, and the American Dream.[63]

NOTES

1. George C. Edwards III, *The Public Presidency: The Pursuit of Popular Support* (New York: St. Martin's, 1983), 69.

2. John Orman, *Comparing Presidential Behavior: Carter, Reagan, and the Macho Presidential Style* (New York: Greenwood Press, 1987), 16.

3. Larry Berman, ed., *Looking Back on the Reagan Presidency* (Baltimore, Md.: Johns Hopkins University Press, 1990), 7.

4. Terry L. Deibel, *Presidents, Public Opinion and Power: The Nixon, Carter and Reagan Years*, Headline Series no. 280 (New York: Foreign Policy Association, 1987), 49; Garry Wills, *Reagan's America: Innocents at Home* (Garden City, N.Y.: Doubleday, 1987), 385.

5. Aaron Wildavsky, "President Reagan as a Political Strategist," in *The Reagan Legacy: Promise and Performance*, ed. Charles O. Jones (Chatham, N.J.: Chatham House, 1988), 3. See also David Mervin, *Ronald Reagan and the American Presidency* (New York: Longman, 1990), 96.

6. William E. Pemberton, *Exit with Honor: The Life and Presidency of Ronald Reagan* (New York: M. E. Sharpe, 1997), 198, 202; Schlesinger quoted in T. E. Mann, "Thinking about the Reagan Years," in Berman, ed., *Looking Back*, 20.

7. Michael Foley, "Presidential Leadership and the Presidency," in *The Reagan Years: The Record in Presidential Leadership*, ed. Joseph Hogan (Manchester: Manchester University Press, 1990), 38. See also Fred I. Greenstein, "Reagan and the Lure of the Modern Presidency: What Have We Learned?" in *The Reagan Presidency: An Early Assessment*, ed. Fred I. Greenstein (Baltimore: Johns Hopkins University Press, 1983), 158–76.

8. Richard E. Neustadt, *Presidential Power and the Modern Presidents: The Politics of Leadership from Roosevelt to Reagan* (New York: Macmillan, 1980), xiii.

9. Ibid., 40.

10. Raymond Tatalovich and Byron W. Daynes, "Toward a Framework to Explain Presidential Power," in *The American Presidency: Historical and Contemporary Perspectives*, ed. Harry A. Bailey, Jr., and Jay M. Shafritz (Pacific Grove, Calif.: Brooks/Cole, 1988), 438–51.

11. Craig A. Smith and Kathy B. Smith, *The White House Speaks: Presidential Leadership as Persuasion* (Westport, Conn.: Praeger, 1994), 3.

12. Ronald W. Reagan with Richard G. Hubler, *Where's the Rest of Me?* (New York: Duell, Sloan, and Pearce, 1965), 302; Broder quoted in Michael Schaller, *Reckoning with Reagan: America and Its President in the 1980s* (New York: Oxford University Press, 1992), 12.

13. Kurt Ritter and David Henry, *Ronald Reagan: The Great Communicator* (New York: Greenwood Press, 1992), 118.

14. Ronald W. Reagan, *Speaking My Mind: The Public Speeches of Ronald Reagan* (New York: Simon and Schuster, 1987), 36. See also Schaller, *Reckoning with Reagan*, 12.

15. Paul D. Erickson, *Reagan Speaks: The Making of an American Myth* (New York: New York University Press, 1985), 30.

16. James MacGregor Burns, *The Power to Lead* (New York: Simon and Schuster, 1984), 56. See also Mary E. Stuckey, *Getting into the Game: The Pre-Presidential Rhetoric of Ronald Reagan* (New York: Praeger, 1989).

17. Robert Dallek, *Ronald Reagan: The Politics of Symbolism* (Cambridge, Mass.: Harvard University Press, 1984), 32; Stuckey, *Getting into the Game*, 13; Burns, *Power to Lead*, 45.

18. Giambattista Vico, *On the Most Ancient Wisdom of the Italians: Unearthed from the origins of the Latin Language*, ed. and trans. Lucia M. Palmer (Ithaca: Cornell University Press, 1988), 161–62; Michael Mooney, *Vico in the Tradition of Rhetoric* (Princeton, N.J.: Princeton University Press), 135–58.

19. Berman, ed., *Looking Back*, 7.

20. John K. White, *The New Politics of Old Values* (London: University Press of England, 1988), 36. See also Berman, ed., *Looking Back*, 9; Hugh Heclo, "Reaganism and the Search for a Public Philosophy," in *Perspectives on the Reagan Years*, ed. John L. Palmer (Washington, D.C.: Urban Institute Press), 42.

21. Jane Blankenship, Marlene G. Fine, and Leslie Smith, "The 1980 Republican Primary: The Transformation of Actor-Scene," *Quarterly Journal of Speech* 69 (Feb., 1983): 25–36; Mary E. Stuckey, *Playing the Game: The Presidential Rhetoric of Ronald Reagan* (New York: Praeger, 1990), 4; Pemberton, *Exit with Honor*, 204.

22. Bob Schieffer and Gary Paul Gates, *The Acting President* (New York: E. P. Dutton, 1989), 171; Ronald R. Reagan, "Inaugural Address, Jan. 20, 1981," in *Public Papers of the Presidents of the United States*, book 1, *Ronald Reagan* (Washington, D.C.: GPO, 1982), 2; Heclo, "Reaganism," 44.

23. Berman, ed., *Looking Back*, 7; Richard Reeves, *The Reagan Detour* (New York: Simon and Schuster, 1985), 22.

24. David Zarefsky, C. Miller-Tutzauer, and Frank E. Tutzauer, "Reagan's Safety

Net for the Truly Needy: The Rhetorical Use of Definition," *Central States Speech Journal* 35 (summer, 1984): 113–19.

25. Foley, "Presidential Leadership," 35; White, *New Politics*, 38.

26. Matthew R. Kerbel, *Beyond Persuasion: Organizational Efficiency and Presidential Power* (New York: State University of New York Press, 1991), 48.

27. Nigel Ashford, "A New Public Philosophy," in *Reagan's First Four Years: A New Beginning?* ed. John D. Lees and Michael Turner (Manchester: Manchester University Press, 1988), 9; Ritter and Henry, *Ronald Reagan*, 5; Foley, "Presidential Leadership," 47.

28. Stuckey, *Playing the Game*, 16; Dallek, *Ronald Reagan*, 57.

29. Jeff Fishel, *Presidents and Promises: From Campaign Pledge to Presidential Performance* (Washington, D.C.: Congressional Quarterly Press, 1985), 170; Foley, "Presidential Leadership," 40; Mann, *Thinking about the Reagan Years*, 21.

30. Richard P. Nathan, "Institutional Change under Reagan," in Palmer, ed., *Perspectives on the Reagan Years*, 124; Smith and Smith, *White House Speaks*, 159; Amos Kiewe and Davis W. Houck, *A Shining City on a Hill: Ronald Reagan's Economic Rhetoric, 1951–1989* (New York: Praeger, 1991), 252.

31. Arthur M. Schlesinger Jr., *The Imperial Presidency* (Boston: Houghton Mifflin, 1989), 439; Dallek, *Ronald Reagan*, 53.

32. Dallek, *Ronald Reagan*, 65.

33. Burns, *Power to Lead*, 67; White, *New Politics*, 54; Martin J. Medhurst, "Postponing the Social Agenda: Reagan's Strategy and Tactics," *Western Journal of Speech Communication* 48 (summer, 1984): 262–63.

34. Berman, ed., *Looking Back*, 5.

35. Erickson, *Reagan Speaks*, 117; Schlesinger, *Imperial Presidency*, 438; Bert A. Rockman, *The Leadership Question: The Presidency and the American System* (Westport, Conn.: Praeger, 1984).

36. Berman, ed., *Looking Back*, 5.

37. Schaller, *Reckoning with Reagan*, 29.

38. Schieffer and Gates, *Acting President*, 175.

39. Ibid., 181; Schlesinger, *Imperial Presidency*, 438; Kathryn M. Olson, "The Controversy over President Reagan's Visit to Bitburg: Strategies of Definition and Redefinition," *Quarterly Journal of Speech* 75 (May, 1989): 129–51.

40. H. W. Brands, *TR: The Last Romantic* (New York: Basic Books, 1997).

41. Ritter and Henry, *Ronald Reagan*, 28.

42. David E. Green, *Shaping Political Consciousness: The Language of Politics in America from McKinley to Reagan* (Ithaca, N.Y.: Cornell University Press, 1987), 269.

43. Robert Scheer, *With Enough Shovels: Reagan, Bush and Nuclear War* (New York: Random House, 1982); Richard Smoke, *National Security and the Nuclear Dilemma: An Introduction to the American Experience* (Reading, Mass.: Addison-Wesley, 1984).

44. "U.S.-Soviet Relations: Reagan Joke during Radio Voice Check Ill-Received," in *Editorials on File* (New York: Facts on File, 1984), 889.

45. Dusko Doder, "President said to voice 'his secret dream': Moscow calls Reagan's quip 'self-revealing'," *Washington Post*, Aug. 15, 1984, A26.

46. Editorial, *Newsday*, in *Editorials on File*, 886.

47. Editorial, *The Forum*, in *Editorials on File*, 885; Paul Taylor, "Mondale Says President's Joke Wasn't Fully: Reagan's Ad-Lib on Bombing Gives His Foes Ammunition," *Washington Post*, Aug. 14, 1984, A6.

48. G. Thomas Goodnight, "Reagan, Vietnam, and Central America: Public Memory and the Politics of Fragmentation," in *Beyond the Rhetorical Presidency*, ed. Martin J. Medhurst (College Station: Texas A&M University Press, 1996).

49. Heclo, "Reaganism," 39.

50. G. Thomas Goodnight, "Rhetoric, Legitimation, and the End of the Cold War: Ronald Reagan at the Moscow Summit, 1988," in *Reagan and Public Discourse in American*, ed. Michael Weiler and W. Barnett Pearce (Tuscaloosa: University of Alabama Press, 1992).

51. Smith and Smith, *White House Speaks*, 16; Fred I. Greenstein, "The Reagan Personality," in *American Presidency*, ed. Bailey and Shafritz, 414.

52. See, for example, Pendleton Herring, *Presidential Leadership: The Political Relations of Congress and the Chief Executive* (New York: Farrar and Rinehart, 1940); Colin Seymour-Ure, *The American President: Power and Communication* (New York: St. Martin's, 1982); Samuel Kernell, *Going Public: New Strategies of Presidential Leadership*, 2d ed. (Washington, D.C.: Congressional Quarterly Press, 1993); Theodore J. Lowi, *The Personal President: Power Invested, Promise Unfulfilled* (Ithaca: Cornell University Press, 1985); Clinton Rossiter, "The Presidency: Focus of Leadership," in *Perspectives on the Presidency*, ed. Stanley Bach and George T. Sulzner (Lexington, Mass.: D. C. Heath, 1974); Jeffrey K. Tulis, *The Rhetorical Presidency* (Princeton, N.J.: Princeton University Press, 1987); Tatalovich and Daynes, "Toward a Framework to Explain Presidential Power," 449; James W. Ceaser, Glen E. Thurow, Jeffrey Tulis, and Joseph M. Bessette, "The Rise of the Rhetorical Presidency," *Presidential Studies Quarterly* 11, no. 2 (spring, 1981): 158–71.

53. Edwards, *Public Presidency*, 71.

54. Ibid., 42; Thomas E. Cronin, "The Presidency and Its Paradoxes," in *The Presidency Reappraised*, 2d ed., ed. Thomas E. Cronin and R. G. Tugwell (New York: Praeger, 1977), 74; Kernell, *Going Public*, 4.

55. George C. Edwards III and Stephen J. Wayne, *Presidential Leadership: Politics and Policy Making* (New York: St. Martin's, 1985), 1.

56. Robert E. Denton and Dan F. Hahn, *Presidential Communication: Description and Analysis* (Westport, Conn.: Praeger, 1986), 8; Amos Kiewe, ed., *The Modern Presidency and Crisis Rhetoric* (Westport, Conn.: Praeger, 1994), xvi; Smith and Smith, *White House Speaks*, 51.

57. William W. Lammers, *Presidential Politics: Patterns and Prospects* (New York: Harper and Row, 1976), 4; James A. Thurber, ed., *Rivals for Power: Presidential-Congressional Relations* (Washington, D.C.: Congressional Quarterly Press, 1996), 7.

58. Roderick P. Hart, *The Sound of Leadership: Presidential Communication in the Modern Age* (Chicago: University of Chicago Press, 1987), 201.

59. George A. Kennedy, *The Art of Rhetoric in the Roman World, 300 B.C.–A.D. 300*

(Princeton, N.J.: Princeton University Press, 1972), 323–26; A. F. Sochatoff, "Basic Rhetorical Theories of the Elder Seneca," *The Classical Journal* 34 (Mar., 1939): 345–54.

60. Robert Hariman, *Political Style: The Artistry of Power* (Chicago: University of Chicago Press, 1995), 93.

61. Schaller, *Reckoning with Reagan*, 180.

62. David Ray Griffin and Richard Falk, eds., *Postmodern Politics for a Planet in Crisis: Policy, Process, and Presidential Vision* (New York: State University of New York Press, 1993).

63. Mervin, *Ronald Reagan*, 215.

CHAPTER 10

Cunning, Rhetoric, and the Presidency of William Jefferson Clinton

John M. Murphy

N JANUARY 14, 1960, Sen. John F. Kennedy stood before the National Press Club and proclaimed, "The history
of this nation—its brightest and its bleakest pages—has
been written largely in terms of the different views our Presidents have
had of the Presidency itself." Citing Jefferson, Lincoln, Wilson, and
the two Roosevelts, he exalted the presidency and said that it must
become "the vital center of action in our whole scheme of government."[1] Perhaps more fascinating than the speech was the reaction.
James Reston praised Kennedy's scorn for riding "the current popular
waves of illusion."[2] *Newsweek* called the speech "bold and audacious,"[3]
and Richard Strout of the *New Republic* granted the "slight, boyish,

patrician figure" the highest praise a liberal could give: "Kennedy's style oddly recalled FDR."[4]

The resemblance was neither odd nor accidental. We should not attribute the nearly ecstatic reaction solely to Kennedy's eloquence. This era witnessed a confluence of forces extolling the presidency, a romantic impulse that remains within us today.[5] From Richard Neustadt's *Presidential Power* to Kennedy's rhetoric, from Arthur M. Schlesinger Jr.'s account of the Roosevelt presidency to Theodore H. White's *The Making of the President, 1960*, academicians and politicians "discovered" that the key to presidential success rested in the president's "zest for power," his "joy for the office," and his willingness "to be as big a man as he can." Whether due to the Cold War, the ennui of the fifties, or the model provided by "James Arness as Marshal Matt Dillon," Americans longed for a hero. John Kennedy read the public mood.

He might well have read the current public mood. We speak of a more cynical time, but with a few exceptions, Senator Kennedy has set the research program for studies of presidential rhetoric: George Washington, Thomas Jefferson, Abraham Lincoln, Theodore Roosevelt, Franklin Roosevelt . . . Bill Clinton. One of these things is not like the other. As a student of mine plaintively wrote: "How can a man lie multiple times, cheat on his wife, commit perjury, and become one of the most popular presidents of recent history?"

Therein lies the rub. How indeed? The romantic longing for heroic presidents cannot explain Bill Clinton. Popular accounts of his survival sound notes of awe and wonder, despair and disgust. In the view of some commentators, call them the Merlin school, the president casts spells in ways that leave them straining for metaphors. *Time* magazine: "Like a weasel, Bill Clinton emerges from the drainpipe shinier than when he went in."[6] Jonathan Alter claims that Clinton has become "the Gipper" by developing "a relaxed Reagan-like mastery over political set-pieces."[7] *Newsweek* proclaimed on January 25, 1999, that the president was, in effect, defying nature by "Basking Under a Cloud."

Magic, of course, is just another word for seduction, and there are those, known now as the neo-Puritans, who rail against this president's corruption of the American people. Led by William "Where is the Outrage" Bennett, the criticism of Clinton has crossed into the land of self-caricature and hatred, revealed nicely by the January, 1999, issue of *Commentary* magazine. In a special forum, pundits proclaim that we are becoming a "society of libertines" (Robert Bartley), as we embrace "moral rot, decadence, relativism disguised as sophistication, [and] 'enlightened' liberalism" (William Bennett), as well as a "depressing sexual and cultural shambles" (Midge Decter), due to a "Clintonism" that "specifically exempts one sphere of life from all moral judgments: sex" (William Kristol). Clintonism results from "the various cultural viruses let loose in the '60s [that] have by now infected the American people as a whole" (Norman Podhoretz). The metaphor of Clinton as AIDS proves well nigh irresistible to these conservatives. William F. Buckley notes darkly that the stakes of the Clinton debate include "the expansion of gay rights to the point of subverting natural liaisons." This, of the president who signed the Defense of Marriage Act—and that president should reflect upon the fact that his signature was no protection; they eventually came for him. As we "degenerate" (William Kristol), the virus spreads. Clinton's popularity is the sexually transmitted disease of the body politic.[8]

The realists have little use for purple prose. They point to a booming economy, a happy electorate, and most important, the lemming-like desire of the aforementioned conservatives to hurl themselves off political cliffs. *Newsweek* entitled an article "With Foes Like These," and said the president, "always lucky in his enemies," reigns as "the consummate campaigner of his generation."[9] Joe Klein writes, "he has been truly blessed among politicians, blessed by the nature of his opposition . . . (it is as if Muhammad Ali never had to fight anyone more taxing than Jerry Quarry)."[10] Margaret Carlson explains that we "all have a little Clinton inside us," but notes tartly, "those who hate Clinton the most seem to have more than the average share of him inside them, which may be one reason why spittle forms at the corners of Representative Bob Barr's mouth when he talks about the President."[11] These are not attractive people, but good politicians, like good generals, always seem lucky in their enemies. One suspects that they craft their own enemies.

As a relatively old-fashioned rhetorical critic, then, I turn to the ways in which Bill Clinton crafts his friends and enemies—to his political context and to the texts that select, reflect, and deflect that context. I argue that the surest interpretive route into the kaleidoscopic Clinton lexicon is to embrace its protean character. Paradoxically, the one unchanging element in Clinton's oratory is its mutability—his ability to shift political positions, to change primary colors, and to steal the Republicans' fire even as he gives them a bipartisan Trojan horse.

My allusions are no accident. Marcel Detienne and Jean-Pierre Vernant point to Prometheus and Odysseus as exemplars of *metis*, of *Cunning Intelligence in Greek Culture and Society*.[12] This "way of knowing," they contend, flows through the "skills of a basket-maker, of a weaver, of a carpenter, the mastery of a navigator, the flair of a politician, the experienced eye of a doctor, the tricks of a crafty character such as Odysseus, the back-tracking of a fox and the polymorphism of an octopus, the solving of enigmas and riddles and the beguiling rhetorical illusionism of the sophists."[13] This lovely iconic rendering of *metis* gives us a glimpse into its character—it is a wily and expansive sort of intelligence. Like the octopus, Clinton embraces the political landscape. To understand such rhetorical leadership, we must begin with that landscape. I then turn to the rhetorical cunning that marks the president's performances and conclude by musing upon his tendency to focus on particular acts rather than mythic ends, on multiple identities rather than a heroic role, and on ideological flexibility rather than political dogma. I suggest that the president's way of knowing accounts at least partly for his popularity and his leadership; friends and enemies alike identify with and model their words upon the *metis* of William Jefferson Clinton.

THE NOVELIZATION OF AMERICAN LIFE

Metis, Detienne and Vernant note, moves most effectively through "a shifting terrain, in uncertain and ambiguous situations."[14] We do not lack for such characterizations of our postmodern, hyper-real, fragmented, third sophistic, late capitalist, radically contingent, or, in my preferred metaphor, novelized era. Drawing on the work of Mikhail Bakhtin, I have argued that the contemporary American community is marked by multiplicity—by a variety of languages and voices interacting with and illuminating one another.[15] Such conditions, Bakhtin contends, define the novel—thus, the metaphor of a novelized era. Too often, however, we are given to pronouncements, not detail: What is it that makes our experience different from past generations and presidents? While I cannot approach a comprehensive account, I suggest a few factors that might connect the dots. Any discussion of difference must begin with similarity.

Clinton's cunning, Stephen Skowronek might explain, emanates not only from him, but also from his presidential context. Skowronek, in his admirable *The Politics Presidents Make*, rethinks presidential leadership by situating it within a recurrent narrative. He argues that heroic presidents come to power at moments open to a decisive repudiation of "the established government formulas"; they succeed because of a "general political consensus that something ha[s] gone fundamentally wrong in the high affairs of state."[16] These "reconstructive" presidents are followed by affiliated presidents—leaders who extend the accomplishments of their predecessors—and, finally, by "disjunctive" presidents—men unable either to repudiate or affiliate with the existing order and thus "often singled out as political incompetents."[17] As the order collapses about the disjunctive president, the hero waits in the wings and the cycle begins again.

Floating through his analytical scheme are the preemptive presidents. Lacking the general consensus that something has gone fundamentally wrong, they attempt to preempt the moment of reconstruction. They push and push hard against the still powerful status quo. Skowronek's language is revealing; these presidents "intrude" into the polity as an "alien force." They "aggravate" existing cleavages and travel a "treacherous" political "terrain." "Probing for reconstructive possibilities," they "get caught in a showdown of constitutional proportions."[18] John Tyler, Andrew Johnson, Woodrow Wilson, Richard Nixon and Bill Clinton each share these qualities. They came to power upon the death of an incumbent or with the aid of a third party. They could not point to the support of a majority of the people (at least in their first terms). They provoked the disdain of many in Washington for political and personal reasons. They engaged in serious constitutional debates concerning the prerogatives of the office and/or their fitness for the post. The political culture has some difficulty accounting for these controversial presidents.

Skowronek, too, appears befuddled by the presidential "wild cards." He recognizes their importance, but he cannot fit them into his cyclical turning of the presidential seasons, so they remain largely exiled to the opening and closing chapters. Yet he suggests that they may well serve as the model for future presidential action because we face the waning of political time. American democracy, he claims, is growing old. Its arteries are clogged by interest groups, its kidneys shutting down under the growing abuse they suffer from the natural opponents of reconstructive presidents—the Congress, the media, the bureaucracy, think tanks, blue ribbon commissions, special prosecutors and even, as we have discovered of late, rogue lieutenant colonels and White House interns. By the waning of political time, Skowronek means the waning of reconstructive possibilities. Each successive heroic president faces a more complex and confusing field of action. Opponents can find refuge in a growing variety of institutions, call upon an increasing array of resistant ideological resources, and rely confidently upon the natural oppositional tendencies of the media.[19]

In addition, each successive reconstructive president acts within the interpretive frames set by his predecessors; each struggles ferociously to reenact the *ethos* of presidential heroes.[20] In 1980, for instance, we were treated to the surreal spectacle of Ronald Reagan slashing away at the New Deal even as he called upon the specter of FDR. In the past few years we have seen a House Speaker raising the ghosts of presidents past as he fomented revolution. The fact that Newt Gingrich dared to make such an effort from the House is compelling evidence for the "thickening" of political life. If a representative can wield such power, then a president faces a Herculean task when he or she attempts to clean out the national stables. There is simply too much stuff out there; they are all becoming preemptive presidents.

This thickening of the political context for presidential action parallels the novelization of American culture. If there ever was a single metanarrative, it has gone by the boards. The resulting cultural anxiety percolates through the nation. The past few years alone have seen a spate of books decrying the twilight of common dreams, the disuniting of America, and the closing of the American mind. No longer can one story tell the American story. Instead, there are powerful centrifugal forces whirling through our lives.

For instance, the traditional family has nearly disappeared. Andrew Hacker reveals, "Among the country's 35 million married couples aged twenty-five to fifty-four, [both spouses work] in 73 percent of the households."[21] *The New York Times Almanac* for 1999 contains twelve different listings for various household permutations.[22] Immigration has exploded in the United States; during the 1980s, there were 7.3 million legal immigrants into this country, "the largest number of legal immigrants in any decade in U.S. history, except for 1901–1910."[23] Bruce Cain notes that the key difference from the past is clear: "It [is] now possible to speak of protecting *an ethnic and racial group's equal right to its distinctive language and culture.*"[24] That difference explains why the most popular name for baby boys in Texas and California last year was Jose.[25] It may also explain why the leading Republican at the turn of the last century, Theodore Roosevelt, denounced the hyphenated American as un-American and the leading Republican at the turn of this century, George W. Bush, speaks Spanish whenever and wherever politically useful. The country has changed. New communication technologies add to the cacophony and spread the stories. In 1990, 23 percent of U.S. homes had a computer; in 1998, 42 percent. In 1990, virtually no one accessed the Internet; in 1997, approximately 42 million people accessed it.[26]

There is no longer a "typical" American family nor a single set of virtues that can encompass diverse experiences. Nonetheless, the "Silent Majority" seems willing to piece it together, if we are to trust Alan Wolfe's *One Nation, After All.* Wolfe's Middle Class Morality Project poses a refreshingly humble question: Does the suburban middle class, as opposed to the pundit class, believe in a culture war? Wolfe says no. Middle-class Americans, he reveals, are a tolerant people, judging not lest they be judged, pulling together a moral code out of their own hard experiences, assorted stories and canonical texts, and recognizing that while "rules are not meant to be broken," they are surely "made to be bent."[27]

Three important conclusions emerge from Wolfe's study. First, suburban Americans believe in "morality writ small." For that reason, they are deeply suspicious of the sweeping claims of the Christian Coalition and the apostles of political correctness. Good works in local communities define their ideals.[28] Second, these ideals percolate up from a variety of sources. According to Wolfe: "Most Americans know at least a few stories from the Bible, have some sense of the Constitution's basic principles, remember stories read to them as children, have become familiar with other stories as they bring up their own children, and understand such crucial episodes in American history as the Civil War, the Great Depression, World War II and the struggle against totalitarianism, and the civil rights movement. . . . From this myriad set of sources, Americans develop a hybrid language for speaking about moral obligation."[29] Finally, that hybrid language is internally inconsistent, shot through with inescapable conflicts and contradictions, yet tested by experience. For instance, Wolfe notes that the languages of work and home both have claims on Americans:

you should work hard and you should spend time with your children. Recognizing the conflicts between these imperatives, most of Wolfe's respondents muddle through as best they can, judging these claims on a contingent basis and maneuvering through the obstacles of contemporary life.[30]

It is the new economy that provides many of these obstacles. Much has been written about the new class of knowledge workers. A good deal of that is true, and yet many Americans have not been touched by such changes. More significant is the fact that Daniel Bell was right.[31] The relentless little engine of capitalism is churning away, creating cultural contradictions, dismantling institutions, and disrupting relationships between downsizing companies and downsized workers. How do Americans cope? We invent new lives. As *Newsweek* reported in a recent cover story, 92 percent of workers laid off in 1998 found jobs with equivalent or better salaries. In 1997, 28 percent of all workers were on flextime, 8 million people held down more than one job, 10.5 million workers were self-employed, and better than one-quarter of those in the workforce had held their current jobs for less than a year.[32] I suspect that few of the scholars reading this chapter currently hold the position in which they began their academic careers and possess tenure. Americans move.

Our successful students will likely lead a life that looks something like this: They will graduate in heavy debt, start jobs at somewhere around $30,000 a year, feel frustration because that salary cannot get them what they want, leave that job to start a small business, pile up more debt, succeed in the business, get swallowed by a larger business, use their skills to move on to another couple of jobs, get downsized when they reach the upper-middle level of management, and end their careers as relatively well-paid private consultants. Along the way they will move in with roommates of varying sexual orientations and interests, spend time back in their parents' home, delay marriage, children, and home ownership, develop their own personally tailored home entertainment centers, and plan their own pension plans, health-care plans, work schedules, and compensation packages.[33] They will do so without a clear idea of what they are doing, if recent surveys of our "investor illiteracy" are correct,[34] and with a clear feeling that unknown, powerful, and hostile forces are out to get them if *The Firm,* the *X-Files, JFK, Enemy of the State, Blade,* and *Millenium* are correct. Welcome to the world of Ken Starr and Bill Clinton.

THE RHETORICAL CUNNING OF BILL CLINTON

I have conducted this whirlwind tour of contemporary life in order to claim that the cunning logic flowing through the former president's speeches flows through the culture. We dance as he dances and vice versa. His popularity results in part from our recognition of his style. His leadership, in turn, results from the trust we develop for the judgment of a crafty Odysseus. We may not love such a cunning character, but we believe that he will lead us through trouble.

Explaining cunning is a difficult task. Detienne and Vernant note that the ancient Greeks did not provide "any theoretical examination" of *metis*. They hasten to add that it "is not difficult to detect the presence of metis at the heart of the Greek mental world. . . . But there is no text which reveals straightforwardly its fundamental characteristics and its origins."[35] Clearly, its kissing cousin is *phronesis* or prudential conduct; Janet Atwill, in fact, tends to collapse the two.[36] Michelle Ballif draws a distinction and her argument makes sense.[37] As Forbes Hill and Eugene Garver note, Aristotle assumes a stable social order, homogenous cultural values and ethical masters of rhetorical *techne*.[38] These ideals cut against the unknown terrain and chameleon-like speakers that characterize *metis;* such normative ideals also discount the notion that we can only navigate, not dominate, rhetorical contexts. As Ballif contends, we must conceive of "a rhetorical situation negotiated by metis rather than mastered by techne."[39]

In the remainder of this chapter I explore three negotiation strategies that characterize the rhetoric of this preemptive president. First, the president metaphorically cast his programs as a journey and sought to prepare the American people for the trip. Second, as he traveled the route, he changed shape; he spoke through a variety of voices and languages in order to find a way for all Americans. Finally, he used dissociation to set traps for his opponents and escape their efforts to bind him in place.

When President Clinton spoke of our tasks, he did so in metaphorical terms that implied an expedition into the future. In his 1995 State of the Union address, for instance, he said we must "enter a new era" and "embark upon this new course," because we "are moving from an industrial age built on gears and sweat to an information age demanding skills and learning and flexibility."[40] He opened his 1993 health-care reform address with the "journey" metaphor,[41] the "march" of

Martin Luther King often appeared as a model in his rhetoric, and in his first nomination acceptance address, Clinton wanted to give his daughter a "country that is coming together and moving ahead."[42]

He was a president who could not hold still. Clinton filled his speeches with metaphors of movement, activity, and progress. To some extent, these are political clichés, part of the American lexicon. Yet the sheer volume suggests something else. Like John Kennedy, Bill Clinton campaigned for the presidency in the belief that the country had lost its confidence and direction; it needed to get moving again. Unlike John Kennedy, Bill Clinton did not specify a destination—such as the New Frontier—nor did he materialize his spiritual commitments in a concrete program—such as the race to the moon. Rather, he wanted to "equip our people" for the unknown road ahead.[43]

Two kinds of equipment recur throughout Clinton's addresses. First, he calls for new abilities to meet new demands. Coincident with "morality writ small," he emphasizes little accomplishments. Each step builds the skills needed for the journey. No president in recent history has been as interested in the minutiae of policy as this one. From school uniforms to V-chips, from microbusiness loans to job-training programs, miniature policies litter his speeches. No problem is too small for a program; no program is too small to advance the journey. We need concrete skills to make the trip.

In a larger sense, each small success comes to comprise a spiritual vision, a new attitude for the twenty-first century, which is the second piece of equipment. Clinton's speeches during his 1995 Northern Ireland tour illustrate this logic beautifully. He praises the ordinary people "who have shown in concrete ways that here the will for peace is now stronger than the weapons of war. With mixed sporting events . . . , women's support groups, literacy programs, job training centers that serve both communities, these and countless other initiatives bolster the foundations of peace." To Clinton, little stuff mattered because the process continues: "I pledge to you that we will do all we can . . . to ease your load. If you walk down this path continually, you will not walk alone."[44] This logic frames his arguments regarding all peacekeeping operations: Stop the shooting, clean up the neighborhoods, put people to work, have some lunch, open some daycare centers—each little step moves us along. The journey is the important thing.

Similarly, when Clinton labeled his domestic program, he called it the "New Covenant." He introduced the phrase in his 1992 nomination-acceptance address and returned to it over the years, usually when he was in trouble. Like other slogans, the New Covenant defined Clinton's "vision." He detailed that vision in the 1992 address, but he also attributes visions to everyone: "I hope no one ever tries to raise a child without a vision. I hope nobody ever starts a business or plants a crop in the ground without a vision—for where there is no vision, the people perish."[45] The visions of people planting crops, raising children, and starting businesses accumulate into the sacred vision. Each activity amplifies the New Covenant in a slightly different way. Yet they are all beginnings and they require new understandings of unknown horizons. How do I go about raising a child?

A covenant can chart the way. The most famous covenant in American history, the Mayflower Compact, came into being during a journey. The colonists faced an unknown shore, a treacherous terrain, and could only specify their determination to act in a charitable fashion—rather like raising a child. The New Covenant, Clinton explained, was "a new set of understandings" for the march across that now-infamous bridge.[46] Similarly, Robert Reich and Tony Blair define the Clinton program as the "Third Way."[47] It is a "way," not a place, and it is not a specific philosophy (e.g., "conservative") but a number that can only mark out the difference from past programs, not the substance of new initiatives. Those who believe in a third way will find their way along the way. Bill Clinton consistently elevated movement and work over product and destination: "Work organizes life. It gives structure and discipline to life. It gives meaning and self-esteem to people who are parents. It gives role models to children."[48] Work is a consummatory not an instrumental act. It provides its own rewards, as does the journey. In Clinton's view, we cannot know the future of those children, specify a single vision, or determine absolute results. But if we learn to learn, develop the skills, and take the first step, all will eventually be well.

Foremost among those skills is the power of metamorphosis. In the new America, we must learn to invent and reinvent the self. On a prosaic level, that claim makes perfect sense. If each American is to hold eight or ten jobs in his or her lifetime, then we must constantly be born again. But it is not only the jobs; as we take on New Covenants, we change and he changes. *Metis*, Detienne and Vernant claim, is "not one, not unified, but multiple and diverse." *Metis* "produces an effect of irridescence, shimmering, an interplay of reflections which the

Greeks perceived as the ceaseless vibrations of light." The goddess Metis "is endowed with the power of metamorphosis . . . she can take on the most widely differing appearances."[49] Michelle Ballif draws on Donna Harraway's figure of the shape-shifting cyborg.[50] Why this shiftiness? If *metis* is to negotiate "a changing situation, full of contrasts, it must become even more supple, even more shifting, more polymorphic than the flow of time: it must adapt itself constantly to events as they succeed each other."[51] Clinton put metamorphosis into rhetorical play. He displayed for us the invention and reinvention of self.

That power reveals itself fully in his November 13, 1993, speech at Memphis, Tennessee. He used his presence "in this hallowed place where Martin Luther King gave his last sermon" to speak of King's influence. In an extraordinary performance, he did so in King's voice. One section of the speech, for instance, opens with accomplishments: "'You did a good job, he would say, voting and electing people who formerly were not electable because of the color of their skin.'"[52] The allusion to "I Have a Dream" provides authenticity and Clinton develops that feeling in subsequent sections by repeating, "You did a good job, he would say," "He would say, you did a very good job," and "that is good," in an uncanny rendition of King's style. The *anaphora,* as in "I Have Dream," opens and closes each unit.

Clinton does not explain King's ideas in this speech; he performs King's voice in a form of *prosopoeia.* King, not Clinton, warrants the arguments that the president makes regarding crime, jobs, and communities. He orchestrates the languages of classical liberalism and the black church throughout the address; each melody shimmers through the other and together they light the way toward the future. As Walter Shapiro wrote, Clinton "transformed himself" by speaking in this way.[53] I have written about this speech at length elsewhere.[54] Suffice it to say here that Bill Clinton as president made a fine preacher and a fine liberal.

Similarly, he made a pretty good *bricoleur.* His ability to weave the feelings, words, and styles of others into his own discourse and life is simply astonishing. The willingness to "feel our pain" disturbs some critics. Denton and Holloway worry about the negative effects of "mediated conversation"; Trevor and Shawn Parry-Giles saw the 1992 Clinton campaign biography as American "scopophilia."[55] We are voyeurs at the life of Clinton. When he tells his story, however, something different emerges, a bizarre combination of the archetypal rise of a president, familiar since William Henry Harrison's hard cider and log cabin campaign, and, dare I say it, feminist consciousness-raising.

Take, for instance, Clinton's "remarks" at Georgetown University on July 6, 1995. This speech is important to the Clinton presidency and I will return to it later. It was one of a series given in mid-1995, beginning with the Oklahoma City memorial address, which put the president back in the saddle again after the 1994 disaster. He announces at the opening that he would like to "have more of a conversation than deliver a formal speech."[56] Clinton turns to his life early, noting that what "I believe grows largely out of my personal history, and a lot of it happened to me a long time before I came to Georgetown and read in books things that made me convinced that I was basically right."[57] In one sentence, he asserts his authenticity and the wisdom of the common folk—life taught him his beliefs—and his education and the validity of those beliefs—books told him he was right. Remarkably, he then assumes the audience knows the form of the story. He says: "When I was a boy, I lived for a while on a farm without an indoor toilet. It makes a good story, not as good as being born in a log cabin, but it's true."[58] In this era, Clinton can only tell the log-cabin-and-hard-cider story by letting the audience in on the "joke," much like the way in which David Letterman can only do a talk show by letting the audience know that he knows the conventions of a talk show. At the same time, it is still a talk show or a life story, and Clinton accrues the credit that comes from a hard rise.

Yet he did not do it alone. The life story broadens into a cultural narrative over the next two pages. Unlike Richard Nixon in his 1968 nomination-acceptance address or Clarence Thomas at his confirmation hearings, President Clinton distributes the credit for his rise: "But I also had a lot of opportunity that was given to me by my community. I had good teachers and good schools. And when I needed them, I got scholarships and jobs."[59] It takes a village to raise a president. But this president goes on beyond that assertion. He notes that he "graduated from high school in 1964, and we had about 3-percent unemployment, about 3–4-percent real growth, and very modest inflation. And we all just assumed that the American dream would work out all right if we could ever whip racism."[60] The mention of racism is not isolated; he also says, "I saw what happened to good people who had no opportunity because they happened to be black or because they happened to be poor and white and isolated in the hills and hollows of the mountains of my state."[61]

It was not only the community that made this president's rise possible; it was the structure of society. In his view, he made it when talented African Americans did not because the political and economic structures of the country lifted him up and held them down. Clinton connects the personal to the political in ways unusual for mainstream American politicians. Bonnie Dow and Lisa Maria Hogeland argue that the key difference between soft or therapeutic consciousness-raising (CR) and hard or political CR is the willingness to connect personal success or failure to larger political structures.[62] Clinton does precisely that; he acknowledges that he made it and others did not for reasons far beyond personal talent or effort. He nests the archetypal story in the CR narrative. His life becomes an argument for an active government to create for everyone those conditions that made his rise possible. He invents himself as Horatio Alger and Alix Kates Shulman; each voice shimmers through the other and each informs and transforms the other.

Preacher and president, feminist and capitalist, Bill Clinton reinvented himself and those stereotypes in virtually every speech. Some critics disliked him for his power of metamorphosis, but it played a major role in saving his presidency. When Bill Clinton spoke of community, he displayed community. He extended his respect to all Americans by speaking in their languages, voices, and forms. People tend to return such trust. More important, he weaved those traditions together; he revealed a chorus of harmony. "In a chorus of harmony," Clinton explained to his Georgetown audience, "you know there are lots of differences, but you can hear all the voices. And that is important."[63] That chorus, by the way, is a metaphor borrowed from Gov. Zell Miller's 1992 Democratic keynote address. And the beat goes on. All move forward together and listen to each other.

In something else that just keeps going and going, we have also listened to Clinton the lawyer. The president not only played a lawyer, he is a lawyer—depending on what "is" is. It is undoubtedly true that Bill Clinton's verbal dexterity saved him from conviction in the Senate. The rhetoric of the House managers was filled with phrases such as, "The President must have known," "we can only believe," and "the only reasonable conclusion to draw is" because they could never find the equivalent of that lovely unambiguous Nixonian statement: "We can get a million dollars." For a month, we listened to thirteen (the number must be significant given the outcome) white, male, mostly southern conservatives argue passionately for civil rights law, for sexual harassment law, and for the idea that the president, a government official, the sort of person they otherwise believe could not run a one-car parade without screwing it up, the president is the primary role model for children. In a bizarre moment, Henry Hyde asked the Senate to "speak truth to power." To my disappointment, he failed to rise and give the black power salute. In their desire to take action against the president, they affirmed precisely the sort of active government they otherwise professed to deplore. In short, they affirmed President Clinton's primary political commitment.

This sort of thing was not unusual during the presidency of William Jefferson Clinton. Let me be clear. I am not saying that he planned catastrophe; I am saying that he navigated treacherous terrain better than most. His opponents seemed always to help him along. While I cannot explain this quality completely, his texts display part of the answer. His ability to shape the debate, to make what Plato and the Republicans would call the weaker case into the stronger case, marks his rhetoric. The budget battle in the summer of 1995 was just such a moment. In his Georgetown address of that summer, Clinton consistently "associates himself with the founding fathers and Constitutional principles and he dissociates rival candidates and factions from those fathers and that principle."[64] That phrase comes from the fine analysis Michael Leff and the late G. P. Mohrmann performed on Abraham Lincoln's Cooper Union address, a speech that bears a striking resemblance to Clinton's effort.

Like Lincoln, Clinton begins with the founders. He cites the Declaration of Independence, emphasizing the phrase "for the support of this Declaration, with a firm reliance on the protection of Divine Providence, we mutually pledge . . . our lives, our fortunes, and our sacred honor."[65] Mutuality is the key. His life story follows the scriptural text. Argumentatively, Clinton's life story reveals the mutuality and the community that created, sustained, and spread the American Dream. Without help, he would not have made it. But today, he says, "Politics has become more and more fractured, just like the rest of our lives: pluralized. It's exciting in some ways. But as we divide into more and more and more sharply defined organized groups around more and more and more stratified issues . . . ., as we see politicians actually getting language lessons on how to turn their adversaries into aliens, it is difficult to draw the conclusion that our political system is producing the sort of discussion that will give us the kind of results that we need."[66] Who could be giving such "language lessons"? Newt Gingrich is firmly and enthymematically dissociated from the mutuality of the founders.

Beyond the obvious, however, this passage persuasively set the national debate in the sort of way most amenable to a Clintonian solution. Most Americans recognized those problems. They were likely to accept the diagnosis of the experienced eye of this political doctor, a doctor who *knew* that particular disease. In addition, the current context is taken as a given; we must navigate through our present circumstance. How can we do so? The president shows the way by displaying his "chorus of harmony." Come let us reason together.

Examples dominate the rest of the speech, but one possesses particular resonance in light of subsequent events, such as Columbine and Atlanta. The president turns to "the NRA's position on gun violence, the Brady bill, and the assault weapons ban."[67] Like Lincoln speaking to the South at Cooper Union, Clinton rehearses their arguments and he does so in the first person: "Why are you making me wait five days to get a handgun? What do you care if I want an AK-47 or an Uzi to go out and engage in some sort of sporting contest to see who's a better shot? I obey the law. I pay my taxes. I don't give you any grief. Why are you on my back? The Constitution says I can do this. Punish wrongdoers. I am sick and tired of my life being inconvenienced for what other people do."[68] The colloquial language and the first-person performance lend authenticity to Clinton's words. At the same time, however, his rehearsal makes the NRA about as attractive to most Americans as Lincoln's highwayman, the South, appeared to the Republicans at Cooper Union. That is cool, sir.

In a rather creative move, the president then disagrees with his own eventual position. He notes, "forgetting about [the] examples, this argument is self-evidently right." The NRA is right? "There is nothing the Government can do for anybody that will displace the negative impact of personal misconduct." Yes, even the NRA can add a line to the chorus of harmony. He then makes sure that the audience recognizes that it is only a line: "But" (there is always a "but" in Clinton's rhetoric) "they're not just single problems. If there's a big crime rate and a whole lot of people getting killed with guns, that affects all the rest of us because some of us are likely to get shot." He compares the "minor inconvenience" of the assault-weapons ban to metal detectors: "You don't gripe when you go through a metal detector at an airport anymore, because you are very aware of the connection between this minor inconvenience to you, and the fact that the plane might blow up." Similarly, he says, "I don't have a problem with saying, 'Look, these assault weapons are primarily designed to kill people. That's their primary purpose. And I'm sorry if you don't have a new one that you can take out in the woods somewhere to a shooting contest, but you'll get over it. Shoot with something else . . . , but remember, the other people [the NRA members] are good people who honestly believe what they say. That's the importance of this debate."[69] The president immediately rolls into an encomium to the NRA of his Arkansas youth. What he taketh away with one hand, he giveth with the other—as long as you follow the conductor.

The colloquial style, the vivid examples, and the argumentative structure dissociate the Republicans from the founders and American principle and associate Clinton with those founders and that principle. Republicans are welcome in the chorus because they are right in that argument for personal responsibility, but they do not see the whole. As a result, they misbehave. The children are griping about minor inconveniences and throwing temper tantrums. He diminishes them and, in particular, he diminishes the speaker with these enthymematic images. The president, believe it or not, appears mature next to Newt Gingrich's public persona. Clinton takes full advantage of that fact. His opponent, he says in effect, does not understand the American symphony, he does not understand it as the founders understood it, and he does not understand it as Lincoln understood it. Clinton closes with a quote from Lincoln's first inaugural address: "We are not enemies but friends. We must not be enemies."[70] Holding his friends close and his enemy closer, Clinton offered Gingrich the chance to follow the president's baton or start a civil war. By the end of 1995, the game was up. By the end of 1998, Gingrich had left public life.

Detienne and Vernant tell the story of the race between Odysseus and Ajax.[71] Odysseus, slower and weaker than his opponent, prayed to Athena and watched for the main chance. Athena nicely dropped a bit of dung where it would do the most good. However, these scholars argue, "if the swift Ajax came a cropper in the dung it is because he has failed to foresee an obstacle which Athena's protégé certainly does nothing to help him avoid and which he no doubt did all that he could to manoeuvre into Ajax's path . . . the fact is, without metis, a man [*sic*] cannot foresee the narrowing of the track which will provide an opportunity for taking the lead over a rival, nor recognize in advance the muddy area which can cause the competitor out in front to slip." President Clinton, politically slower and weaker than his opponent, could not alter the deleterious results of the 1994 elections nor could he foresee that the Republicans would shut down the government. He could only survey the track, seize the opportunity, and maneuver Gingrich into the dung.

CONCLUSION

If imitation is a form of flattery, then Bill Clinton should feel good about his rhetoric. Any number of nations—from Great Britain to France, from Germany to Texas—have elected leaders who speak of a New Britain, a "Third Way," or a "compassionate conservatism." We should not lightly dismiss such a trend. Contemporary life has led some pretty bright men and women to approach public problems in a manner akin to Bill Clinton. His determination to focus on little agreements rather than mythic ends, on shifting identities rather than rigid roles, and on room to maneuver rather than adherence to dogma struck a responsive chord in diverse communities. His record of accomplishment is also clear. Jonathan Alter recently wrote, "A surprisingly high percentage of his original campaign promises have been fulfilled. As Vernon Jordan might say: Mission accomplished."[72]

Alter's sarcastic surprise captures nicely the ambivalence that some critics felt about Clinton's leadership. His style made little sense to them. They longed for a man of principle, a romantic hero who would make of the presidency the "vital center of action" rather than the vital center of reaction. I am not sure that such a president has ever existed, and I suspect that the John Kennedy of 1963 would support my position. Yet the Clinton presidency was different. There is no doubt that his private actions diminished the office, but his rhetorical leadership did so as well. That is the more intriguing phenomena. His willingness to acknowledge the existence of unknown terrain, the mutability of contemporary life, and the inability of the president to determine the course of the nation embraces the backtracking of the presidential fox and discards the roar of the presidential lion. As scholars continue to ponder the Clinton presidency, we should consider his legacy and sort out the personal predilections as well as the cultural forces that led to this style of leadership. Much like Clinton's own "Third Way," the cunning mode of leadership weaves together elements of the Imperial President and the Imperiled President. The president finds ways to act, but they are not always admirable. He moves through his obstacles, but aims ultimately at survival. He achieves his ends, but will those ends matter? A human president, for good or for ill, marks a significant moment in the journey of democracy.

NOTES

1. John F. Kennedy, "The Role of the President," in *Representative American Speeches 1960*, ed. L. Thonssen (New York: H. W. Wilson), 124, 127.

2. James Reston, "Primary Issue Explored," *New York Times*, Jan. 20, 1960, 14.

3. "Kennedy the candidate," *Newsweek*, Jan. 18, 1960, 34.

4. Richard Strout, "TRB," *New Republic*, Jan. 25, 1960, 1.

5. Bruce Miroff, "From 'Mid-Century' to Fin-de-siecle: The Exhaustion of Presidential Image," *Rhetoric & Public Affairs* 1, no. 2 (summer, 1998): 185–200.

6. Nancy Gibbs, "The Last Campaign," *Time*, Feb. 1, 1999, 22.

7. Jonathan Alter, "Playing the Gipper Card," *Newsweek*, Feb. 1, 1999, p. 29.

8. "Clinton, the Country, and the Political Culture: A Symposium," *Commentary*, Jan., 1999, 20–42.

9. Howard Fineman and Daniel Klaidman, "With Foes like These," *Newsweek*, Feb. 1, 1999, 24.

10. Joe Klein, "Foreword," in Evan Thomas, *Back From the Dead: How Clinton Survived the Republican Revolution* (New York: Atlantic Monthly Press, 1997).

11. Margaret Carlson, "The Clinton in Us All," *Time*, Jan. 4, 1999, 94.

12. Marcel Detienne and Jean-Pierre Vernant, *Cunning Intelligence in Greek Culture and Society*, trans. J. Lloyd (Sussex: Harvester Press, 1978).

13. Ibid., 2.

14. Ibid., 15.

15. John M. Murphy, "Critical Rhetoric as Political Discourse," *Argumentation and Advocacy* 32, no. 1 (summer, 1995): 1–15; John M. Murphy, "Inventing Authority: Bill Clinton, Martin Luther King, Jr., and the Orchestration of Rhetorical Traditions," *Quarterly Journal of Speech* 83, no. 1 (Feb., 1997): 71–89.

16. Stephen Skowronek, *The Politics Presidents Make* (Cambridge, Mass.: Harvard University Press, 1993).

17. Ibid., 39.

18. Ibid., 43–44.

19. Thomas E. Patterson, *Out of Order* (New York: Alfred A. Knopf, 1993).

20. Skowronek, *Politics Presidents Make*, 409–14.

21. Andrew Hacker, *Money* (New York: Touchstone Books, 1997), 59.

22. *The New York Times Almanac*, ed. J. W. Wright (New York: Penguin Reference, 1998).

23. Bruce Cain, "Racial and Ethnic Politics," in *Developments in American Politics*, ed. G. Peele, C. Bailey, B. Cain, and B. G. Peters, vol. 2 (Chatham, N.J.: Chatham House, 1995), 49.

24. Ibid.

25. Maria Puente, "What's in a Name? USA's Changing Face," *USA Today*, Jan. 15, 1999, 8A.

26. *New York Times Almanac*, 793, 798.

27. Alan Wolfe, *One Nation, After All* (New York: Viking, 1998), 300.

28. Ibid., 275–322.

29. Ibid., 301.

30. Ibid., 88–132.

31. Daniel Bell, *The Cultural Contradictions of Capitalism* (New York: Basic Books, 1976).

32. Daniel McGinn and John McCormick, "Your Next Job," *Newsweek*, Feb. 1, 1999, 45.

33. This scenario is drawn from ibid., 43–45; Wolfe, *One Nation*; and Hacker, *Money*.

34. Bernard Roshco, "Behind the Numbers: Investor Illiteracy," *The American Prospect*, Mar.–Apr., 1999, 69–74.

35. Detienne and Vernant, *Cunning Intelligence*, 3.

36. Janet Atwill, *Rhetoric Reclaimed* (Ithaca, N.Y.: Cornell University Press, 1998).

37. Michelle Ballif, "Writing the Third Sophistic Cyborg: Periphrasis on an [In]Tense Rhetoric," *Rhetoric Society Quarterly* 28, no. 4 (fall, 1998): 51–72.

38. Forbes Hill, "The *Rhetoric* of Aristotle," in *A Synoptic History of Classical Rhetoric*, ed. J. J. Murphy (Davis, Calif.: Hermagoras Press, 1983), 19–76; Eugene Garver, *Aristotle's Rhetoric: An Art of Character* (Chicago: University of Chicago Press, 1994).

39. Ballif, "Writing the Third Sophistic," 67.

40. William J. Clinton, "Address before a Joint Session of the Congress on the State of the Union," *Public Papers of the Presidents of the United States, 1995*, vol. 1 (Washington, D.C.: GPO, 1995), 76–77 (hereafter PPOP followed by year and volume number).

41. William J. Clinton, "Address to a Joint Session of the Congress on Health Care Reform," *PPOP, 1993*, vol. 2 (Washington, D.C.: GPO, 1993), 1556–57.

42. Bill Clinton and Al Gore, *Putting People First* (New York: Times Books, 1992), 231.

43. Clinton, "State of the Union," 77.

44. William J. Clinton, "Remarks to Mackie International Employees in Belfast, Northern Ireland," *PPOP, 1995*, vol. 2, 1805.

45. Clinton and Gore, *Putting People First*, 227.

46. Clinton, "State of the Union," 77.

47. Robert B. Reich, "We Are All Third-Wayers Now," *The American Prospect*, Mar.–Apr. 1999, 46–51; Tony Blair, *New Britain* (Boulder, Colo.: Westview Press, 1996).

48. William J. Clinton, "Remarks to the Eighth Annual Holy Convocation of the Church of God in Christ," in *Selected Speeches of President William Jefferson Clinton* (Washington, D.C.: GPO, 1993), 25.

49. Detienne and Vernant, *Cunning Intelligence*, 18.

50. Ballif, "Writing the Third Sophistic," 67–68.

51. Detienne and Vernant, *Cunning Intelligence*, 20.

52. Clinton, "Remarks to the Eighth Annual," 23.

53. Walter Shapiro, "Bully Bill, or Just What Can a President Do to Stop a Twelve-year-old with an Uzi?" *Esquire*, Feb. 4, 1994, 34.

54. Murphy, "Inventing Authority."

55. Robert E. Denton, Jr., and Rachel L. Holloway, "Clinton and the Town Hall Meetings: Mediated Conversations and the Risk of Being 'in Touch'," in *The Clinton Presidency*, ed. R. E. Denton Jr. and R. L. Holloway (Westport, Conn.: Praeger, 1996); Trevor Parry-Giles and Shawn Parry-Giles, "Political Scopophilia and the Intimacy of American Politics," *Communication Studies* 47, no. 3 (fall, 1996): 191–205.

56. William J. Clinton, "Remarks at Georgetown University," *PPOP*, 1995, vol. 2, 1047.

57. Ibid., 1048.

58. Ibid.

59. Ibid., 1049.

60. Ibid.

61. Ibid.

62. Bonnie J. Dow, *Prime-Time Feminism* (Philadelphia: University of Pennsylvania Press, 1996); Lisa Maria Hogeland, *Feminism and Its Fictions* (Philadelphia: University of Pennsylvania Press, 1998).

63. Clinton, "Remarks at Georgetown," 1056.

64. Michael C. Leff and Gerald P. Mohrmann, "Lincoln at Cooper Union: A Rhetorical Analysis of the Text," *Quarterly Journal of Speech* 60, no. 4 (Nov., 1974), 348–49.

65. Clinton, "Remarks at Georgetown," 1047.

66. Ibid., 1050.

67. Ibid., 1051.

68. Ibid.

69. Ibid., 1052.

70. Ibid., 1056.

71. Detienne and Vernant, *Cunning Intelligence*, 228–29.

72. Alter, "Playing the Gipper Card," 29.

Afterword

Rhetorical Leadership
and Presidential Performance

Leroy G. Dorsey

LEADERSHIP REVOLVES around being rhetorical. Leaders do not command allegiance or direct action simply based on their status in some organization. Neither do they sustain converts or empower followers by some psychological or cosmological process that is beyond human ken. Leaders must actively engage in that process of investigation that will allow them to sift among available options for their audience, determine what might be best among those options, and construct a message of some kind that would help the audience to align itself with that alternative. In some ways it is remarkable that a chief executive, or anyone else for that matter, can effectively lead given such a complex and dynamic process.

These essays illustrate that, for the president, the heart of rhetorical leadership is prudence. At one level, executive leaders must be reasoned deliberators who can sensibly apply their knowledge to the furtherance of the community's goals. At another level, the president must be of a decent enough character so that any decisions reached are not just practical in a technical sense, but also appropriate in an ethical sense. More importantly, however, is the realization that the president must have the skill to express these inner virtues of thought and character as well as the awareness of how to balance them in a public performance. This performative aspect of prudence does not mean that the president's reasoning ability and force of character are just an "act" in the pejorative sense. Rather, it means that chief executives must seize public moments to demonstrate their understanding of that confluence of people, goals, opportunities, and other contingent elements before their audience would be willing to be led toward some goal.

As these essays reveal, successful rhetorical leadership by presidents is distinguished by their performance, an unobtrusive performance given during moments transformed by their inventiveness to balance the expression of their decision-making skills and their sense of good will. In his historical overview of presidential prudence, David Zarefsky's essay concludes that some of the most successful presidential leaders showcased their intelligence and character by transforming staid political moments into memorable ones that united the nation. Steven Lucas's essay on George Washington depicts the first president's ability to convey his heroism, humbleness, and command of history on the public stage as a means to lead the nation. For H. W. Brands, the public's perception of Theodore Roosevelt's rugged character lent credibility to his shows of force, causing his intractable opponents to rethink their positions. James Andrews writes that Woodrow Wilson's legacy of character and rhetorical leadership comes from the president's articulation of a vision that sought to transform individuals into a morally responsible nation. In his essay on Franklin Roosevelt, Thomas Benson argues that the president successfully promoted his ideas about the New Deal by demonstrating his practicality and his graciousness. G. Thomas Goodnight observes that Ronald Reagan articulated a revised American Dream that allowed Reagan to display his virtue of thought and to endear his virtue of character on the world stage. And for John Murphy,

Bill Clinton's demonstration of "cunning" as a means of survival, as well as his protean ability to take on the roles of revered figures, resonates with audiences and makes them more receptive to the president's leadership.

But presidents do not always succeed. If judged wanting in a performance to balance artfully the twin virtues of practical knowledge and character, the president cannot successfully influence others. Such instances are also instructive for a deeper understanding of rhetorical leadership.

James Farrell argues that John Adams was concerned with the public's recognition of his performance as president, particularly on the issue of French-American relations. So much so that Adams vigorously defended his presidency in his letters, essays, and memoirs to ensure that his audiences then and later would see him as the Ciceronian ideal of a prudent leader. This begs the question: If Adams felt the need to defend his presidency to the extent that he did, was his actual performance somehow lacking? Farrell implies a weak performance by Adams when he writes that Adams's recollection of his administration made him "certain he had done the right thing, whether or not we, as his posterity, would be prepared to recognize his prudence." Farrell's statement reflects a disconnect between Adams's performance and at least a contemporary audience's judgment of it. In other words, how good could the performance be if the actor himself feels compelled to tell the audience about its merits? If anything, Adams's performance comes across as self-serving and not necessarily in service to the situation. As Farrell notes, "for Adams, fame remained a powerful motive, and drove him always to conduct himself with an eye toward posterity and the historical record." Perhaps the lesson here for rhetorical leaders is to be prudent in the moment for that moment. Attempting to speak to the ages, at least in Adams's case, calls into question his performance as a rhetorical leader.

Lawrence Kaplan's essay on Thomas Jefferson clearly delineates the third president's failure of rhetorical leadership. Admittedly, Kaplan believes that certain external forces, what Lloyd Bitzer would call exigencies that cannot be modified, were beyond Jefferson's rhetorical control.[1] Such forces helped as well as hindered Jefferson. However, according to Kaplan, the president did not perform well in those moments that were open to his influence. Due to some combination of pride over-whelming his practical reasoning ability and his underestimation of Napoleon Bonaparte's duplicitous machinations, Jefferson failed to account for that convergence of ideas, events, and opportunities to which a rhetorical leader must respond thoughtfully. As Cicero wrote, a leader "anticipates the future, calculates the chances for good or for evil, decides how to meet every contingency, and is never reduced to the necessity of saying: 'That is not what I expected.'"[2] On this occasion, Jefferson did not meet that challenge.

According to Meena Bose and Fred Greenstein, most of Dwight Eisenhower's presidency was a study of successful rhetorical leadership. He adapted to his moments and thrived in the public and political arenas. However, Bose and Greenstein recognize that Eisenhower failed to perform artfully during the missile-gap controversy. His usual public performance of ambiguity, they conclude, seemed to dismiss the rising level of American anxiety over the Soviet launch of *Sputnik.* Instead of demonstrating the virtue of compassion in public, Eisenhower seemed oblivious to the public's concerns. Eisenhower failed to use all of the available means of persuasion: Bose and Greenstein note that the president should have revealed certain of his private deliberations that would have helped him to improve the nation's attitude. Because Eisenhower did not balance his sense of rationality with a show of concern for the feelings of others, he missed the opportunity for successful prudential leadership.

Each of the essays in this collection demonstrates that presidents obviously need to assess any number of variables during the process of leadership. That complex constellation of issues, precedence, timing, auditors, culture, and other exigencies require leaders who can find the points of convergence, choose rationally and ethically among those points, and demonstrate that balance of reason and character in a moment defined by them. Successful episodes of persuasion, and those less so, reflect an important lesson about prudence and rhetorical leadership: it is about performance at a particular moment. It is about a seized moment or a missed opportunity. For presidents to be successful rhetorical leaders, they must, at the very least, be able to differentiate between the two.

NOTES

1. Lloyd Bitzer, "The Rhetorical Situation," *Philosophy and Rhetoric* 1, no. 1 (1968): 1–14.

2. Cicero, "On Moral Duties," trans. by George B. Gardiner in *The Basic Works of Cicero,* ed. Moses Hadas (New York: Modern Library, 1951), 32.

CONTRIBUTORS

James R. Andrews is a professor of communication and culture and adjunct professor of American studies at Indiana University. He is author or coauthor of several books, including *The American Ideology: Reflections of the Revolution in American Rhetoric* and *A Choice of Worlds: The Practice and Criticism of Public Discourse.* He received the National Communication Association's Winans-Wichelns Award for Distinguished Scholarship in Rhetoric and Public Address, twice won the American Forensic Association's Award for Outstanding Research, and received the Douglas Ehninger Distinguished Rhetorical Scholar Award.

Thomas W. Benson is the Edwin Erle Sparks Professor of Rhetoric at Pennsylvania State University. He is the author or coauthor of several books, including *Readings in Classical Rhetoric, American Rhetoric: Context and Criticism,* and *Rhetoric and Political Culture in Nineteenth-Century America,* as well as many scholarly essays. He is a recipient of the Distinguished Scholar Award, the Kibler Award, the Ehninger Distinguished Rhetorical Scholar Award, and the Mentor Award of the National Communication Association.

Meena Bose is an assistant professor of political science at the United States Military Academy, West Point, New York. She is the author of *Shaping and Signaling Presidential Policy: The National Security Decision Making of Eisenhower and Kennedy.* An earlier version of the book received the first annual Best Dissertation on the Presidency Prize from the Center of Presidential Studies, Texas A&M University, in 1997. Her teaching and research interests include the American presidency, American foreign policy, American politics, and political leadership.

H. W. Brands is Distinguished Professor of History and Ralph R. Thomas '21 Professor in Liberal Arts at Texas A&M University. He is the author of *TR: The Last Romantic, The Reckless Decade: America in the 1890s,* and other works of American history.

Leroy G. Dorsey is an associate professor of speech communication at Texas A&M University. He writes on Progressive Era politics and on the rhetoric of Theodore Roosevelt. His work has been published in the *Quarterly Journal of Speech, Rhetoric and Public Affairs, Western Journal of Communication,* and *Presidential Studies Quarterly.* In 1998 he received the Teacher/Scholar Award from the University Honors Program at Texas A&M.

James Farrell is an associate professor of communication at the University of New Hampshire, where he teaches rhetoric and public address. He has published numerous articles on the career and public discourse of John Adams and has lately turned his attention to study of Daniel Webster's oratory and to investigation of American discourse about the Great Irish Famine. Farrell received the 1991 Karl R. Wallace Memorial Award from the Speech Communication Association and the 1994 Excellence in Teaching Award from the College of Liberal Arts at the University of New Hampshire.

G. Thomas Goodnight is a professor of communication studies at Northwestern University, where he has directed the departmental graduate program. He is currently a visiting professor at the Annenberg School for Communication, University of Southern California. He has written on Reagan administration foreign policy for the *Quarterly Journal of Speech* and a number of research volumes. His interests include studies in the public sphere from contemporary and historical perspectives.

Fred I. Greenstein is a professor of politics emeritus at Princeton University. He is the author of many books and articles, including *Children and Politics, Personality and Politics, The Hidden-Hand Presidency: Eisenhower as Leader,* and *The Presidential Difference: Leadership Style from FDR to Clinton.*

Lawrence S. Kaplan is currently an adjunct professor of history at Georgetown University, and director emeritus of the Lyman L. Lemnitzer Center for NATO and European Union Studies at Kent State University. He has authored a number of books on American diplomatic history, including *A Community of Interests: NATO and the Military Assistance Program, 1948–1951, American Historians and the Atlantic Alliance,* and *The Long Entanglement: NATO's First Fifty Years.*

Stephen E. Lucas, a professor of communication arts and Evjue-Bascom Professor in the Humanities at the University of Wisconsin, is the author of numerous books and articles on American political discourse, including *The Quotable George Washington* and *Portents of Rebellion: Rhetoric and Revolution in Philadelphia, 1765–1776.*

John M. Murphy is an associate professor of speech communication at the University of Georgia. He writes on contemporary political rhetoric and rhetorical theory. His work has appeared in such outlets as the *Quarterly Journal of Speech, Communication Monographs, Rhetoric & Public Affairs,* and *Rhetoric Review,* and he has provided political commentary for the Cable News Network and National Public Radio. He is currently working on a book about the Clinton administration.

David Zarefsky is a professor of communication studies and John Evans Professor of Speech at Northwestern University. From 1988 to 2000 he was dean of the School of Speech. He is a past president of the National Communication Association and a recipient of its Distinguished Scholar Award. He also received the association's Winans-Wichelns Award for Distinguished Scholarship in Rhetoric and Public Address for *President Johnson's War on Poverty: Rhetoric and History* and *Lincoln, Douglas, and Slavery: In the Crucible of Public Debate.*

INDEX

PRESIDENTIAL RHETORIC SERIES
Martin J. Medhurst, General Editor

Beer, Francis A. *Meanings of War and Peace.* 2001.

Houck, Davis W. *Rhetoric as Currency: Hoover, Roosevelt, and the Great Depression.* 2001.

Medhurst, Martin J., ed. *Beyond the Rhetorical Presidency.* 1996.

Medhurst, Martin J., and H. W. Brands, eds. *Critical Reflections on the Cold War: Linking Rhetoric and History.* 2000.

Pauley, Garth E. *The Modern Presidency and Civil Rights: Rhetoric on Race from Roosevelt to Nixon.* 2001.

Volume editor LEROY G. DORSEY is an associate professor of speech communication at Texas A&M University. He holds the Ph.D. from Indiana University. Dorsey has published a number of articles in scholarly journals and is working on a book on the rhetoric of Theodore Roosevelt.

ISBN 1-58544-178-3